Praise for Scott Turow and *One L*

"A profoundly gifted author."
—*The New York Times*

"An elegant report from the graduate school battlefield
and from the heart."
—*The Boston Sunday Globe*

"Absorbing . . . for the layman as well as lawyers, *One L*
is compelling and even suspenseful reading."
—*Business Week*

"A fascinating account."
—*Dallas-Fort Worth Star-Telegram*

"Gripping . . . candid and straightforward."
—*The Portland Oregonian*

"An important document . . . For those who have not been
to law school, Turow makes the experience breathe; for those
who have, he recalls it vividly."
—*Chronicle of Higher Education Review*

"A sensitive, dramatically paced account."
—*The New York Times*

"Exciting."
—*The Kansas City Star*

PENGUIN BOOKS

ONE L

Scott Turow is the international best-selling author of nine novels, including *The Burden of Proof*, *Pleading Guilty*, *The Laws of Our Fathers*, and *Presumed Innocent*, as well as its sequel, *Innocent*. His essays and op-ed pieces have appeared in many publications, including *The New York Times*, *The Washington Post*, *The New Yorker*, *Vanity Fair*, and *The Atlantic*. He holds degrees from Amherst College, Stanford University, and Harvard Law School and lives outside of Chicago where he is a partner in the international law firm SNR Denton.

SCOTT TUROW

ONE L

THE TURBULENT TRUE STORY
OF A FIRST YEAR AT
HARVARD LAW SCHOOL

PENGUIN BOOKS

PENGUIN BOOKS

Published by the Penguin Group

Penguin Group (USA) Inc., 375 Hudson Street, New York, New York 10014, U.S.A.
Penguin Group (Canada), 90 Eglinton Avenue East, Suite 700, Toronto,
Ontario, Canada M4P 2Y3 (a division of Pearson Penguin Canada Inc.)
Penguin Books Ltd, 80 Strand, London WC2R 0RL, England
Penguin Ireland, 25 St Stephen's Green, Dublin 2, Ireland (a division of Penguin Books Ltd)
Penguin Group (Australia), 250 Camberwell Road, Camberwell,
Victoria 3124, Australia (a division of Pearson Australia Group Pty Ltd)
Penguin Books India Pvt Ltd, 11 Community Centre,
Panchsheel Park, New Delhi – 110 017, India
Penguin Group (NZ), 67 Apollo Drive, Rosedale, North Shore 0632,
New Zealand (a division of Pearson New Zealand Ltd)
Penguin Books (South Africa) (Pty) Ltd, 24 Sturdee Avenue,
Rosebank, Johannesburg 2196, South Africa

Penguin Books Ltd, Registered Offices:
80 Strand, London WC2R 0RL, England

First published in the United States of America by G. P. Putnam's Sons 1977
Published in Penguin Books with a new afterword 2010

1 3 5 7 9 10 8 6 4 2

THE LIBRARY OF CONGRESS HAS CATALOGED THE HARDCOVER EDITION AS FOLLOWS::
One L : an inside account of life in the first year at Harvard Law School / by Scott Turow.
p. cm.
ISBN 0-374-22647-4 (hc.)
ISBN 978-0-14-311902-9 (pbk.)
1. Turow, Scott.   2. Law students—Massachusetts—Biography.
3. Harvard Law School.   I. Title.
KF373.T88A33   1988
340'.073—dc19   88-19845

Printed in the United States of America
Designed by Kathryn Parise

CONTENTS

It is Monday morning, and when I walk into the central building, I can feel my stomach clench. For the next five days I will assume that I am somewhat less intelligent than anyone around me. At most moments I'll suspect that the privilege I enjoy was conferred as some kind of peculiar hoax. I will be certain that no matter what I do, I will not do it well enough; and when I fail, I know that I will burn with shame. By Friday my nerves will be so brittle from sleeplessness and pressure and intellectual fatigue that I will not be certain I can make it through the day. After years off, I have begun to smoke cigarettes again; lately, I seem to be drinking a little every night. I do not have the time to read a novel or a magazine, and I am so far removed from the news of world events that I often feel as if I've fallen off the dark side of the planet. I am distracted at most times and have difficulty keeping up a conversation, even with my wife. At random instants, I am likely to be stricken with acute feelings of panic, depression, indefinite need, and the pep talks and irony I practice on myself only seem to make it worse.

I am a law student in my first year at the law, and there are many moments when I am simply a mess.

PREFACE

In baseball it's the rookie year. In the navy it is boot camp. In many walks of life there is a similar time of trial and initiation, a period when newcomers are forced to be the victims of their own ineptness and when they must somehow master the basic skills of the profession in order to survive.

For someone who wants to be a lawyer, that proving time is the first year of law school. There are many obstacles to becoming a successful attorney. Getting *into* law school these days is far from easy. And following graduation three years later, you must pass the bar exam in your state, find a job, or set out on your own, build and maintain a practice. Yet none of those steps is thought to possess the kind of wholesale drama of the first year of law school. Not only is it a demanding year—the work hugely difficult and seemingly endless, the classroom competition often fierce—but it is also a time when law students typically feel a stunning array of changes taking place within themselves. It is during the first year that you learn to read a case, to frame a legal argument, to distinguish between seemingly indistinguishable ideas; then that you begin to absorb the mysterious language of the law, full of words like *estoppel* and *replevin*. It is during the first year, according to a saying, that you learn to think like a lawyer, to develop the habits of mind and world perspective that will stay with you throughout your career. And thus it is during the first year that many law students come to feel, sometimes with deep regret, that they are becoming persons strangely different from the ones who arrived at law school in the fall.

This book is about my first year as a student at the Harvard Law School in Cambridge, Massachusetts. The fact that the year's events took place at Harvard—the oldest, largest, and perhaps most esteemed of America's law schools—does not in the end differentiate my experience much from that of the nearly 40,000 Americans who begin their legal education every fall. The first year at American law schools tends to be remarkably uniform. The course of study has changed little in the past century. Almost every first-year student is required (as I was) to take what are generally thought of as the basic subjects—the law of Contracts, Torts, and Property, the Criminal Law, Civil Procedure. Nor does the manner of instruction vary much from place to place. Study focuses on selected court cases from which students are expected to deduce legal principles, and the classes are usually conducted by the so-called "Socratic method," in which individual students are interrogated at length about their impressions of the material. These days, students at all law schools are usually bright and accomplished, and the struggle for jobs in the future and for first-year honors leads at most schools to the same emphasis on grades and the same atmosphere of tension, competition, and uncertainty in which I found myself during the past year at Harvard. For all of us who have made it through the first year,

I am sure that it was a similar undertaking, overwhelming, sometimes frightening, always dizzyingly intense.

In writing this book, I have sought to show that intensity, and the process of change, as they made themselves felt day by day upon my classmates and me. I kept a journal throughout the year and often I've taken passages directly from it when my thoughts and feelings seemed especially clear and important. For the most part, however, I've attempted to shape those reflections in light of the experience of the complete year and the knowledge that first impressions did not always prove an especially reliable indicator of either the way things would turn out, or even the general course of my feelings.

This book is one person's perspective on an experience that is viewed in widely varying ways. I make no claims that any of my reactions are universal. And it is also a book, written as soon as the year had concluded, which has little of the mellowing of time. No doubt, I would write a different book ten years from now, emphasizing different events, expressing more or less concern about certain elements of my education. For better or for worse, I have tried in the immediate aftermath of that demanding, rewarding, turbulent year to produce a coherent account of what it feels like to go through it. I have written in the belief that the law, like any other field, is little more than the people who live it, and that lawyers—as well as the law they make and practice—are significantly affected by the way they were first received into the profession. If I am right about that, then the first-year experience should be of interest to everyone, for it bears on the law that bounds and guides our whole society.

I should add two special notes.

First, this book is not a novel. Everything I describe in the following pages happened to me. But the people about whom I speak are not the same as the friends and professors with whom I spent the year. I have combined and altered personalities in order to represent more adequately the general character of my experience. And because the people around me did not know that I would undertake this project, I have changed names, backgrounds, and sometimes other details, to avoid any potential sacrifice of their privacy.

Finally, I should say once, forthrightly, that I am proud to be a student at Harvard Law School ("HLS" is the abbreviation I'll often use). I'm sure that much of this book bespeaks that pride, but I make this declaration in order to insure that my occasional criticism of HLS will not be misunderstood. Since its founding in 1817, through its graduates and as a scholarly resource, the Harvard Law School has had an extraordinary impact on the growth and enrichment of the American law and the American legal profession. I am glad to be among the inheritors of its traditions. That both the law and HLS can be made richer, more humane, more just institutions is more than a personal assumption—it is an institutional one as well, an idea taught and reinforced at HLS. It is ultimately out of the belief in reasoned change, for which the law school in many ways stands, that any criticism grows.

S.T.

ONE L

REGISTRATION
Meeting My Enemy

9/3/75
(*Wednesday*)

. . . a warm place, a good place . . . I think.

They called us "One Ls," and there were 550 of us who came on the third of September to begin our careers in the law. For the first three days we would have Harvard Law School to ourselves while we underwent a brief orientation and some preliminary instruction. Then, over the weekend, the upper-year students would arrive, and on Monday all classes would officially commence.

A pamphlet sent in August to all first-year students—the

One Ls (1Ls) as they are known at HLS—instructed me to be at the Roscoe Pound Classroom and Administration Building at 10 A.M. to register and to start orientation. I took the bus into Cambridge from Arlington, the nearby town where my wife and I had found an apartment.

I had been to the law school once earlier in the summer when David, a close friend who'd recently graduated, had given me a tour. HLS occupies fifteen buildings on the northern edge of the Harvard campus, and is bounded on one side by Massachusetts Avenue, Cambridge's clogged main thoroughfare. The architecture is eclectic. The student commons and dormitories are square and buff-colored and functional. Old Austin Hall, a classroom building, looks like a sooty fortress with arches. Langdell, the school's largest building, is a long gray expanse of concrete. When I toured the law school in the summer, it had all looked so solid, so enduring, that I'd felt a majestic thrill to think I'd soon be allied with this and the time-ennobled traditions of the law. Now, getting off the bus, I felt mostly my nerves, which were lit all the way down to my knees.

In the Pound Building, a modern affair with exposed brick walls and a lot of glass, I was handed a thick packet of registration materials as soon as I came through the door. Then I was directed down the hall to a classroom where my section—Section 2—was being loosely assembled for the first time to fill out the variety of cards and forms in the packets.

Every year at Harvard the 1Ls are divided into four sections of 140 students each. With that same group, I would have all my classes throughout the year, except a single elective course in the spring. The members of my section, I'd been told, would become my friends, my colleagues, the 140 people on earth who would know best the rigors I was going through daily. They would also be the individuals with whom I would be constantly compared, by the faculty and probably by myself. Relations within the section would be close. Most 1Ls, even those who

live in the on-campus dorms—about half the first-year class—
have only passing contact with the members of the other three
first-year sections or with upper-class students. For the most
part, friends had said, it would seem as if I were in a separate
school, a tiny universe centered on the professors, with the 140
of us in a dense and hectic orbit about them.

My first view of my section mates was inauspicious. In the
classroom most of the people were seated, dutifully emptying
their packets and filling out cards. A few students who seemed
to have known each other, probably as undergraduates, stood
about in clusters or called to one another across the room. I had
few distinct impressions. For the most part, they were a little
bit younger than I'd expected. There were a number of women,
a number of blacks. Most of the men wore their hair quite short.

On the blackboard a notice had been written, naming the
cards and forms in the pack and giving the order in which they
were to be received by the representatives of the registrar's office who awaited them on the far side of the room. When I finished, I looked at the man seated beside me. I watched him
count his cards three times. Then I did the same thing myself.
When I looked up he was watching me.

"They're all here," I told him. He nodded. I introduced myself and we shook hands. His name was Hal Lasky and he was
from Ashtabula by way of Ohio State. He asked if I knew anything about our professors. Their names had been announced
in the August pamphlet. I told him I didn't.

"What do you hear?" I asked.

"Not much," he said, "except about Perini in Contracts.
He's supposed to be pretty tough. And Morris in Civil Procedure—people like him."

After handing in our cards, all of us, in a peculiar ceremony,
were required to "sign in" to the law school, registering our
name, age, and previous degrees in a large ledger. As I wrote, I
scanned the page to see about my classmates. Two listed their

undergraduate college as Oxford. Another person had a Ph.D. The woman who'd signed above me was an M.D.

That's only one page, I told myself.

When I finished signing, a woman handed me a plastic ID card. I was enrolled.

I walked outside for a moment. It was a fine day, sunny and mild. I sat down on a brick retaining wall near the Pound Building.

So here you are, I told myself, the famous Harvard Law School, alma mater to many of the great men of American law—Supreme Court justices, senators, a President—and more persons influential in contemporary life than I could remember or keep count of.

"*El numero uno*," a friend of mine had called HLS the spring before, in trying to persuade me to come here. Every detail about the place suggested its prominence. HLS is the oldest law school in the nation. It has the largest full-time enrollment—1,800, including graduate students. The more than sixty-five professors constitute the biggest full-time law faculty in the country, and perhaps the most illustrious. As a place actually to undertake a legal education, Harvard is sometimes criticized, especially when compared to schools, like Yale, that have more flexible curricula and lower ratios of students to faculty. But for whatever it was worth, I knew that a poll the previous winter of the deans of all the law schools in the country had revealed that among them, Harvard was still most often thought of as the best.

But despite having become part of that lustrous setting, as I sat there on that wall I did not feel entirely self-satisfied. Doubt—about themselves, about what they are doing—is a malady familiar to first-year law students and I arrived already afflicted. I was not sure that I was up to that tradition of excellence. And I was still not absolutely positive that law school was the place where I should be. For me, the route to law school had been somewhat roundabout. I was twenty-six, three or four years older than most of the other 1Ls, for it had taken me somewhat longer than it had taken them to realize that I wanted to study law.

For the past three years I had been a lecturer in the English department at Stanford where, before that, I was a graduate student. I had spent my time as lecturer teaching courses in creative writing and doing my best to write on my own. It was not a bad life. But I found myself with a deepening interest in law. Some of the writing I was doing had involved a good deal of legal research, and contrary to my expectations I found much of the work intriguing. In college, at Amherst, in the era of Vietnam and the civil-rights struggle, the law had seemed to me the instrument by which the people in power kept themselves on top. When many of my friends had decided to go to law school, I had been openly critical of their choices. Now, five years later, I saw the law less as a matter of remote privilege, and more a part of daily affairs. Getting married, renting an apartment, buying a car—legal matters were all around me. I was fascinated by the extent to which the law defined our everyday lives. And the friends whose decisions I'd criticized were now in practice, doing things which pleased them and also seemed absorbing to me.

In the spring of 1974—purely speculatively, I told myself— I took the Law School Admissions Test (LSAT), the nationally administered exam required of all law-school applicants. I did well on the test—749 out of 800, a score near the ninety-ninth percentile—but I was still reluctant to give up my career in writing and teaching. It was only later that spring, when I was offered a better job as an assistant professor at another university, that I forced myself to think about the lifelong commitments I wanted to make. I came to realize how much I would regret allowing my interest in law to go unfulfilled.

The following fall, I filed applications at law schools across the country. When it became apparent that I would have a

choice among schools, there was another period of hard decision. I had many college friends who had gone to law school at
Harvard and most had found the place large, harsh, and stifling.
But I admired Harvard's reputation and its resources. I often
told myself that my friends had been younger and less mature
law students than I would be, that at the end of the 1960s they
had brought different expectations to law school than I would
now. Nevertheless, my doubts remained. Ultimately, I shunned
any ideal choice among schools and let the decision rest on the
prestige of a Harvard degree and the fact that the job market for
my wife, Annette, a schoolteacher, was far the best in Boston.

Now and then as the year ran down at Stanford, I worried
that I had made the wrong choices—in giving up teaching, in
going to Harvard. I talked about it one day to a friend, a graduate student in the department who I knew had thought seriously of going to law school himself.

"Look," he told me, "if I was going to law school, I would be
going because I wanted to meet my enemy. I think that's a
good thing to do. And if I wanted to meet my enemy, I would
go to Harvard, because I'd be surest of meeting him there."

I smiled weakly at my friend. I was not sure what he meant
by "meeting my enemy." It seemed like one of those cleverly am-
biguous things people were always saying around the English
department. But in the following weeks the phrase recurred to
me often. I realized that somehow it summed up the feelings I
had about law school: the fear, the uncertainties, the hope of
challenge, triumph, discovery. And somehow with that name on
what was ahead I became surer that my decisions were correct.

Thinking it over once more as I sat on the wall, I felt that
sureness again. Meeting my enemy. It was what I wanted to
do. I could only hope I would come out all right.

The schedule I'd found in my registration pack directed me
next to the third floor of Pound, where coffee and doughnuts

were being served and the representatives of various student organizations sat behind banks of tables, introducing themselves to the 1Ls milling by. I joined the married students' group, as Annette had requested. We had already received mail from them which promised that they would run a number of activities for the husbands and wives of first-year students. The 1Ls' spouses, the letters had said, often found themselves spending long periods alone.

With that done, I moved next door to Harkness Commons, where there is a student lounge and a sundries store and, on the second floor, a dining hall where I was heading for lunch. As I started up, I saw a tall, blond-haired man who I thought was a friend from college. I called out. I was right—it was Mike Wald.

"I had no idea you were here," I told him, and pumped his hand enthusiastically. The last I'd heard, he was a graduate student at Yale. It was good to see a friend, especially on the first day.

With our meals, we sat down together. Mike told me he'd come to law school last year, after concluding that the condition of the academic job market meant that he would never get the kind of work he wanted, as a historian. On the whole, he said, he still felt law school was the right choice.

He explained that he was in school now, before other upper-year students, because he was a member of the Board of Student Advisors, the group of second-year and third-year students—2Ls and 3Ls—who traditionally helped steward 1Ls through the year. BSA people would assist in the teaching of our Legal Methods classes, the small informal course on legal writing and other lawyering skills, which would meet for the first time this afternoon. BSA would also be in charge of the Moot Court competition, in which all first-year students were required to take part, in the spring.

When we finished lunch, Mike asked me what section I was in. When I told him Section 2, he looked at me.

"You've got Perini?" he asked.

I nodded. "I hear he's tough."

"You said it. I had him last year," Mike said. "He's something else."

"What does he do—beat his students?"

"You'll see." Mike smiled, but he shook his head as if someone had given him a blow. "You'll live through it. Besides, a lot of people think he's a great teacher."

I asked Mike about my other professors. He did not know much, except about Nicky Morris, the Civil Procedure professor. He was young, Mike said, progressive, well liked by students.

At two, I left Mike and went to the first meeting of Legal Methods. Rather than a full-blown law-school course, Methods was regarded as an introductory supplement to the first-year curriculum. It would run for only ten weeks, a little longer than half of the first term, and the instructor would be a teaching fellow, instead of a member of the faculty. For the next three days, though, Methods would be at the center, concentrated instruction aimed at bringing us to the point where we could start the work of our regular courses, which would begin meeting on Monday.

Normally, Legal Methods would gather in classes of twenty-five, but today for the introductory session three groups had been joined and the small classroom was crowded. There was a lot of commotion as people went about introducing themselves to each other. I sat down next to a man who was glad-handing everybody around him. It was only a moment before he got to me.

"Terry Nazzario," he said, grasping my hand. He was a tall, slim man in his mid-twenties, coarse-skinned but quite handsome. His black hair was combed back behind his ears and he reminded me a lot of the kids we'd called "greasers" when I was growing up in Chicago. He looked a little out of place amid the Ivy League ease of Harvard Law School. Apparently, he thought so himself. When I asked where he was from, he told me Elizabeth, New Jersey, and Montclair State College, then added, "Hey, man, the only reason I got in here was 'cause they thought I was Puerto Rican."

I looked at him.

"No jive," he told me. "My mailbox is full of stuff from the Latin Students Organization."

He might have been serious, I decided, but he did not appear disturbed. A character, I figured. Your basic hustler. I smiled cautiously. Nazzario watched me a moment, then laughed out loud and gave me a wink. I had passed.

At the front of the room the instructor was calling us to order. "I'm Chris Henley," he said. He was short and had a full beard. He looked to be in his early thirties. "I'd like to welcome you to Harvard Law School. This'll be a brief session. I just want to give you a few ideas about what we'll be doing for the next few days and then in the rest of the course."

Before he went on, Henley told us a little about himself. He had been a lawyer with OEO in Washington for seven years. Now he was here, working on a graduate law degree; next year he would probably move on to another school to become a law professor. Then he introduced the three members of the Board of Student Advisors who would be working with each of the Methods groups. A lean, dark man named Peter Geocaris, a 3L, had been assigned to mine. After that, Henley described the course.

"In the Legal Methods program," he said, "you'll be learning skills by practicing them. Each of you will act as attorney on the same case. You'll assume the role of a law-firm associate who's been asked to deal with the firing of an employee by a corporation."

It would all be highly fictionalized, but we'd follow the matter through each of its stages, gaining some taste of many aspects of a lawyer's work. Among other things, Henley said we would be involved with a client interview, the filing of suit,

preparing and arguing a brief for summary judgment. At the
very end we would see how two experienced attorneys would
handle the suit in a mock trial. I had only the vaguest idea of
what many of the words Henley used meant—*depositions* and
interrogatories and *summary judgment*—and perhaps for that reason alone, the program sounded exciting.

Henley said our first assignment would be handed out at the
end of class. It consisted of a memo from our mythical law-firm
boss and a "case" the boss had asked the associate to consult.
"Case" here means the published report of a judge's resolution
of a dispute which has come before him. Typically, a case report
contains a summary of the facts leading up to the lawsuit, the
legal issues raised, and what the judge has to say in resolving
the matter. That portion of the case report in which the judge
sets forth his views is called an "opinion." Cases and opinions
form the very center of a law student's world. Virtually every
American law school adheres to the "case-study method,"
which requires students to learn the law by reading and discussing in class a steady diet of case reports. Most of those are
the decisions of appellate courts, designated higher courts to
which lawyers carry their objections to some point of law ruled
on by a trial judge. Because they deal with closely defined legal
questions, appellate opinions are considered especially apt tools
for teaching students the kind of precise reasoning considered
instrumental to a lawyer's work.

The case Henley assigned us was from the Supreme Court of
New Hampshire. He asked us to read it and to be ready to discuss it the next time the Methods group met. That did not
sound like much.

Before letting us go, Henley reminded us of our schedule for
today and the rest of the week: this afternoon an address by the
dean and a beer party with our section, tomorrow, for my
group, more meetings, classes, a lecture by the librarian. Then
Henley added a word of his own.

"I hope you will all take some time off during the year," he said. "I know you'll have your hands full. But it's so important, *so important* to get away from the law now and then. Just so that you can maintain some perspective. Don't get so caught up in all of this that you forget to leave it once in a while. Your work will always be there when you get back."

This seemed advice I hardly needed. After five years in California, one thing I'd thought I'd learned was how to relax.

When Henley finished, people swelled to the front to collect the memo and the case report. I picked up copies, then followed most of my classmates as they headed toward the basement, where Henley had said our first regular class assignments would be posted.

In law school there would be no "introductory day" like the ones I'd experienced in college and graduate school, none of that business of the professor's displaying himself to prove he does not have a mumble and hoping that students won't drop. "Lectures begin on the opening day of the year," the catalog sternly announced. Assignments were posted in advance so that we would be fully prepared when we entered class Monday.

In Criminal Law, Professor Mann had simply assigned the first chapter of the casebook. But Professor Perini's announcement was longer:

> For Monday's class, please read pages 1-43 in the casebook, Baldridge and Perini, *Selected Cases in the Law of Contracts*. Also read, at page 46, the case of *Hurley v. Eddingfield* and the case of *Poughkeepsie Buying Service, Inc. v. Poughkeepsie Newspaper Co.* at p. 50.
>
> Do not forget to bring your casebook and supplement to class.
>
> Be certain to read all material CAREFULLY.

It was not a good sign. As I copied the announcement, one man beside me said he had looked at the casebook and that the assignment would take hours. And as I finished writing I also noticed that Professor Perini had underlined the last word, CAREFULLY, twice.

Back upstairs, the dean was already in the midst of his welcoming address. It was a typical first-day speech, full of anecdotes and general advice and muted efforts at inspiration, but the dean delivered it with verve. He reminded us that almost all attorneys regard their first year of law school as the most challenging year of their legal lives and he urged us to use the year well. Then he released us to the green behind Harkness where beer was being served to the sections, each of which was gathering on a different corner of the lawn.

It was our first chance to mingle, aside from the quick handshakes and introductions that had been taking place in the hallways, and the members of my section sought each other out eagerly, inquiring into backgrounds, exchanging accounts of what had brought each of us to law school. I met a former Senate aide, another man who'd been U.S. karate champion while in the army. I introduced myself to a number of people: a group standing together who had been undergraduates at Harvard; a man who'd been a paralegal in New York City; the M.D. whose name I'd noticed in the entry ledger. She had interrupted her residency at the University of California, she told me, because she thought law school "might be fun."

As I met my classmates that day and in the next few weeks I was often amazed by the range of achievements. About two fifths of them had been out of college for at least a year and few had wasted the time. Around twenty of the people in the section had other advanced degrees, and many more had been successful in previous careers. There was an inventor, an architect, a research scientist, a farmer, mothers, a number of business-

men, three women who'd been social workers, many former
college instructors, three reporters, ex-servicemen, people
who'd had significant jobs in government. Nor were the men
and women who'd come direct from college less impressive. If
anything, their undergraduate records were more outstanding
than those of us who'd been out, many of the younger people,
if not most, *summa cum laude* from the best-known universities
in the country.

But more than the array of résumé glories that each person
could present, I was taken in those first few weeks with the
personal force of those around me. After ten years in universities I was accustomed to being surrounded by bright people.
Yet I had never been in a group where everybody was as affa-
ble, outgoing, articulate, as magically able to make his energy
felt by others. I had been told that my classmates would be
academic privateers and cutthroats, but as I wandered around
the Harkness green, sun-dazed and excited and a little bit
drunk, I felt a little like one of the astronauts, headed for ad-
venture with the most prime and perfect companions anyone
could choose.

Indeed, that impression was not far from the truth. The
process of selection which brought each of us to that green was
rigorous. In the past decade, the race for admission to all the
law schools in the country has grown remarkably thick and
heated. The number of persons enough interested in law school
each year to take the LSAT has quadrupled since 1964, and
since 1971, when the crunch became especially pronounced,
there have been more than twice as many law-school applicants
each year as there have been places.

The reasons for the incredible law-school boom are varied.
Certainly the birthrates after World War II, the end of the
draft, and the drought in university-level teaching jobs, which
has discouraged enrollment in other graduate schools, are all
significant factors. So too are national episodes like Vietnam

and Watergate, which have inspired many to look to law as a means by which change can be accomplished. Probably most important in accounting for the sudden rise in applications is the fact that minorities, and especially women—groups virtually excluded in the past—are now seeking legal education in large numbers.

One of the results of this boom in interest has been a boom in the number of lawyers. Law-school enrollments have grown rapidly, and in 1974 there were nearly 30,000 young lawyers graduated, three times more than were graduated ten years earlier and far too many for the legal job market to absorb. The Department of Labor estimated that there were only 16,500 positions available that year for new attorneys.

In consequence, the battle has grown ever more intense for admission to "name" law schools; Harvard, Yale, Michigan, Columbia, Chicago, Stanford, University of California (Boalt Hall), Penn, NYU, and Virginia are most often listed as the top flight. It is only the graduates of those schools, and law-review editors at some others, who continue to have job opportunities as extensive as those commonly available to all law-school graduates a few years ago. Harvard each year receives between 6,000 and 7,000 applications for a class of 550. At Yale and Stanford the disparities are even more dramatic: 3,000 applicants for only 165 spaces.

In making their selections, admissions officers generally place the greatest weight on two factors—the student's college grades and his score on the LSAT. The emphasis on those criteria is often criticized. Because of variations from college to college in academic standards, law schools tend to favor applicants from undergraduate schools whose marks have proved reliable in the past. At law schools like Harvard, that means a continued influx from the Ivy League colleges, with candidates from smaller and lesser-known schools at a disadvantage. The sole leveler is the LSAT—the only measure common to all applicants—but its accuracy is often doubted. The test is administered in a session which lasts only four hours, and many persons question the fairness of allowing the results of so short an exam to be so crucial. A grade below the median of 500 makes it difficult to get in at most American law schools, and each year many college students who have long planned on a legal career must change objectives when the LSAT results come back.

Admissions officers, however, discount the failings of grades and test scores and point instead to their utility in speeding the selection process and also in foretelling law-school success. By now the average grades and test scores of those admitted to the most selective schools have hit astronomical levels. In recent years, at Harvard, Yale, Stanford, and Chicago, the entering class has boasted medians near a solid A average and LSAT scores of around 720, close to the ninety-eighth percentile among all those taking the test nationally.

No matter what criteria were used, though, my guess would be that most of my HLS classmates would have arrived there or someplace similar anyway. They had been jumping hurdles all their lives, impressing teachers and counsellors and admissions officers, leading, succeeding, achieving. There were moments when I wished for greater diversity in the group. Nearly a third were from Ivy League colleges—and it was hard not to notice how many of my classmates were plainly the children of privilege and wealth, now acquiring more of the advantages they had started with. But those observations applied just as well to me—eastern-educated, a son of the well-to-do—and if advantages became a basis for exclusion then I might well have been the first to go. As it was, there were many moments during those initial days when, awed by the geniality and talents of my classmates, I felt proud, and sometimes startled, that I had been included at all.

9/3/75
(near midnight)

Tried tonight to read a case for the first time. It is harder than hell.

When I started, I thought the Legal Methods assignment would be easy. The memo from the boss was straightforward. A man named Jack Katz is "our firm's" client. Katz, who had worked for years as the comptroller of a company that makes raincoats, was fired a few months ago by the president of the corporation. His name is Elliot Grueman and he is the son of the man, now dead, who hired Katz ages ago. Grueman and Katz differed about expansion plans for the company; when Katz carried his objections to a member of the board of directors, Grueman showed Katz the door.

The memo from the boss indicates that Katz probably doesn't have a leg to stand on. It looks like Grueman had every right to fire him, since Katz did not have an employment contract. But still, the boss says, read this New Hampshire case, *Monge* v. *Beege Rubber Company*, which may indicate some limitations in an employer's right to discharge a worker.

OK. It was nine o'clock when I started reading. The case is four pages long and at 10:35 I finally finished. It was something like stirring concrete with my eyelashes. I had no idea what half the words meant. I must have opened *Black's Law Dictionary* twenty-five times and I still can't understand many of the definitions. There are notations and numbers throughout the case whose purpose baffles me. And even now I'm not crystal-clear on what the court finally decided to do.

Even worse, Henley asked us to try our hand at briefing the case—that is, preparing a short digest of the facts, issues, and reasoning essential to the court in making its decision. Briefing, I'm told, is important. All first-year students do it so they can organize the information in a case, and the various student guide books make it sound easy. But I have no idea of what a good brief looks like or even where to start. What in the hell are "the facts," for instance? The case goes on for a solid page giving all the details about how this woman, Olga Monge, was fired primarily because she would not go out on a date with her foreman. Obviously, I'm not supposed to include all of that, but I'm not sure what to pick, how abstract I'm supposed to be, and whether I should include items like her hourly wage. Is a brief supposed to sound casual or formal? Does it make any difference how a brief sounds? Should I include the reasoning of the judge who dissented, as well? Is this why students hate the case-study method?

Twenty minutes ago, I threw up my hands and quit.

I feel overheated and a little bit nervous. I wouldn't be quite so upset if I weren't going to be reading cases every day and if understanding them weren't so important. Cases are the law, in large part. That fact came as news to me when David explained it this summer. I had always thought that the legislature makes all the rules and that judges merely interpret what has been said. I'm not sure where I got that idea, either in high-school civics or, more likely, from TV.

Anyway, that is not right. When the legislature speaks, the judge obeys. But most of the time, nobody has spoken to the point, and the judge decides the law on his own, looking to what other judges have done in similar circumstances. Following precedent, that's called. Much of what lawyers do in court, apparently, is to try to convince judges that the present situation is more like one precedent than another.

This system of judges making law case by case is called the "common law." I am a little embarrassed that I did not understand what that meant when I applied to law school, particularly since the first page of the HLS catalog says that the law school prepares lawyers to practice "wherever the common law prevails."

Well, tonight, the common law has prevailed over me, beaten me back. I suppose it will not be the last time, but I feel frustrated and disturbed.

I am going to sleep.

The Methods class the next morning made me feel more at ease. We met in a small group of twenty-five and Henley's teaching manner was casual. He first handed out a sample brief of the *Monge* case. It resembled the brief I had done only in that both were written on paper, but I felt some comfort in knowing that I now had a model to work from. Then he slowly led us through the case itself, unpacking the mystery of many of the details which had so confused me the night before.

Henley explained that there are fifty-one independent court systems in the country, those of each of the states and that of the federal government. Most of the systems, however, are constructed the same way, with three levels of ascending authority. On the first level are the trial courts, where a judge or a jury initially decides each dispute. Above, there are the appeals courts, composed only of judges, where all losers by right can seek review of the trial record and reversal of the trial decision. Finally, on the highest level in both the state and the federal systems, are supreme courts in which selective review is made of appellate decisions. Typically, a supreme court will hear only cases of broad significance or ones in which the law on point is especially murky.

Henley told us that almost every appellate and supreme court decision made in the United States, whether in state or federal courts, is published, and he showed us the various shorthand citations used to indicate where each case can be found in the endless series of report volumes issued by the states and by private publishers. By the time Henley had finished those explanations, and had gone briefly over the *Monge* opinion itself, he had made things clear enough for me to feel some real pleasure in recognizing how much order had followed on what had previously seemed befuddling and complex.

And yet the experience of having been so confounded the night before had a definite effect on me. The first year of law school was no longer something I'd heard tales about and was trying to imagine. I knew for myself now how frustrated, how sheerly incapable of doing what I was supposed to, I was liable to feel. I tried to take it with good humor but that realization also touched me with the first genuine wisps of fear.

At one o'clock, the Methods group met with our BSA advisor, Peter Geocaris, to hear his suggestions on what we should expect in the next few days. Peter attempted to lay things out fairly, advantages and drawbacks, and in light of my experience the night before, I tried to pay some attention to his occasional warnings. Regarding classmates, for instance, he reminded us of our mutual talents and the amount we could learn from each other. But he also described the peer pressures which would soon develop, to perform well in class, and the race which he said would begin in each section to make the Law Review.

Among our teachers, too, Peter indicated that we would find both dark and bright spots. The overall quality of teaching was high, Peter said, but certain individuals were more agreeable than others. On the more positive side seemed to be Nicky Morris.

"He's thirty-one and he's easygoing," Peter said, "and he is very, very smart." Morris, Geocaris told us, had graduated from the Harvard Law School when he was twenty-three years old. He had been first in his class, president of the Law Review, and had attained the highest academic average since Felix Frankfurter was a law student. After that, he had been a clerk to one of the justices of the U.S. Supreme Court for a year, then counsel to United Farm Workers, before he'd begun teaching. "Nobody has ever called him a slow learner," Peter added.

About our Torts professor, William Zechman, Peter knew

almost nothing, except that he was returning to teaching after
a long absence. But Peter had had a class the year before with
our Criminal Law teacher, Bertram Mann, and he was not enthusiastic. Mann was the former United States Attorney for the
Southern District of New York. He was well-informed, Peter
said, yet often confusing in class.

But the direst warning of all was reserved for Perini.

"He's a great teacher," Peter told us, "but not an easy one.
When I was a 1L, the first person he called on was a national
champion debater and Perini had him on his back in forty
seconds."

Always be prepared for that class, Geocaris advised. Know
what every word in a case means; and if your study has been
shoddy, don't bother to show up: It would be a long time before you forgot the humiliation of being caught unready.

The lecture on the library which we heard next was full of
the same mixture of good news and bad omens. The librarian
nimbly described where the important books were located and
when and why we would want to use them—the sets of state
laws, the volumes of case reports, the treatises and encyclopedias and journals, the gargantuan indices which could help you
sort your way through all of that. If you knew what you were
doing in the library, you could solve the most complex legal
problems in the world. But it was plain in listening that that
kind of skill would not be developed merely by taking the
walking tours of the stacks which the librarian suggested or
doing the reading on legal research. You would have to go up
there and work with the stuff, fail, get frustrated, try again.

I was willing to do it. I was determined to do it. By the end
of the day, that had become my reaction to all of the signs of
hard things ahead—a new purposefulness, hardy resolve.
Everything I'd encountered so far—the law, my classmates, the
great pace of discovery—had left me in deep thrall and I was

bent on making sure that continued. I would have the best of it, I decided, whatever the obstacles.

Over the weekend, I studied hard. I did not want to feel again the helpless ignorance of the other night. I outlined carefully the chapters of text assigned in both Criminal Law and Contracts, then I went over the two cases Perini had given us, a number of times. I did scrupulous briefs for both cases, each word weighed, every angle considered. I rehearsed what I would say if called on. I paged through the law dictionary until I had virtually memorized the definition of every term important in the opinions. I was going to be ready for Perini, *totally* prepared.

I was too absorbed to notice that I had already been lured onto enemy ground.

SEPTEMBER AND OCTOBER
Learning to Love the Law

9/8/75
(Monday)

Just a note before I leave for school.

Today is the start of regular classes. We will now commence "normal" law-school life. The 2Ls and 3Ls will be present and the section will begin the schedule we'll be on for much of the year. This semester we'll have Contracts, Civil Procedure, Criminal Law, and Torts. The latter two courses last only one term and they'll be the subjects on which we'll take our first exams in January. Second semester, Contracts and Civil Pro continue, Property will be added, and we'll each be allowed to choose an elective.

We've been warned that today's classes—Criminal and Contracts—will not seem much like Legal Methods. The courses we begin now are considered the traditional stuff of law school, analytical matter, rather than mere how-to. Unlike Methods, these courses will be graded, and they'll be taught by professors, not teaching fellows. The classes will be made up of the whole 140-person section instead of a small group. And, most ominous to me, the instruction will be by the noted "Socratic method."

In a way I'm looking forward to Socratic instruction. I've heard so much about it since I applied to law school—it will at least be interesting to see what it's like.

The general run of student reaction is most succinctly expressed in a comment I heard from David this summer, the day he showed me around the law school. He was kind of mimicking a tour guide, whining out facts and names as he took me from building to building. When we reached Langdell, he stood on the steps and lifted his hand toward the columns and the famous names of the law cut into the granite border beneath the roof.

"This is Langdell Hall," he said, "the biggest building on the law-school campus. It contains four large classrooms and, on the upper floors, the Harvard Law School library, the largest law-school library in the world.

"The building is named for the late Christopher Columbus Langdell, who was dean of Harvard Law School in the late nineteenth century. Dean Langdell is best known as the inventor of the Socratic method."

David lowered his hand and looked sincerely at the building.

"May he rot in hell," David said.

The Socratic method is without question one of the things which makes legal education—particularly the first year, when Socraticism is most extensively used—distinct from what students are accustomed to elsewhere. While I was teaching, it was always assumed that there was no hope of holding a class discussion with a group larger than thirty. When numbers got that high, the only means of communication was lecture. But Socraticism is, in a way, an attempt to lead a discussion with the entire class of 140.

Generally, Socratic discussion begins when a student—I'll call him Jones—is selected without warning by the professor and questioned. Traditionally, Jones will be asked to "state the case," that is, to provide an oral rendition of the information normally contained in a case brief. Once Jones has responded, the professor—as Socrates did with his students—will question Jones about what he has said, pressing him to make his answers clearer. If Jones says that the judge found that the contract had been breached, the professor will ask what specific provision of the contract had been violated and in what manner. The discussion will proceed that way, with the issues narrowing. At some point, Jones may be unable to answer. The professor can either select another student at random, or—more commonly—call on those who've raised their hands. The substitutes may continue the discussion of the case with the professor, or simply answer what Jones could not, the professor then resuming his interrogation of Jones.

Professors' classroom procedures differ so widely that this description cannot be called typical. Some professors never ask for a statement of the case, commencing discussion with a narrower question instead. Some interrogate students for thirty seconds—others leave them on the hot seat for the entire class. A few professors never do any more than ask questions, disdaining any direct statement. Most, however, use a student's response as the starting point for a brief lecture on a given topic before returning to more questioning.

However employed, the Socratic method is often criticized. Ralph Nader has called it "the game only one can play," and there have been generations of students who, like David, have wished curses on Dean Langdell. The peer pressures which Peter Geocaris described to my Methods group during orientation often make getting called on an uncomfortable experience. You are in front of 140 people whom you respect, and you would like them to think well of you.

Despite student pain and protest, most law professors, including those who are liberal—even radical—on other issues in legal education, defend the Socratic method. They feel that Socratic instruction offers the best means of training students to speak in the law's unfamiliar language, and also of acquainting them with the layered, inquiring style of analysis which is a prominent part of thinking like a lawyer.

For me, the primary feeling at the start was one of incredible exposure. Whatever its faults or virtues, the Socratic method depends on a tacit license to violate a subtle rule of public behavior. When groups are too large for any semblance of intimacy, we usually think of them as being divided by role. The speaker speaks and, in the name of order, the audience listens— passive, anonymous, remote. In using the Socratic method, professors are informing students that what would normally be a safe personal space is likely at any moment to be invaded.

That feeling might well have made me more attentive in class, but it also left me quite agitated when I went for the first time to take my place in Criminal Law, that day last September. It was a little after 9 A.M., and I hunted down the rows to find my seat. At most law schools, Harvard among them, class seats are assigned in advance. The allotment is random and there is a different seat for each course. Every student's seat number is recorded on a diagram of the classroom which professors normally have before them at all times. Many professors cut students' pictures out of the first-year students' handbook and place them on the chart as well. Students are more easily recognized when called on, and they are also prevented from sitting in the back of the class, out of their assigned seats, a practice called "backbenching."

Seat assignment is a requirement of the Socratic method. The seating chart allows professors to select students freely throughout the classroom for questioning, rather than awaiting volunteers. I understood the rationale, but still I chafed. I was twenty-six years old, a grown-up, and here I was being told exactly where to place my fanny come 9:10 A.M. And beyond that remained the disquieting thought of getting called on, and, even worse, the paralyzing little possibility, no matter how remote, that I might be the initial victim. Ineptness could make me a legend. "Remember Turow? Mann called on him and he passed out cold." I was giddy and ill at ease when I finally took my seat.

As it happened, there was no need for great concern. Professor Mann spent the period making introductory remarks. He called on no one and I'm certain we were all grateful.

About 9:12 he mumbled to himself, "I think we should start." Then he looked at the ceiling and began to speak. He was a man near sixty, quite meticulous, with a large pomp of white hair and a still, humorless face. He wore a pin-striped suit. As he talked, he moved back and forth, somewhat stiffly, behind the podium.

I had not listened to Professor Mann long before I recognized that he was not a great teacher. Given what Peter had said, that was no surprise. It was not any secret that every section was planned so that the distribution of teaching talent between them was relatively equal, which usually meant that each would have its good teachers and bad. Like other academic institutions, Harvard Law School does not place sole premium on teaching ability in developing a faculty.

The men and women who are professors of HLS have proved their brilliance many times. In just a few days, I had seen that they were treated as lofty, superior beings, the students plainly in awe of their intelligence and, especially, of their achievements. Most of the HLS professors are themselves graduates of the law school. Wherever they were educated, virtually all were members of the Law Review, and most also ranked at the very tops of their classes. Many were law clerks to members of the U.S. Supreme Court, a very high honor. After graduation, nearly all practiced law for some time, often with great success, and a number have interrupted their teaching careers at points to take on prominent positions in government—assistant cabinet secretaries, presidential advisors, high-ranking bureaucrats. But the capacity for legal scholarship—the ability to speculate about and research the law—remains a primary criterion for hiring faculty, and publication is indispensable. Bertram Mann, I'd been told, had written a wealth of well-regarded studies on victimless crimes—prostitution, narcotics use, gambling—and after the first hour I became certain that his best efforts with the law were there.

I had been told that he taught as if he were talking to himself; that proved to be a telling description. Now and then he would twist himself around and look at us, as if to make sure that he still had an audience; then he would stare back at the ceiling and continue. His comments were only vaguely tied to each other and every remark seemed offhand.

"Of course, I want you to be prepared each day," he said at one point, "very well prepared. As if this were a tutorial, me and you, me and each one of you. But of course"—he shot out a hand, glancing down momentarily from the acoustical tiles— "of course if you're not prepared occasionally, now and then, why you should come to class anyway; no need to stay away. If it's one of those days, well, then, just say it—just say, 'I'm unprepared'—and I'll give you another chance, in a day or two— soon after that. No need to worry."

He paced, nodding now and then to himself. Eventually he began talking about the course. He said that Criminal Law would be unique in many ways. It was the only course that would concentrate expressly on the relationship between government and private citizens. And he also said that it would be the single class in which we would do close reading of statutes as well as cases. Much of our time would be spent on the Model Penal Code, a criminal statute drafted in the '60s by the American Law Institute, a group of legal scholars, and since adopted by a number of states.

I found Terry Nazzario after class. He asked me what I thought about Mann and I told him you couldn't win them all.

"Seemed like a nice dude, at least," Terry said. "The thing about not being prepared?"

I agreed.

We had half an hour before our first meeting with Rudolph Perini in Contracts. Terry said he wanted to buy a book in the meantime and I volunteered to go with him. I had bought all mine the week before, but I wanted to get a look at the Lawbook Thrift Shop, where he was heading—a store in the law school where used books are bought and sold.

I'd had lunch with Terry on Thursday and had gotten to know him better. The route he'd taken to law school was a lot different than most everybody else's. He was near my age—twenty-five—but he'd finished college only the preceding June. After high school, by his own account, he'd been a "bum," hanging around the tracks, but at twenty he'd gotten married, borrowed the money to open a store selling stereos, and started college at night. He prospered. His wife gave birth to twin boys; he opened a second store and hired people to run both while he transferred to the college's day division, where he did phenomenally well. Last December, a large chain had offered him too much money for his stores for him to turn down.

"We had enough," he told me, "to live good for three, four years. I figured we could do anything—go to Europe, move to California and lay on the beach. But hell, man, I *like* school; I get off on that stuff. I didn't see the odds in grad school. I mean, there're no jobs there and I wanted to be able to do

something besides run a store when I finished. So I decided to
go to law school. After I aced the LSAT, I said, Hey, try Harvard, you're as good as anybody else. And bingo! Donna's parents, mine—man, they think there's something almost wrong,
that they let me in."

He laughed as he told the story. He was tough, proud, fero-
ciously independent, bright with that incredible city quick-
ness. I admired him.

The Lawbook Thrift Shop was crowded when we arrived. It
is run by the wife of one of the law students out of a small office
in Austin Hall and it was full of 2Ls and 3Ls hunting course
books on their first day back. I told Terry I'd wait outside.

I should say a word or two about law books, since they are
plainly the focus of so much of a law student's attention. There
are three general categories. The first are the casebooks, the
thousand-page volumes out of which class assignments are regularly made. The cases in the book are usually edited and have
been selected for their importance in the development in given
areas of the law. In the second category, a kind of academic
purgatory, are the "hornbooks," brief treatises produced by
well-known legal scholars which summarize leading cases and
which provide general descriptions of the doctrines in the field.
Professors discourage hornbook reading by beginning students. They fear that hornbook consultation will limit a 1L's
ability to deduce the law himself from the cases and also that it
will decrease a student's interest in class, since the hornbooks
often analyze the daily material in much the same way that the
professors do themselves. In the final category, the nether
world well beneath academic respectability, are the myriad
study aids, commercially prepared casebook and course and
subject-matter outlines, and other kinds of digests. The best-
known series is the Gilbert Law Summaries. Although law students have gotten by for generations with the aid of these and
other prepared outlines, there are members of the faculty who

claim to have never heard the word "Gilbert's" from a student's lips. Before I started, I myself was somewhat incredulous that students would buy a course guide rather than prepare it themselves. It seemed to border on plagiarism.

Whatever category, two generalizations about law books usually hold true. They are quite large—I'd already had to invest in a big orange knapsack to haul all of them around. And they are expensive. The casebooks are especially dear, $16 to $25 when bought new, the prices probably inflated because the publishers recognize that casebooks are required reading and have to be purchased. Faculty agitation for lower prices would probably do little good and in any event is unlikely, since the professors are most often the editors or authors of the books they assign. In all but one of my first-year classes, the required casebook had been produced by either that professor or another member of the HLS faculty. Used-book exchanges like the Lawbook Thrift Shop are the only means students have to lessen costs.

Terry emerged with a heavy green book which he showed me at once. "Got that yet?"

I examined the title page. It was a Contracts hornbook, written, as was our casebook, by Gregory Baldridge and Rudolph Perini.

"Two buddies of mine say that the dude's whole course is in there," Terry told me.

"He wrote a hornbook, huh?" I asked, still fingering the cover.

"'Wrote a hornbook?' Hey, man this guy *is* Contracts—he is *the* authority. That is *the* hornbook."

"I thought profs say don't read hornbooks for a while."

"That's what they say, man—that's not what people do. At least, that's what I hear."

I shrugged and handed him the book back. But I worried. How did I know what was right? I felt my faith should be in the professors, but I didn't want to fall behind my classmates, either.

"I'll wait," I said.

"Your choice," Terry answered.

"I want to see how bad Perini really is, first."

He nodded and we went off together toward the classroom in Austin where we would both find out.

Most law-school classrooms are arranged in roughly the same way. Broken usually by two aisles, concentric semicircles of seats and desks issue back from the podium, resulting in a kind of amphitheater. In Pound, where we had met Mann, the newly constructed classrooms had been built with remarkable compactness. But in Austin the rooms were ancient and enormous. The seats and desks were in rows of yellowed oak, tiered steeply toward the rear. At its highest, the classroom was nearly forty feet, with long, heavy curtains on the windows and dark portraits of English judges, dressed in their wigs and robes, hanging in gilt frames high on the wall. It was an awesome setting, especially when its effect was combined with the stories we had all heard about Perini. There was a tone of tense humor in the conversations around me, most voices somewhat hushed. As I headed for my seat, I overheard a number of people say, "I don't want it to be me," referring to whom Perini would call on.

I introduced myself to the men sitting on either side of me. One was a former marine from Ohio, the other a kid named Don, just out of the University of Texas. The three of us gossiped about Perini, exchanging what little information we knew. Don said that Perini was a Texan. He had graduated from the University of Texas Law School, but he had been a professor at HLS for twenty years. Only in the late '60s had he interrupted his teaching, when he had briefly been some kind of counsellor to Nixon.

It was already a few minutes after ten, the hour when we were supposed to start. The class was assembled and almost everyone was in his seat. Don asked me what Perini looked like.

"I don't know," I answered. "No idea."

Greg, the ex-marine on the other side, said, "Just take a look."

Perini moved slowly down the tiers toward the lectern. He held his head up and he was without expression. My first thought was that he looked softer than I'd expected. He was around six feet, but pudgy and a little awkward. Although the day was warm, he wore a black three-piece suit. He held the book and the seating chart under his arm.

The room was totally silent by the time he reached the lectern. He slapped the book down on the desk beneath. He still had not smiled.

"This is Contracts," he said, "Section Two, in case any of you are a little uncertain about where you are." He smiled then, stiffly. "I have a few introductory comments and then we'll be going on to the cases I asked you to look at for today. First, however, I want to lay out the ground rules on which this class will run, so that there will be *no* confusion in the future."

He spoke with elaborate slowness, emphasis on each word. His accent was distinctly southern.

Perini picked up the casebook in one hand.

"The text for this class is *Selected Cases in the Law of Contracts.* The editors are Baldridge and"—Perini lifted a hand to weight the silence—"et cetera." He smiled again, without parting his lips. Around the room a few people snickered. Then he said, "Needless to mention, I hope you bought it new," and got his first outright laugh.

"We will proceed through the book case by case," Perini told us. "Now and then we may skip a case or two. In that event, I'll inform you in advance, or you will find a notice on the bulletin boards. You should stay three cases ahead, each day."

Between the desk on which the lectern sat and the students in the front row, there was a narrow area, a kind of small proscenium. Perini began to pace there slowly, his hands behind his back. I watched him as he came toward our side of the room, staring up harshly at the faces around him. He looked past fifty, coarse-skinned and dark. He was half-bald, but his black hair was styled carefully. There was a grim set to his mouth and eyes.

"This class will deal with the law of obligations, of bargains, commercial dealings, the law of promises," Perini said. "It is the hardest course you will take all year. Contracts has traditionally been the field of law of the most renowned intellectual complexity. Most of the greatest legal commentators of the past century have been Contracts scholars: Williston, Corbin, Fuller, Llewellyn, Baldridge—" He lifted his hand as he had done before. "Et cetera," he said again and smiled broadly for the first time. Most people laughed. One or two applauded. Perini waited before he began pacing again.

"Some of your classmates may find the Property course in the spring the hardest course *they* take. But you will not feel that way, because you will be taking Contracts with me. I am not"—he looked up—"an easy person.

"I expect you to be here *every* day. And I expect you to sit where the registrar has assigned you. On the so-called back benches, I should see only those persons who are visiting us seeking a momentary glimpse of something morbid." Laughter again from a few places.

"I expect you to be very well prepared, *every* day. I want to be absolutely clear on that. I have *never* heard the word 'pass.' I do not *know* what 'unprepared' means. Now and then, of course, there are personal problems—we all have them at times—which make full preparation impossible. If that is the case, then I want a written note to be handed to my secretary at least *two* hours before class. You can find her on the second floor of the Faculty Office Building in room two eighty-one."

I wrote it all down in my notebook: "No absence. No pass. No unprepared. Note to sec'ty 2 hrs. b-4 class, FOB 281."

Holy Christ, I thought.

As expected, Perini told us to read nothing aside from class assignments for the first few months—not even "a certain hornbook" we might have heard of. For the present, he assured us, we would have our hands full. Then he described the course in some detail. In that discussion too, Perini maintained that tone of barely veiled menace. We may have been Phi Beta Kappas and valedictorians, but this was Harvard Law School now—things would not be easy.

There were moments when I was certain that Perini was only half serious. There was such obvious showmanship in all of this, the deliberateness of the gestures, the archness of his smile. It was almost a parody of the legendary tough professor, of the Perini of rumor. But if it was an act, it was one which he was determined would be compelling. He revealed no more than a trace of irony and there were often moments, as when he had looked up at us, that he seemed full of steel.

As he went on describing the subjects with which we would soon be dealing—offer, acceptance, interpretation; the list was extensive—I began to think that, like Mann, he would let the hour slip away. No one would be called and we'd all be safe for one more day. But at six or seven minutes to twelve he returned to the lectern and looked down at the seating chart.

"Let's see if we can cover a *little* ground today." Perini took a pencil from his pocket and pointed it at the chart. It might as well have been a pistol. Please, no, I thought.

"Mr. Karlin!" Perini cried sharply.

Nearby, I heard a tremendous thud. Five or six seats from me a man was scrambling to grab hold of the books that had been piled before him, two or three of which had now hit the floor. That, I was sure, was Karlin who had jolted when he heard his name called. He was a heavyset man, pale, with black eyeglasses. He was wearing a yarmulke. His eyes, as he struggled with his books, were quick with fright, and at once I felt terribly sorry for him and guilty at my own relief.

"Mr. Karlin," Perini said, ambling toward my side of the room, "why don't you tell us about the case of *Hurley* v. *Eddingfield*?"

Karlin already had his notebook open. His voice was quavering.

"Plaintiff's intestate," he began. He got no further.

"What does *that* mean?" Perini cried from across the room. He began marching fiercely up the aisle toward Karlin. "In-*tes*-tate," he said, "in-*tes*-tate. What is that? Something to do with the *stomach*? Is this an anatomy class, Mr. Karlin?" Perini's voice had become shrill with a note of open mockery and at the last word people burst out laughing, louder than at anything Perini had said before.

He was only five or six feet from Karlin now. Karlin stared up at him and blinked and finally said, "No."

"No, I didn't think so," Perini said. "What if the word was 'testate'? What would that be? Would we have moved from the stomach"—Perini waved a hand and there was more loud laughter when he leeringly asked his question—"*else* where?"

"I think," Karlin said weakly, "that if the word was 'testate' it would mean he had a will."

"And 'intestate' that he didn't have a will. I see." Perini wagged his head. "And who is this 'he,' Mr. Karlin?"

Karlin was silent. He shifted in his seat as Perini stared at him. Hands had shot up across the room. Perini called rapidly on two or three people who gave various names—Hurley, Eddingfield, the plaintiff. Finally someone said that the case didn't say.

"The case doesn't *say!*" Perini cried, marching down the aisle. "The case does *not say*. Read the case. *Read* the case! *Carefully!*" He bent with each word, pointing a finger at the class. He stared fiercely into the crowd of students in the center of the room, then looked back at Karlin. "Do we really care who 'he' is, Mr. Karlin?"

"Care?"

"Does it make any *difference* to the outcome of the case?"

"I don't think so."

"Why not?"

"Because he's dead."

"He's *dead!*" Perini shouted. "Well, that's a load off of our minds. But there's one problem then, Mr. Karlin. If he's dead, how did he file a *law*suit?"

Karlin's face was still tight with fear, but he seemed to be gathering himself.

"I thought it was the administrator who brought the suit."

"Ah!" said Perini, "the ad*min*istrator. And what's an administrator? One of those types over in the Faculty Building?"

It went on that way for a few more minutes, Perini striding through the room, shouting and pointing as he battered Karlin with questions, Karlin doing his best to provide answers. A little after noon Perini suddenly announced that we would continue tomorrow. Then he strode from the classroom with the seating chart beneath his arm. In his wake the class exploded into chatter.

I sat stunned. Men and women crowded around Karlin to congratulate him. He had done well—better, it seemed, than even Perini had expected. At one point the professor had asked where Karlin was getting all the definitions he was methodically reciting. I knew Karlin had done far better than I could have, a realization which upset me, given all the work I had done preparing for the class. I hadn't asked myself who was suing. I knew what "intestate" meant, but not "testate," and was hardly confident I could have made the jump while under that kind of pressure. I didn't even want to think about the time it would be my turn to face Perini.

And as much as all of that, I was bothered by the mood which had taken hold of the room. The exorbitance of Perini's manner had seemed to release a sort of twisted energy. Why had people laughed like that? I wondered. It wasn't all good-natured. It wasn't really laughter *with* Karlin. I had felt it too, a sort of giddiness, when Perini made his mocking inquiries. And why had people raised their hands so eagerly, stretching out of their seats as they sought to be called on? When Socratic instruction had been described for me, I had been somewhat incredulous that students would dash in so boldly to correct each other's errors. But if I hadn't been quite as scared I might have raised my hand myself. What the hell went on here? I was thoroughly confused, the more so because despite my reservations the truth was that I had been gripped, even thrilled, by the class. Perini, for all the melodrama and intimidation, had been magnificent, electric, in full possession of himself and the students. The points he'd made had had a wonderful clarity and directness. He was, as claimed, an exceptional teacher.

As I headed out, Karlin, still surrounded by well-wishers, was also on his way from the classroom. I reached him to pat him on the back, but I had no chance to speak with him as he went off in the swirl of admiring classmates. A man, and a woman I'd met, a tall blonde who had gone to Radcliffe, Karen Sondergard, had stayed behind. I asked them about Karlin.

"He's a rabbi," Karen said, "or else he trained for it. He was at Yeshiva in New York."

"He did quite a job," I said.

"He should have," the man told me. "He said he read Perini's hornbook over the summer."

I stared for an instant, then told the guy that he was kidding.

"That's what he said," the man insisted. "I heard him say so." Karen confirmed that.

Nazzario came up then and I had the man tell Terry what he had said about Karlin.

"Over the *summer*," I repeated.

Terry glanced at me, probably suppressing "I told you so," then shook his head.

"Folks around here sure don't fool around," he said.

We all laughed and the four of us went off together for lunch. Afterward, I went back to the Lawbook Thrift Shop. I wasn't sure if it made me feel better or worse when I bought Perini's hornbook.

———————

Why did I bother? Why did I care? Why didn't I write Perini off as a bully or a showman? Why was I afraid?

Imagine, is all that I can answer.

You are twenty-six or twenty-two, it makes little difference. Either way you have a stake. You have given up a job, a career, to do this. Or you have wanted to be a lawyer all your life.

All your life you've been good in school. All your life it's been something you could count on. You know that it's a privilege to be here. You've studied hours on a case that is a half page long. You couldn't understand most of what you read at first, but you have turned the passage inside out, drawn diagrams, written briefs. You could not be more prepared.

And when you get to class that demigod who knows all the answers finds another student to say things you never could have. Clearer statements, more precise. And worse—far worse—notions, concepts, whole constellations of ideas that never turned inside your head.

Yes, there are achievements in the past. They're nice to bandage up your wounded self-esteem. But "I graduated college *magna cum laude"* is not the proper answer when the professor has just posed a question and awaits your response with the 140 other persons in the class.

The feeling aroused by all of that was something near to panic, a ferocious, grasping sense of uncertainty, and it held me, and I believe most of my classmates, often during that first week and for a long while after. On many occasions I discovered that I didn't even understand what I didn't know until I was halfway through a class. Nor could I ever see how anyone else seemed to arrive at the right answer. Maybe they were all geniuses. Maybe I was the dumbest guy around.

But I knew I needed help—somebody, something to show me the way through. And if my shepherd was someone like Perini who was also a little bit a wolf, well, then, I couldn't practice much discrimination. For the lambs of this world there have always been tough breaks.

I grabbed at anything which could make the law surer, more clear. I became a kind of instant sucker. The hornbook I bought that first day was soon joined by outlines and prepared briefs on my desk at home. They all sat there, barely opened, for they proved not much easier to understand than the cases. But somehow their mere sight made me feel more at ease. I was suddenly not much concerned about plagiarism or intellectual integrity. I wanted to understand.

Early in that first week I hit on my most bizarre scheme for making things clearer. In one of the student handbooks I had read that there were those who took class notes in different colored inks. The idea had stayed with me because I found it so extreme. Yet by the second day of classes I recognized that my notes looked as if they had been sprayed on the page. So I marched to Harvard Square and bought a number of expensive pens, each a different shade. I did my briefs in black, took class notes in blue. Specific legal rules were inscribed in red and what I couldn't understand was written down in green. I kept the pens, two in each color, in the pockets of my knapsack, where they showed like the arrows in a quiver. Nazzario at once began to call me the "Rainbow Kid." Classmates looked at me strangely. I was not concerned. My notes were gradually beginning to take on some kind of order. When someone would suggest that that was only natural with the passage of time, I would of course agree. But I didn't stop carrying the pens in the knapsack or quit taking notes in black, red, blue, and green.

It's obvious, in looking back, that one of the things which made me feel most at sea initially was the fact that I barely understood much of what I was reading or hearing. Before we'd left for the East, one California lawyer-friend advised me to remember that in many ways a legal education was just the learning of a second language. In those first days, I saw exactly what he meant. What we were going through seemed like a kind of Berlitz assault in "Legal," a language I didn't speak and in which I was being forced to read and think sixteen hours a day. Of course Legal bore some relation to English—it was more a dialect than a second tongue—but it was very peculiar. It was full of impossible French and Latin terms—*assize, assumpsit, demurrer, quare clausum fregit*, thousands more. Moreover, throughout Legal I noted an effort to avoid the normal ambiguities of language and to restrict the meaning of a word. "Judgment," for instance, has a variety of senses in ordinary speech. "What's your judgment of him?" "I think he has good judgment." "He'll come out right on the Judgment Day." In Legal, "judgment" means only the final and determinative utterance by a court on a lawsuit.

And beyond new words employed in novel ways, there was a style of written argument with which we had to become familiar. In reading cases, I soon discovered that most judges and lawyers did not like to sound like ordinary people. Few said "I." Most did not write in simple declarative sentences. They wanted their opinions to seem the work of the law, rather than of any individual. To make their writing less personal and more impressive, they resorted to all kinds of devices, "whences" and "heretofores," roundabout phrasings, sentences of interminable length.

This is from *Batsakis* v. *Demotsis*, the first case we read in Civil Procedure:

" . . . under the circumstances alleged in Paragraph II of this answer, the consideration upon which said written instrument sued upon by plaintiff herein is founded is wanting and has failed to the extent of $1975.00, and defendant pleads specially under the verification hereinafter made the want and failure of consideration stated, and now tenders, as defendant has heretofore tendered to plaintiff, $25.00 . . ."

To wade through stuff like that took time—astonishing amounts of time. Before I'd started school, I could not believe that reading a few cases every day in each course could possibly absorb more than a couple of hours. In the first week, none of the cases was longer than two or three pages, but between the drawing of case briefs and my frequent detours to the dictionary, I did not have a moment to spare. Every instant I was not in class, I was studying—early in the morning, late in the afternoon, far into the night—and always in the fierce, determined manner in which I had begun over the weekend.

And still I was not sure I could get through it all. By Tuesday night, the work had mounted to an alarming level. Wednesday and Thursday were our heaviest days—three classes on each; and Zechman and Morris, both of whom we'd be meeting the following morning, had posted substantial assignments. In addition, there was continuing work in Contracts and Criminal Law; and in Legal Methods that day, Henley had handed out a sheaf of cases on which we'd have to prepare an eight-page memo due a week from Thursday. It looked endless. Annette went to sleep and I stayed up for hours trying to finish Torts.

But, for all of that, I loved it.

That has to be said. "Learning to love the law" is a phrase which, with its undertone of coercion, is used ironically by first-year students to describe their education. But for me it fit. Harried, fearful, weary, I nonetheless never resisted that sensation of being taken, overwhelmed. The sense which brought me to law school, that a knowledge of the law would somehow amplify my understanding of the routines of daily life, was instantly fulfilled. In Contracts, for example, Perini used the first two cases, *Hurley* v. *Eddingfield* and *Poughkeepsie Buying*, to begin an examination of the conflict between personal freedoms and public duties. What kind of obligation, he asked us, should a society force on individuals like Eddingfield, a physician who refused to treat a patient? Were his responsibilities different from those of the Poughkeepsie Newspaper Company, which turned down advertisements without apparent cause? Could a society coerce any commercial relationship and preserve the right of other citizens to do business in whatever manner they chose?

I didn't think those were worthier questions than others which people could puzzle over—when man first wandered through the Olduvai Gorge, or how to build a better carburetor, or whether goods can be moved to Omaha in a shorter time. But they were the kinds of questions I seemed to have been wondering about always and I was exhilarated now by their systematic contemplation. Sitting in class, struggling with cases, talking to classmates, I had the perpetual and elated sense that I was moving toward the solution of riddles which had tempted me for years.

———————

At the end of the week, we met Zechman and Morris. Zechman's Torts class immediately followed Contracts on Wednesdays and that day Perini had held us over the hour. When we

filed into the classroom Zechman was already standing behind
the podium, a small man in a black suit, a series of moles along
one temple and his hair grown long so that it would comb over
the bald spot in the middle of his head. I thought he looked a
lot like the younger Adlai Stevenson.

As the week had gone on, I had gathered more information
about him. He was returning to the Harvard faculty after an
absence of about a dozen years. He had taught at HLS while in
his early thirties, then had moved to one of the English universities. For a few years now, he had been back in the States,
practicing law privately, but his manner remained decidedly
English. He was quiet-spoken, impassive, and somewhat formal. He did not move from behind the podium except to jot
an occasional notation on the board.

Zechman made only brief introductory remarks. He did not
mention the casebook or class preparation. He paused merely
to say that the course would concern legal theory (the broad
conceptions of purpose underlying an area of law) as well as legal doctrine (the structure of rules); then he called on a man far
in the back of the class to state the first case.

"Torts" more or less means "wrongs" and the subject is the
study of the kinds of injuries done by private citizens to one
another for which the law offers relief. In a tort suit, a private
party—the plaintiff—seeks a monetary payment to compensate for harms supposedly done by the defendant. The cases
concern virtually the entire range of misfortune and hurts
which human beings can blame on one another—auto wrecks,
beatings, medical malpractice, injuries from defective prod-
ucts—and the narratives of fact in the cases often offer accounts of bizarre calamities. One of my friends said during the
year that Torts is the course which proves that your mother was
right.

Much of the thinking in Torts revolves around a theoretical
struggle to define the minimal duties which the law should

force citizens to assume toward one another. Just how careful of each other's rights must we be? When we started the first case, Zechman made it plain that the task of definition can be quite perplexing. The suit had been brought by an old woman who had broken her hip when a chair was pulled out from under her by a five-year-old boy who was the defendant. The case turned on the question of whether the little boy had intended to hurt the old woman. The trial judge eventually decided he had.

"And what does the court mean by 'intent to harm'?" Zechman asked the tall, blond man who had stated the case. "Is it the kind of moral wickedness of a man who has a grudge against another and deliberately runs his enemy down in the street with his auto?"

The man in the back said he thought the court meant something different from that.

"Perhaps so," Zechman said, "perhaps so, but what exactly does the court mean then? What state of mind is sufficient to make this little boy liable for battery? What kind of judgment is it that we make? If he's not wicked, why do we blame him? Was he merely not paying attention? Is that intent to harm?"

The questioning was gentle, soft-spoken. But by the end of the period there had been no answers. Nor were there any firm resolutions to the series of questions Zechman put to us in the next few days, inquiries about what courts meant by "negligence" or why the injuries caused by certain kinds of activities had to be compensated, whether there had been negligence or not. How could it be, Zechman asked us, that in some situations you could run a pedestrian down and not pay a penny, and yet be forced to bear all the losses when a toaster which you'd merely sold exploded in a freak accident?

The responses from the class were puzzled, tentative. Zechman would digest each, then frame another question. Usually they centered on elaborate hypothetical situations Zechman had devised ("hypo" for short, a term which for weeks re-

minded me, a doctor's son, of syringes); and the hypos themselves sometimes seemed wildly peculiar, only adding to our
confusion. Was it assault if a midget took a harmless swing at
Muhammad Ali? Was it negligent to refuse to spend $200,000
for safeguards on a dam which could wash away $100,000
worth of property?

When bewilderment on a subject seemed to have peaked,
often with the class baffled into silence, Zechman would move
on to another topic. But he never made a positive statement,
never gave anything which resembled an answer, not even a
hint. He just stood up there in his black suit with an expression of muted concern and kept asking questions; and as confusion grew, so did dissatisfaction. No one was quite sure what
Zechman wanted from us. Were we stupid? Were the questions bad? What were we supposed to be learning? It was almost as if Zechman had set out to intensify that plague of
uncertainty which afflicted us all.

By Friday, the level of anxiety in the class had mounted to a
kind of fury. Most people were willing to agree that Zechman
was earnest and extremely patient. He was kindly in his interrogations. He'd never once told a student he or she was wrong,
and he seemed almost reluctant to call on us off the chart, preferring to question the class as a whole. But a number of people
claimed that they had not taken a single intelligible note in the
three days of class. Karen Sondergard, the tall blonde with
whom I'd spoken after Perini's first class, told me that she had
been so anxious and confused after Thursday's class that she had
gone home and wept. Everyone seemed to have arrived at an assessment like the one that Terry gave me after Friday's meeting.

"The guy can't teach," Terry said. "No wonder they laid him
off for twelve years."

Nicky Morris, on the other hand, was a hit at once. From
the start it was obvious that we would be on a different footing
with him than with the other professors.

"I'm Nicky Morris," he said when he started the first class, "and I'm very glad to be here. I like teaching Civil Procedure." He was the only teacher who took the trouble to introduce himself, although perhaps he did it because there were students in the room who still did not believe he was the professor. When I'd pointed Morris out before class to the man who sat next to me, he'd been incredulous. Morris had been an all-Ivy halfback at Dartmouth and he still looked the part, tanned and trim and strongly built. He came to the first class in a pair of blue jeans and a red polo shirt; his dark hair, although smoothly styled, was long. He leaned against the podium, talking with a group of students, looking like a jock chatting with the cheerleaders as he rested confidently on the coach's Chevy.

In front of the class, he remained casual, hands in his pockets, idly strolling as he talked. It was plain that in this class there would not be the same atmosphere of adversity, nor the same distance. Nicky was young—in fact, at thirty-one, he was younger than two or three students in the section. He dressed as we did. He even spoke colloquially—he said "thing" and "dealie" and "y'know." And besides the affinity of shared manners, there was a subtler alliance struck between Morris and the class. From the start it was apparent that Nicky was an outsider at HLS, just as we were as newcomers. He was freely critical of the law school and of legal education in general.

"You are going to have an enormous power to do bad things when you finish your education here," he said. "When you get into practice, you'll be shocked at the incredible opportunities you have to mess up other people's lives. That's not funny," he told us, "although for some reason most law-school professors don't like to talk about the destructive capacity you'll all hold as lawyers. I hope we can talk about that in here, and I also hope we can talk about some of the good things you can do, which, unfortunately, are often a little harder to accomplish."

As for the running of his own class, it was unorthodox. Morris said that he preferred to select students off the seating chart because that equalized the opportunity to speak in class. But if we didn't want to talk for whatever reason, we merely had to say "pass" when called on.

"I won't hassle you," Morris promised. "Don't feel you have to make any excuses. I don't believe in coercing you into having something to say." The only thing he did ask was that we try not to raise our hands when other students were talking.

Morris had a reputation as a theorist, often high-flown and abstract in his teaching. Civil Procedure deals with the uniform set of rules courts use to conduct their business in all noncriminal actions, and Morris, according to what Peter Geocaris had said during registration week, tended to teach the course as a kind of philosophical inquiry into the nature of rules themselves. But in the first few days he was graciously down to earth. He understood how lost we felt, the struggle we were having with language. Through much of the first session, Morris simply threw the floor open to questions. Most dealt with cases we had read for Procedure, but queries on any topic were in order and it was not surprising that many people asked questions about Contracts, where we had all felt far too intimidated by Perini to risk exposing our ignorance.

And the section was grateful. "I love him," Karen Sondergard told me after our last class of the week on Friday. "He's just wonderful." There was general assent that Morris's class had been a relief. For many of the members of Section 2, their first week as full-fledged law students had not been a period of exhilaration anything like the one I had gone through. A number—even most—seemed to have found it sheer oppression. The work, the pressure, the gnawing uncertainty had been too much. During the week, I had heard complaints of insomnia, fatigue, stomach trouble, crying bouts, inflated consumption of food, liquor, cigarettes. Nor did I feel remote from everybody else's troubles. It was easy to see how my high could have been translated into something as extreme but not as pleasant. We listened to each other sympathetically. That was the one consolation. We were all in this together.

In general, that kind of good feeling had continued to prevail among us, but in the first week there had been some changes in our dealings with each other. For one thing, we were suddenly talking of nothing but law. People stopped asking me about my background or how I liked New England. The classes seemed too stimulating and difficult to allow talk of much else. We were all explaining, comparing, seeking each other's help. Out of class, school became an environment of legal talk, almost all of it well-spoken. I reported to Annette each night my general wonder at how enormously articulate everybody seemed. And people were beginning to inject that new vocabulary into their conversation, speaking Legal to each other. It was strange at first to hear classmates saying in the hallways, "*Quaere* if that position can be supported?" Or employing Legal in other contexts—"Let me add a *caveat*" to mean "Let me give you a warning." People were self-conscious about how oratorical and windy they sounded. They uttered a little hiccup or a laugh when they tried out their Legal, but most of us persisted, practicing on each other.

It was Nicky Morris who most neatly summed up what we were all trying to do in using legalisms. In the last meeting of Civil Procedure that week, a woman answered a question Morris had posed. "The court does not have subject matter jurisdiction over the person," she said.

"I'm not sure I know what that means," Morris told the woman, "but I'm still glad to hear you talking that way. After all," he said, "you can't be a duck until you learn to quack."

9/14/75
(Sunday)

Work, work, work.

I've been at it all weekend, struggling to finish the Legal Methods memo so I can struggle the rest of the week to finish the daily assignments.

I keep waiting for things to relent somehow. I'm blown out. I've never experienced mental exhaustion like what I felt by the end of each day this week. The ceaseless concentration on books and professors, and even on classmates who never went low-key, left me absolutely blithering when I got home each evening. The weekend has not been that much better. I'm still too excited to sleep much and the stuff is always in my head. I feel as if I've been locked in a room where all the walls say "Law."

I enjoy it—I enjoy it. But it's still an emotional merry-go-round. Studying, I often feel as if I'm being borne aloft, high just on the power of enlarging knowledge, making connections, grabbing hold. Then, suddenly, I'm close to dread. Tomorrow we face Perini again; when I picked up my Contracts book, I felt a quiver in my gut. I've just spent the last forty-five minutes marching around the study, rehearsing what I'd say if I were called on for tomorrow's case.

I'm running so hard that I keep putting off even a few minutes for genuine reflection about what I'm up to. I feel as if I am doing some enormous scrimshaw—fine and minute and detailed—from six inches away, without any chance to step back to see the actual design. It's all darkness and eyestrain and a constant chipping away, and I know that the bone I'm working in is my own.

Maybe it'll get easier soon. Last night we went to the orientation dinner of the Harvard Law School Community Association—the married students' group—and the topic of conversation all evening was how hard people work as 1Ls, especially in the beginning. The dean talked about it in the speech he gave, and so did the association secretary. It was the subject of dinner conversation as we ate our meal.

"That first week or so," one man, a 2L, said, "those were the longest days of my life."

A woman sitting at the table said, "Amen."

Amen.

———————

On Monday, Aubrey Drake stopped me in the hallway and asked me if I wanted to join a study group. I had met Aubrey during registration week. He was older, near thirty, and he had introduced himself to me because he had been at Amherst. He'd graduated four years before I had, but we had friends in common and we seemed to take to each other quickly. He was an urbane man, tall, dark-haired, good looking, with a kind of cultivated charm which had been lost on my generation of students in the political chaos of the '60s.

"It's nothing formal yet," Aubrey told me about the study group. "Just some people getting together at lunch to talk it over."

Study groups are another of the basics of the first-year life. A small number of students, usually between four and eight, meet regularly to discuss common difficulties which have arisen with course work. There is no set regime for study-group operation. Some groups merely hash over random questions; others use their time together to work out formal exercises; some spend the year developing long course outlines which are exchanged among group members before exams. Most of the faculty encourage the formation of study groups. They afford each student an opportunity for extensive talk about legal problems, something rarely possible in class. And aside from their educational value, study groups have a kind of therapeutic function, offering a much valued element of stabil-

ity amid the uncertainties of first-year life. The other members
of your study group are the people to whom you can always go
with questions, the only students in the school whom you
know have committed themselves to your support.

As with the prepared study aids which I had been sure I
would be too proud to use, I had also figured before starting
school that I would not join a study group. I was too mature, I
thought, to need that sort of T-group; and besides, I preferred
to do things on my own. By the start of the second week, with
groups forming throughout the section and upper-year students like Mike Wald and Peter Geocaris advising me to join, I
greeted Aubrey's offer eagerly. My only reservations were that I
wanted to be sure there would be room for Terry—we'd discussed a group already—and I was unwilling to saddle myself
with the responsibility of a course outline, a project which I
knew a couple of the groups in the section had already begun,
each member taking on a subject for the term.

Aubrey agreed to both propositions and at lunch, Terry and
I met with him and the other people he'd contacted: six or
seven men and women, none of whom I yet knew well. The
conversation was tentative. In the second week of school,
everyone was naturally leery of a long-run commitment.
Whatever the group would do, however, everyone present
seemed anxious that it include a regular meeting in the hour
before Perini's class to talk over the cases for the day. Perini
was still following that routine of heavy-going inquisitions,
and we all remained powerfully intimidated.

When we met upstairs in the Pound Building the next day
for the first pre-Perini go-round, the group had mushroomed.
It seemed as if each of us had asked along a friend or two and
there were fifteen or sixteen people sitting around a large oval
table. Aubrey found the numbers unwieldy and I preferred to
be in a group that would consider more than Contracts and
erecting defenses against Perini.

By the end of the week, a smaller group had broken away. On Thursday afternoon, the six of us met in the slate-walled lounge in Harkness to work through a statutory problem Mann had assigned in Criminal Law. Aside from Aubrey, Terry, and me, there were three other men. Kyle Schick had just graduated from Harvard the spring before. He was tall and narrow, with a huge corolla of springy blond hair. I didn't know him well—he was someone Aubrey had met. He struck me as a little self-serious and overly ingratiating, but he was also good-humored, quick, and admirably well versed in Civil Procedure, a knowledge gathered in the summers spent working in his father's law offices in Iowa. Sandy Stern had recently finished an engineering degree at MIT. He wore a big walrus moustache and personally had something of the manner of a slow-turning drill. Sandy went straight ahead without self-consciousness or faltering. In class, he had already become quite outspoken. No point was too small for Sandy to give it scrutiny or comment, and always in the same dry, almost toneless, voice. I had no idea how he had arrived in the study group, but once we'd had the aid of his precise analytic skills in working over problems, he became a valuable and accepted member.

Finally, only that afternoon, I had invited Stephen Litowitz into the group. A small, stocky man, Stephen sat behind me in Contracts and I had wanted to get to know him better. We seemed to have an extraordinary amount in common. He'd been raised in the same neighborhood in Chicago as Annette and I had been. He was a Ph.D. in sociology. Like me, he had taught in a university for a couple of years before law school.

The problem Mann had posed for us concerned a complicated hypo in which an accused rapist claimed drunkenness as an excuse for the crime. We were to figure out if such a defense were feasible under the Model Penal Code. The provisions of the code interlocked and cross-referenced so intricately that the job took hours of excruciatingly careful reading, paging back and forth between various sections to reconcile apparent contradictions. It was a wonderful session, though. If I was excited by the process of probing at a legal problem on my own, then I was positively intoxicated by the kind of speed and depth of insight that could be achieved by a group of bright, willing people working together. It was a sort of good-spirited intellectual melee. Except for Aubrey, who was too polite to shout or interrupt, we spent the time half out of our chairs, storming at one another, arguing points—each trying to explain before someone else cut him off.

When the session was over, we were all pleased. We agreed that we were a group, and set up a schedule of further meetings. Sandy and Kyle, who lived in the dorms, went upstairs, and Stephen, Terry, Aubrey, and I sat around for another few minutes. All older, the four of us seemed to feel particularly comfortable together. We talked about what had brought us to law school, each in the midst of another career.

"Man," Terry said, "sometimes I just tell myself, Hey, you didn't wanna be a grown-up. You're not ready yet. You wanna stay loose."

I admitted that I'd had the same thoughts myself.

Aubrey and Stephen, though, disagreed. Each had more tangible reasons for being here. For Stephen, the law degree was a way to find a secure job teaching. Even though he had his doctorate, the academic job market in his field was so clogged that only that kind of acute specialization would guarantee that he could find a teaching position which would lead to tenure.

Aubrey's story was the most interesting, since he had already been through business school and one professional education. In '68 he'd finished at Harvard B School and gone into importing for a while, then opened an art gallery in Los Angeles which specialized in East Asian works. The gallery had folded four years later, but not before consuming every dime he had. So now he was in law school. Aubrey told the story cheerfully. Things, he said, were lower-keyed than the mid-'60s, when many of his law-school friends regularly wore coats and ties to class. At any rate, he felt he could take whatever law school required. He was tired of the boom/bust risks of business. He wanted to work for somebody else with the guarantee of a good living.

When I went home that evening I felt specially satisfied. Not living in the dorms, I had felt, in the first couple of weeks, a little isolated from my classmates. Now, with the group, I knew I'd be having regular contact with some of the people around me. The group met nearly every day. Three mornings a week we gathered to drill each other on the Contracts cases before facing Perini, then on Thursday or Friday afternoon we'd get together for a longer session on Civ Pro or Torts or Criminal.

More important, I became close almost at once with Aubrey and Terry and Stephen. Most often I'd eat lunch with one of them each day. We'd talk on the phone, play squash, often spend time on the weekends. We were frank with each other, personal. The three of them were good friends to me and in many ways they became my year.

Finally during that second week, I began to volunteer in class.

My motives for speaking were complicated. One was a promise I'd made myself. While I was deciding whether to apply to law school, I had made it a point to sit in on a few law classes. When I did, I was bothered by the reticence of the students. One class had disturbed me especially. It was an upper-year Evidence course, and the day I saw it the professor was talking about lawyer-client privilege. The questions he was asking were ones to which even I, as a layman, could have tried an answer. Yet no more than two or three of the students in that room had responded, and by the end of the period I saw that class, stoical, frozen, as emblematic of the state—halfway between being alienated and being cowed—which seemed to have gripped so many of my friends while they were law students. I couldn't understand it and I'd sworn that I wouldn't let that happen to me.

For the most part, though, raising my hand was not the result of any well-thought-out scheme. I am something of a babbler, especially when I'm tense. Outside of class, I was on a kind of oral jet stream, cruising along on my own talk, assailing anyone who would listen, like a drunk on a bus. In class, it was getting increasingly hard to keep my mouth shut. I was so engrossed in each session that I stifled myself only out of fear that I would not perform well.

On the Tuesday of the second week, I finally gave in. It was in Perini's class. We were studying *Hadley* v. *Baxendale*, a famous case which established a limit on the kinds of damages a winning plaintiff in a contract suit could collect. Perini asked us what the rule of Hadley was *not* designed to do. He said there was a one-word answer. People raised their hands offering responses ranging from "work" to "make sense," and Perini toured the room, quickly shooting them down: "No," "Never," "Silly," "You think *that* makes sense?"

When he saw my hand, he whirled and pointed.

"To punish," I said. I was shocked I was speaking. My heart was slamming in my chest.

Perini came closer, tilting his head. "How so?"

"The way the rule works, it doesn't act to punish somebody who breaches a contract."

"What difference does that make?"

"It means that damages aren't awarded to deter breach."

"What are they intended to do, then?" Perini asked.

"Just compensate the loss."

"Right!" said Perini. "Contract damages are merely intended to compensate plaintiff for his loss. You leave all that soul-splitting over punishment behind in Torts and Criminal Law—it's not for Contracts!"

That was the end. Perini was already on his way back to the podium. A trivial incident. Yet I ached with pride. People congratulated me all day. Kyle, a little fulsomely, told me I had seen right inside Perini's head.

In spite of the success of the first venture, I felt ambivalent about volunteering again. For one thing, it seemed a crazy feistiness, if I was scared of Perini and uncomfortable at the idea of being called on, to willingly expose myself to the same kind of interrogation. More important, I'd begun to realize how complicated the personal politics of speaking in class had become.

By the second week, a mood of disapproval had grown up in the section toward any sign of aggressiveness or competitive spirit displayed by a fellow student. Some of that is generational. To want to do better than others is out of keeping with the egalitarian ethic on which most of us who came of age after the 1960s cut our teeth. But part of it too, I thought, had to do with a widespread effort by classmates to suppress their own ambitions. We had all been extremely successful students in the past, but a desire to repeat that success here was not only an unrealistic hope amid so talented a group, but even a dangerous one when you considered the extent to which it could be frustrated. At the end of the term, the professors would examine and then grade us. Given our present incompetence with the law, that was a frightening idea. During the first weeks most people had been struck with the seeming equality of everyone's abilities, and that became an impression many of us were eager to cling to. If everyone was the same, you couldn't come out ahead, as you always had before, but you wouldn't end up behind, either, which would be crushing and which, at the moment, seemed the more real possibility. Parity, then, became a kind of appealing psychic bargain everybody swore with himself, renouncing competitiveness in the process.

I remember a conversation I had with a classmate, Helen Kirchner, late in the second week. She told me she already hated law school.

When I asked her why, she said, "Because the people are so aggressive."

I knew she had been through Exeter and Princeton at the top of each class and I asked if she wasn't aggressive herself.

"I am," she answered, "but I try not to show it."

Trying not to show it became a dominant style of behavior in class. Some people seemed to withdraw almost from the initial sessions. I was surprised a number of times during those first weeks when I'd meet members of the section who proved outside the classroom to be sociable and outgoing. I'd never have guessed that from the look of stony remoteness they had while sitting in class.

The other means of containing competitive feelings was simply to deny them. Many people said they didn't care how they did, what their grades might be, how they were perceived. That was what I often said. Like Helen, those people tended to blame others for the feeling of a competitive atmosphere.

But with the great majority of us, that competitiveness was simply part of our nature. It was what had gotten us through the door of the joint in the first place. There was something, some faith in distinction, which had led us to *Harvard* Law rather than to a less revered school. And we were all gladly training now for an intensely competitive profession in which there are winners and losers every time the jury returns, or the judge speaks. Nor was it unreasonable that we were competitive. Competitiveness had led to recognition and pleasure for many of us in the past; it was an old and rewarding habit.

But we carried those feelings with us at all times. In many ostensibly informal conversations with classmates—in the hallways, the gym, at lunch—I had the feeling that I was being sized up, that people were looking for an angle, an edge on me; I caught myself doing that to others now and then. And especially within the classroom, where the professors' questions acted to pit the 140 of us against each other, our aggressions were bound to be excited, whether they were acknowledged or not.

The only other option in dealing with those feelings was to give in to them—to seek openly to do well and win recognition and favor. Solely the professors had the authority to award those prizes, and right from the start of the year there was a crowd of students, usually the same ones, who rushed to the front of the room to consult with the teacher at the end of every class. But the most obvious way to score with the professor and your classmates was to be able to answer those befuddling questions that were always being asked. By the beginning of the second week there was a noticeable group who seemed to talk in every meeting, people who raised their hands, faced the professor, and proved themselves less fearful and perhaps more competent than the other members of the section. Clarissa Morgenstern had come to law school after the dissolution of a brief marriage. She was still only twenty-three or twenty-four but she was a commanding figure—tall, attractive, and dressed each morning in the best from *Vogue*. She spoke in a high-flown, elocutionary style and when called on she would hold the floor for a lengthy statement, not just a one-line answer. Wally Karlin, inspired, perhaps, by his first-day success with Perini, spoke repeatedly; so did Sandy Stern, the MIT engineer from my study group. Other regulars emerged in the next couple of weeks. And there were also a couple of students from large state universities, so accustomed to succeeding by driving through the masses, that when not recognized by the professor, they would, on occasion, shout out their answers anyway.

In general, those people heard from regularly were regarded

with a kind of veiled animosity. Many people admired and envied their outspokenness, but for the most part, the regular talkers were treated with an amused disdain.

"I can't stand Clarissa," someone told me one day during the second week. "I can't imagine how I'll live through all year listening to her. The way she carries on, you'd think it was opera."

Stephen repeated to me someone else's remark that Clarissa was "a nice guy off the field, but a terror once she gets between those white lines."

Feelings seemed widespread that the people who spoke daily were hotdogging, showing off. They were being egotistical. They were displaying the ultimate bad taste of appearing competitive.

With that background, the idea of continuing to volunteer after my initial face-off with Perini left me feeling a strong conflict. There were advantages. I'd been told by 2Ls and 3Ls that you were less likely to be called on off the chart if you raised your hand. And I'd feel more involved in those large classes if I spoke now and then. But it still seemed childish greed to demand the attention of the professors and my classmates, and given the subtle hostility to everyone who talked regularly, the stakes on performing well were raised considerably. If you spoke too often, or frequently proved uninspired or wrong in what you said, you risked being thought a boor. I felt that way now and then about some of the daily speakers.

And I imagine some people felt that way about me, because in spite of reservations, I did begin to raise my hand often. I fell into a kind of second phalanx behind Clarissa and Wally and Sandy and a few others. I was heard from frequently, but not every day. Yet I never reconciled my ambivalence. Whether I spoke or sat silent, whether I was right or wrong, from the time an idea entered my head until I or someone else had said it, I would sit in class in a state of discomfort.

It seemed a trivial preoccupation, but finally I tried talking to Aubrey about it, since he tended to volunteer as often as I did.

"Two classes out of every five," Aubrey told me at once. He'd worked out a formula, an emotional calculus, to tell him how often it was appropriate to speak.

I had trouble believing he was serious, but he nodded his head. I kidded him a little bit about it, but in the next few days I found myself keeping count.

9/22/75
(Wednesday)

The bad teachers, Mann and Zechman, seem to be getting worse.

Through last week, I tolerated Mann. In fact, I remained somewhat interested in the course. But today I realized that my middling reaction thus far to Criminal Law is the result of what Mann subtracts from a subject that actually fascinates me.

Mann is still wandering around the front of the classroom talking to himself. Half the time his remarks are too disconnected for me to make sense of them, and when I do understand what he's saying I'm disappointed by the sort of cramped, sociological style of his thinking. There are moments when you can see how large and subtle his mind is, but usually he tries to stuff big questions into little boxlike categories. We've spent all this time talking about the use of criminal sanctions in terms of how junkies, madmen, drunks, juvenile delinquents—persons clearly incapacitated—should be treated. Answer? They should not be confined without a fair hearing. Terrific. But what do we do with the unmad, undrunk, unyoung who know what they're doing and who menace us all? How can we protect ourselves from them without losing our sense of principle and decency?—those questions Mann prefers to brush off. Perhaps we'll reach them later in the course, but my impression is that our time for being philosophical is now.

As for Zechman, I'm still lost in there, along with ninety-nine percent of the section. People remain befuddled and angry. Class was called off today and I did not even have to go into the classroom to know. I heard the cheer go up from a hundred yards away.

Last week, we seemed to take a definite turn for the worse in there. Still confused about what "intent" is, we began our study of intentional torts. The first discussed was assault. Zechman took a straightforward case and turned it into a maze. A man pointed a rifle at another's back. The gun hadn't been fired and the victim was unaware that he was in any danger. The court held that there was no assault, which made sense, since there had been no personal injury.

But then Zechman started with his questions.

What if the victim had been facing the gunman? What if the rifle was loaded? What if it wasn't? What if, instead of a gun, a recording of a landslide had been played behind the victim's back? What if the gunman had pointed the rifle at the sky, but fired it? What if the gun had discharged accidentally? What if the gunman had meant to pull the trigger?

No one could even begin to sort through it all. The students again left disgruntled, even outraged, and this time Zechman chose to take notice.

The next morning he came into class and wrote on the board: "Assault: intent to cause harmful or offensive contact or apprehension of that." Facing the class, Zechman strained to seem pleasant, but he was obviously a little bitter.

"I am giving you this definition because the level of anxiety in the class seems to have reached such extreme proportions. I hope you realize how little such a definition tells you."

No matter how little it told, everyone I saw carefully wrote the sentence down. But if Zechman had provided any relief, it didn't last long.

"Now let us commence our discussion of battery," he said, "returning to the gunman of yesterday whom we left shooting at the sky. Let us assume that the gunman intended to frighten the victim and that those actions indeed constituted assault. Imagine now that a duck was flying overhead. The duck was hit by the gunman's bullet, wholly inadvertently, and fell from the sky, striking the victim. Battery?"

For the next two days we talked about that goddamn duck. No answers, of course. No answers!

Amazingly, there are a few people who seem to like what Zechman's doing. I talked on Friday with Leonard Hacker, one of the kids who went to school in England. Len was a philosophy jock at Cambridge and he thinks Zechman is wonderful.

Far more people seem to have given up. There are a number now skipping the cases and reading the hornbook instead, Professor William Prosser's *Handbook on the Law of Torts*, another famous first-year aid, usually known simply as "Prosser." I have a copy I haven't cracked yet, but that may not be true by the end of the week.

9/23/75
(Thursday)

Henley very much liked my memo for Legal Methods. Nice to get the stroking, but after three years as a writing instructor I'd probably have been dismembered if he'd told me I couldn't put a sentence together.

We now have the next chapter in the story of Jack Katz, the fired raincoat-company employee. Henley passed out another memo from our mythical senior partner. Katz has come up with an old letter which may pass for an employment contract with Grueman. It's close enough so that we'll soon be bringing suit in Katz's behalf.

9/25/75
(Saturday)

The student life is still a treadmill, class and books all day, closed up in my study briefing cases every evening. And never enough sleep. The only time I get to see Annette, during the week, is over dinner. On the weekends, thus far, I've managed to take off Friday and Saturday nights for movies, music, restaurants; but even then I'm sure I'm not the best of company. Right now, law's my greatest enthusiasm, yet after losing me to the legal world all week, it's the last thing Annette wants to hear about. Even when she's willing to listen, the strange language and the intricacy of all of it makes it difficult for me to convey just what's so exciting. To A., I'm sure it all seems a jumble and a bore. I continually make resolutions to talk about other subjects, which I somehow never keep.

In those first few weeks, I gradually became aware that second-year and third-year students were moving through a world much different than that of a 1L. Upperclassmen have no required courses and their work load is lighter. Many participate in the numerous law-related extracurricular activities from which 1Ls are usually excluded. Much of the energy of 2Ls and 3Ls does not go into school at all. They are busy looking for work for the forthcoming summer or after graduation, a process with which most 1Ls are not involved.

Yet what made the 2Ls and 3Ls seem most distinct was simply that they had survived their first years. They were initiates, part-way attorneys, people no longer fazed by the things which confused us. All of my classmates seemed to have some second-year or third-year student on whom they relied for advice, and I was no exception.

I often solicited wisdom from Mike Wald. Even more frequently, I would go with questions to our BSA advisor, Peter Geocaris. Peter was a generous guide in acquainting me and my cohorts in our Methods group with the customs of the law school. I was intrigued from the start by the earnestness with which Peter regarded HLS's institutions. Other upperclassmen came on jaded about the school and about studying law. But Peter took Harvard Law School quite seriously.

One day in mid-September I was talking to him about the amazing pace at which the first-year students seemed to be driving themselves, the amount of work we were doing, and the relentless stress we all seemed to place on doing that work well.

"That's what I love most about the law school," he told me. "People want to come here because they think it's the best and they demand the best from themselves. There's a real standard of excellence here, a standard of achievement."

The phrase "standard of excellence" reminded me of a Cadillac commercial and I tended at first to dismiss what Peter had said. But thinking it over, I understood. I had already noted in my classmates, and sometimes in myself, a demand for achievement which went beyond a mere orientation toward success or competition. As Peter suggested, there was something about Harvard Law School which inspired people to use their capacities fully, to do things in a way that would make them proud of what they'd done and of themselves. I regarded that as something affirmative, and in time it was Peter himself whom I began to see as the embodiment of all of that. In Methods class he always spoke of law and lawyer's work as something sober and exalted. He regularly talked of "achievement" and "excellence," and when he did, mention of the *Harvard Law Review* was seldom far behind.

To Peter, the Review seemed the symbol of those things around HLS he most admired, and at times he appeared almost fixated with the subject. In his first meeting with the Methods group during registration week, Peter had explained that he was not a member of the Law Review. I had been struck by his tone of apology, and also that that was nearly the first thing he'd told us about himself. Peter's talk about the Review always sounded that way, half awe, half sadness.

To me as a 1L, the *Harvard Law Review* was an object of deepening mystery. I knew a little bit about it, but I could not understand why the words "the Review" were such a constant, if suppressed, murmur around us. Professors on occasion mentioned "the Review" in class, and there seemed to be an article about the Law Review in the law-school newspaper each week. Before I'd started law school, lawyer friends had teased me by saying they were sure I'd "make the Review." Now and then, even other 1Ls would mention the Law Review. By the end of September, the Law Review had begun to seem the centerpiece of that world of upper-year privilege in which 1Ls were not included.

Finally, one day about that time, Terry and I bumped into Peter in Harkness. I asked him if he'd have time to answer a question: "What's the Law Review?"

Peter looked at me queerly. "It's a magazine," he said, "a legal periodical."

That much I'd come to understand. Law reviews, produced at almost every law school in the country, are the scholarly journals of the legal profession. In the reviews, articles appear which suggest some answer to a particularly troublesome legal problem or which survey a tangled field of law, attempting to set it in some new order. The authors are usually law professors, often members of the faculty of the school publishing the review. Nor are review articles treated as any kind of idle scholarship. I'd already read a number of opinions in which law-review articles were cited as authorities. Because judges and lawyers are apt to rely on them so substantially, review articles are held to an unyielding standard of accuracy. One of the chief tasks in publishing a law review is to make sure each written piece has been scrupulously checked over for errors, right down to the case citations and footnotes—a process generally known as "cite checking" or "subciting." That is a tiresome job, and the reluctance of faculty authors to do that kind of work may account, in part, for the fact that the membership of law-review staffs is made up entirely of students—the only professional journals published by students, as Peter noted during our conversation.

Even knowing much of that, I remained quite fuzzy on many of the simpler details of the Law Review's operation.

"Like how do you get on it?" I asked Peter, after he and Terry and I had sat down together in the lower lounge in Harkness. "It's only 2Ls and 3Ls, right?"

"Right," Peter said, "but you get it for first-year grades." He explained that the top five or six people in each 1L section would be elected the next summer. Then in the fall of our second year, there would be a writing competition for others who wanted to make the Review. "That's going on right now for the 2Ls," he said, "and it's a backbreaker. About ninety people trying—maybe ten, twelve'll make it. At some schools like Yale, law review's all by writing competition, but here it's mostly grades."

"And once you get on," I asked, "what do you do beside cite-checks?"

"Write Notes."

Terry asked what a Note was.

"Sort of a junior version of a faculty article," Peter said. "That's basically it: You're like a junior professor when you're on the Review. You help the faculty with their articles. You do work of your own. You go over each other's work."

"And it takes a lot of time?" I asked. I had heard that.

Peter laughed. "Say, forty, fifty hours a week?"

"Plus classes?"

"If they get time to go."

I said it sounded worse than being a 1L and Peter agreed—much worse. Review members considered a Sunday away from law a cause for celebration.

"So, hey, what's the angle?" Terry asked. "I mean, what do they get out of it?"

Peter shrugged. "Faculty contacts? There are just a lot of things that come your way when you're on the Review."

"Like?"

"Teaching," Peter said. "At all the big-name law schools, you can't get a faculty position unless you were on law review where you went to school. And a lot of them end up with Supreme Court clerkships, too."

A judicial clerkship is a job working for a year or two as a research assistant to a judge. The clerk seeks out the law on various points and helps the judge in writing opinions. Clerkships are prestigious and enviable positions for new law-school graduates, and I recognized that working for a justice of the U.S. Supreme Court would be in a category of its own. Yet to me the rewards of Review membership still sounded meager compared to the obligations, the dry work, and the hours.

"I still don't understand why people treat it as if it's something holy," I said.

"It's an *honor*," Peter answered. "It's the honor society around here. The cream of the cream. The *Harvard Law Review* is the oldest law-school journal in the country. It's respected. It's like being on the Supreme Court of law reviews. If you're a Review member, it just stays with you all your life."

"And did you want to be on it?" Terry asked.

Peter wound his head around, nodding emphatically a number of times.

"Damn right," he said. "I wanted it first year and I didn't get the grades; then I tried the writing competition and I didn't make that. There are even a few 3Ls who get elected on second-year grades, and believe me, I didn't join the Board until grades were out. Damn right. I wanted it," he said. "You will too. It goes through everybody's mind now and then."

Peter's voice had that sorry edge again and his face was clouded and wistful. Watching him, I realized that there was something about Harvard Law School I didn't yet understand. Maybe something to do with all that striving for achievement. Maybe some part of that enemy that my friend at Stanford had told me I would meet here. I felt baffled, proudly remote, and also a little imperiled.

I shook my head. "I can't see it," I said. I looked at Terry and he said he couldn't understand it either.

Peter said to both of us, "Wait."

10/1/75
(Wednesday)

The heavy trucking, conceptually, seems to be beginning in all our courses now. The first three weeks, the professors sort of showed us the blueprint in each subject, the basic principles and terms we had to master before we could understand anything else. Now we seem to be down to actual lessons in how you put the house together. We've moved into the more detailed study of rules in defined legal subjects in each course. In Procedure, we're reading cases on jurisdiction, the very complicated matter of when and how and over whom a court can exert its power. In Torts, we continue with intentional wrongs—assault, battery, false imprisonment—and excuses like consent and self-defense.

As we proceed with that close work, we seem to have started on the traditional classroom routine described by the catalogs and guidebooks. HLS, like many others, is what's called a "national law school." That means that the laws of no one state are emphasized. Instead, by comparing cases from all over the country we are supposed to get a sense for the general thrust of American common law and the typical methods and strategies of legal thinking. It all sounded like a pretty mysterious process to me when I read about it, but day by day the workings of the basic law-school program and the case method are starting to seem familiar.

In Contracts, for example, we are now studying Interpretation, the ways a judge decides what the words in a contract mean. Does he listen to A, who said those words? Or B, who heard them? Does he try to figure out what a reasonable person standing in one of their shoes might think? Or does the judge just take the words for their plain meaning?

The pattern of each class all week was more or less the same. First Perini would call on a student who would state the facts of the case; then Perini would ask the person under fire to identify the kernel issue in the decision. In one case, the plaintiff was suing for ground rent, so the narrower "issue" was whether the word "house" in the contract of sale meant the house alone, or also the land that sat beneath it. With that established, Perini would have the student consider the case's result, asking from whose point of view the judge seemed to have looked at things and what kind of interpretative standard that suggested. Then Perini would ask whomever he was questioning to compare that standard with what we'd seen in other cases. He'd ask the student to reconcile the decisions, to explain the ways they seemed to establish consistent principles of interpretation, and to account for differences through the varying circumstances and facts of each case. For instance, we saw much different interpretative standards employed in cases where the contract was written down, as compared to those in which the agreement had only been by word of mouth. Finally, Perini would touch on what he sometimes refers to as "the deep-thought issues," and what students usually call "policy questions." How much discretion do we want judges to have in interpreting contracts? Too much, and the judge, in essence, can compose the agreement himself, rather than the parties. Too little, and the judge may have to accept without question all kinds or perjury and injustice.

The other professors do not go at things in exactly the same way as Perini. He usually covers only one case a day, practicing on it that kind of step-by-step analysis. Morris goes over a number of cases, setting them out against each other in a far more straightforward manner, doing much of the work Perini demands from students. Zechman usually transforms a case into another of his peculiar "hypotheticals," which he alters bit by bit, question by question, so we can see the way each fact relates to the controlling principle. Mann tends to lecture. But in each course, that process of comparing and distinguishing in order to flesh out the law is usually somehow repeated. In Criminal, for example, we're now deep in the mire of the Model Penal Code and the deadly work of learning to read a statute. Each day, Mann has us contrast the code with cases on the same subject; we compare and distinguish common law and statute, the provisions of state law and the code.

That jigsaw puzzling, case after case, piece after piece, is a far easier process to describe than it is to practice. The common law is crazy and cases go off in all directions. You can never quite jimmy all of them into place. Today Zechman tied the section in knots by asking us to distinguish between two cases with identical facts and contrary results. Two men had a fist-fight. In one case they were allowed to sue each other for battery; in the other they were not because the court considered both to be "wrongdoers." People suggested every trivial distinction to explain the different holdings: One fight had been with bottles, the other with knives; one fight had been during the day, the other at night. Nobody ever hit on the most obvious distinction: The cases were from two separate states, where the courts simply decided the same question in opposite ways. (I got that from Prosser, not Zechman, who left it all in the air—another example of why that class is like a trip on a runaway carousel.) Usually, though, the contradictions are subtler and the patterns are present if you press hard enough. Up and down, back and forth. Hopping from minutiae to the big picture. That process is now fully in gear which is supposed to teach us to think like lawyers.

When we started jurisdiction in Procedure, Nicky Morris made what seemed an important comment.

"About now," he said, "law school begins to become more than just learning a language. You also have to start learning rules and you'll find pretty quickly that there's quite a premium placed on mastering the rules and knowing how to apply them.

"But in learning rules, don't feel as if you've got to forsake a sense of moral scrutiny. The law in almost all its phases is a reflection of competing value systems. Don't get your heads turned around to the point that you feel because you're learning a rule, you've necessarily taken on the values that produced the rule in the first place."

The remark struck a number of people, and as we left class for lunch, I talked about what Nicky had said with Gina Spitz. Gina came on as the last of the tough cookies. She'd just graduated from Barnard and she was full of the bristle of New York City. She was big, feisty, outspoken, and glitteringly bright. But what Nicky had said had touched her in a way that left her sounding plaintive.

"They're turning me into someone else," she said, referring to our professors. "They're making me different."

I told her that was called education and she told me, quite rightly, that I was being flip.

"It's someone I don't *want* to be," she said. "Don't you get the feeling all the time that you're being indoctrinated?"

I was not sure that I did, but as Gina and I sat at lunch, I began to realize that for her and many other people in the section, there was a crisis going on, one which had not yet affected me as acutely.

On one hand the problem was as simple as the way Nicky had put it. Students felt they were being forced to identify with rules and social notions that they didn't really agree with. In Contracts, for instance, it had already become clear that Perini was an ardent free-market exponent, someone who believed that the national economy should function without any government regulation. Perini quickly succeeded in showing us that many of the common-law contract rules reflected free-market assumptions. When he threw the floor open for comment about whether those free-market rules were desirable or not, Perini's fearsomeness made it hard to contest him.

But there was a subtler difficulty in our education, one which went to the basis of legal thinking itself and which became especially apparent in class. We were learning more than a process of analysis or a set of rules. In our discussions with the professors, as they questioned us and picked at what we said, we were also being tacitly instructed in the strategies of legal argument, in putting what had been analyzed back together in a way that would make our contentions persuasive to a court. We all quickly saw that that kind of argument was supposed to be reasoned, consistent, progressive in its logic. Nothing was taken for granted; nothing was proven just because it was strongly felt. All of our teachers tried to impress upon us that you do not sway a judge with emotional declarations of faith. Nicky Morris often derided responses as "sentimental goo," and Perini on more than one occasion quickly dispatched students who tried to argue by asserting supposedly irreducible principles.

Why, Perini asked one day, is the right to bargain and form contracts granted to all adults, rather than a select group within the society?

Because that was fundamental, one student suggested, basic: All persons are created equal.

"Oh, *are* they?" Perini asked. "Did you create them, Mr. Vivian? Have you taken a survey?"

"I believe it," Vivian answered.

"Well, hooray," said Perini, "that proves a great deal. How do you *justify* that, Mr. Vivian?"

The demand that we examine and justify our opinions was not always easily fulfilled. Many of the deepest beliefs often seemed inarticulable in their foundations, or sometimes contradictory of other strongly felt principles. I found that frequently. I thought, for example, that wealth should be widely distributed, but there were many instances presented in class which involved taking from the poor, for whom I felt that property rights should be regarded as absolute.

Yet, with relative speed, we all seemed to gain skill in reconciling and justifying our positions. In the fourth week of school, Professor Mann promoted a class debate on various schemes for regulating prostitution, and I noticed the differences in style of argument from similar sessions we'd had earlier in the year. Students now spoke about crime statistics and patterns of violence in areas where prostitution occurred. They pointed to evidence, and avoided emotional appeals and arguments based on the depth and duration of their feelings.

But to Gina, the process which had brought that kind of change about was frightening and objectionable.

"I don't care if Bertram Mann doesn't want to know how I *feel* about prostitution," she said that day at lunch. "I *feel* a lot of things about prostitution and they have everything to do with the way I *think* about prostitution. I don't want to become the kind of person who tries to pretend that my feelings have nothing to do with my opinions. It's not *bad* to feel things."

Gina was not the only classmate making remarks like that. About the same time, from three or four others, people I respected, I heard similar comments, all to the effect that they were being limited, harmed, by the education, forced to substitute dry reason for emotion, to cultivate opinions which were "rational" but which had no roots in the experience, the life, they'd had before. They were being cut away from themselves.

Many of the people with these complaints were straight out of college. In thinking about it, I concluded that having survived the '60s, held a job, gotten married—having already lived on a number of principles—made me feel less vulnerable to a sense that what we learned in class would somehow corrupt some safer, central self. But there was no question that my friends' concern was genuine, and listening to them made me more self-conscious about the possible effects our education in the law was having on me.

At home, Annette told me that I had started to "lawyer" her when we quarreled, badgering and cross-examining her much as the professors did students in class. And it seemed to me there were other habits to be cautious of. It was a grimly literal, linear, step-by-step process of thought that we were learning. The kind of highly structured problem-solving method taught in each of Perini's classes, for instance—that business of sorting through details, then moving outward toward the broadest implications—was an immensely useful technical skill, but I feared it would calcify my approach to other subjects. And besides rigidity, there was a sort of mood to legal thinking which I found plainly unattractive.

"Legal thinking is nasty," I said to Gina at one point in our conversation, and I began to think later I'd hit on a substantial truth. Thinking like a lawyer involved being suspicious and distrustful. You reevaluated statements, inferred from silences, looked for loopholes and ambiguities. You did everything but take a statement at face value.

So on one hand you believed nothing. And on the other, for the sake of logical consistency, and to preserve long-established rules, you would accept the most ridiculous fictions—that a corporation was a person, that an apartment tenant was renting land and not a dwelling.

What all of that showed me was that the law as a way of looking at the world and my own more personal way of seeing things could not be thoroughly meshed; that at some point, somehow, I would have to *learn* those habits of mind without making them my own in the deepest sense. I had no idea quite how I'd go about that, but I knew that it was necessary.

"Every time we have one of these discussions in Criminal," Gina said, "I want to raise my hand and say, The most important thing is to be *compassionate*. But I know what kind of reaction I'd get from Mann—he'd tell me, That's nice, or just stare at the ceiling. I mean, am I wrong?"

I agreed that she was not, either in predicting Professor Mann's answer or in the opinion she'd expressed.

"It's a problem," I said, and I realized it was one that nobody yet had shown us how to solve.

10/7/75
(Tuesday)

Perini's class remains the biggest show in town. In the other courses the profs have all backed off a little. In Torts or Procedure or Crim no one has been asked to state the case in full since the second week. When you're called on in those courses the professors ask you only a question or two and then go on to someone else, or fill in with their own comments. Nobody likes getting called on. But with Nicky you can pass when you don't want to speak; and with Zechman, now, you can pass when you don't know the answer. You can always tell Mann that you are unprepared.

But in Contracts there are no excuses once you hear your name called, and being selected for the day's case remains a dramatic event. Despite some detours, Perini usually returns to his chosen interrogatee with more questions, so you remain on the spot throughout the hour; and Perini rarely comes on soft or unimposing. The study group continues the furious cramming and rehearsing in the period before the class in case it turns out to be the day for one of us to give the big performance. "The contract was voided for mistake." "No, no, unilateral mistake." "No, mutual mistake as to essence."

There are, however, rewards for being called on. Word is it only happens once. Perini makes large checks on his seating chart beneath the name of the person whom he selects each day. We all have noticed.

The tension in the class is often terrific as we wait to see who the day's victim will be and then what Perini will do to him or her. Maybe for that reason, there is more laughter in Contracts than elsewhere. Also, in fairness, Perini has quite a sense of humor. He is often brilliantly funny, and he can take a joke as well.

On Monday, he was making a point the long way around and he asked us, "Did anyone see the late movie last night?"

There was a spatter of giggling at once, painfully ironic. I think most of us are still too overwhelmed with work to even glance at a television set or the late movie.

From the back of the classroom, someone yelled, "Was it assigned?"

It was the biggest laugh we've had in class all year and Perini laughed along with us.

Today he called on Hal Wile to state *Boone* v. *Coe*, an old Kentucky case. Hal is one of the easiest-going people in the section, but he struggled today, first with his nerves and then with the case. He obviously didn't have a brief, nor did he appear to have read the opinion very well, if at all. He started out haltingly, reading the facts directly out of the book. He said that the parties had made an oral lease for a year.

"Well, that's the whole case, isn't it?" Perini said.

He had a hard look on his face and it was clear that he was angry. The question he'd asked would be a dead giveaway on whether Hal had read the case at all. One of the points later in the opinion is that oral leases aren't valid if made for a year or longer.

The kid beside me, Don, whispered, "Oh, brother." We'd all heard dark rumors about Perini's reaction when he found a student unprepared.

Hal, across the room, was looking into the casebook, desperately seeking the answer. Finally, he looked up and said almost sweetly, "I did see the late show."

The laughter was wild, partly from the relief. Perini smiled a moment, then waited for the class to quiet. He called on another student; but before he did, he got in a line, tart and a little foreboding, of his own.

"Believe me, Mr. Wile," he said, "it shows."

At the start of October, many of the upper-year students began to appear each day in professional dress. The men moved through the corridors in a phalanx of three-piece suits in pinstripe and flannel and the women put on dresses and nylons and high-heeled shoes.

It was interview season at Harvard Law School, the two-month period when representatives of about 800 law firms and government agencies from all over the country arrive to present themselves and to choose the 2Ls and 3Ls who will soon join them. The third-year students were seeking permanent jobs, to commence as soon as they had taken the bar exam the following summer. Most would become associate attorneys in large urban law firms. The 2Ls were looking for summer work as clerks—again, most often in big private firms.

Ostensibly, the job search of the upperclassmen has little to do with the experience of first-year law students. The administration discourages 1Ls from seeking jobs for the summer after their first year, going so far as to deny 1Ls the services of the Pound Placement Office, which coordinates interviews and career counseling for upper-year students. The traditional wisdom is that 1Ls profit by a rest from the law after the trial of the first year. Additionally, many employers are reluctant to hire first-year students because they do not yet know enough law.

Despite those obstacles, most of my classmates sought and eventually found summer work, and many even had interviews at the law school with prospective employers just as the 2Ls and 3Ls did. There were a large number of first-year students, however, who never went near the placement office, and I was among them. I remain unclear on the detailed procedures of interviewing and looking for work.

Yet as I watched my senior colleagues march through the school on their way to the outside world, like many 1Ls I felt my concerns over the future sharpening. I realized that important decisions were hardly as far away as they might have seemed. Though we were still nearly three years away from graduation, in only twelve months my classmates and I would begin our first round of interviews. And at that point we would be looking for more than a way to make pocket money. Traditionally, the job that a student takes for the summer at the end of his second year—the job we'd be interviewing for next fall—is a kind of tryout with a permanent employer. Many—probably most—Harvard students end up as associates in the law firms with which they worked the previous summer. Thus, a year from now I'd need some idea where Annette and I wanted to live and the kind of law I wanted to practice.

Throughout interview season, therefore, I made it a point to talk to 2Ls and 3Ls about the general shape of things on the job front. I learned at once that it was easier to find work in Chicago, Cleveland, Pittsburgh, New York; far more difficult in San Francisco, Boston, Seattle. I also learned that many upperclassmen did not much enjoy the search for employment. Although virtually every Harvard student who makes a serious effort finds work—a remarkable fact given the state of the legal job market—there are nevertheless pains and pressures to the interviewing process. You have to present yourself well in a brief period of time—twenty minutes an interview—and also face the possibility of defeated hopes. There are other tensions as well. Mike Wald, my college friend, had a bad time during interview season while looking for a summer clerkship.

"The atmosphere is really something," he told me one day at lunch. "People go bananas about ZYX firm and XYZ firm. All this pressure begins to mount to take *any* job supposedly 'better' than another. You feel as though if you don't take the 'better' jobs then you're blowing all the advantages you built up by going to Harvard Law School."

I asked Mike what made one job better than another.

He shrugged. "If it's a firm, maybe bigger-named clients, salaries that are a little higher. If it's a government agency, the amount of power it wields and how much of it you'll have when you get there. It's hard to tell, really. All you know for sure is that 'better' jobs go to people with better grades."

One of the clearest messages that emerged to me as a member of the first-year class, just watching and listening during interview season, was of the paramount importance of grades. During the first weeks of school, I had thought that our marks were used only to measure off the lofty types fit for Law Review. But as interviews progressed and upperclassmen talked, it became apparent to me and my classmates that grades were a king of tag and weight fastened to you by the faculty which

determined exactly how high in the legal world you were going to rise at graduation.

"There are firms and agencies which only hire people with
A's, and ones that only hire people with A-minuses, and right
on down on the line," Mike said. "Not all of them are like that.
But grades still count."

That meant there was an undercurrent sense of exclusion
and lost opportunity. A few upperclassmen seemed to feel that
they could not really get the jobs they wanted. And there was
another, equally unhappy group, who seemed to feel the jobs
they wanted were not really there.

Most of the employers who interview at Harvard Law
School are large private law firms. A law firm is a group of attorneys who share clients, profits, and responsibilities, very
much like a group practice among M.D.'s. Firms range in size
from two-man operations to the biggest in New York, Washington, Chicago, LA—some of which employ well over two
hundred attorneys. The lawyers in firms are either partners—
essentially part owners of the practice—or associates, salaried
employees. The firms that interview at Harvard are among the
biggest and best-known in the country, and their clients are often some of the wealthiest and most powerful businesses and
individuals around—people who can pay for highly valued legal services. The big firms usually bill at between $60 and
$100 an hour, and sometimes as high as $200.

There are many advantages to big law-firm practice, especially
to someone coming out of school. The large firms can more easily
afford the time to train a new associate thoroughly; and because
there is often no sharp limit on what clients can spend in legal
fees, the work that is done usually meets the highest professional
standards for thoroughness and care. The problems which are the
mainstay of most firm practices—those of large businesses (contracts, merger or loan agreements, securities matters, tax difficulties)—are at times highly challenging and complex.

But it is not an easy life. Young attorneys starting out as associates usually hope to "make partner," a process that generally takes between four and eight years. For them, the combined effort of mastering law practice and impressing seniors often requires a grueling pace. Many of my friends in private firms think nothing of working sixty to eighty hours each week, and with firms billing clients for fifteen-minute or even six-minute portions of an hour, little of that time is spent idly.

Yet the kind of objections to big-firm practice which I heard from students like Mike Wald really had less to do with hard work than with moral and political values. To Mike, an old '60s activist, it was discomforting to think of being part of a law firm which assisted individuals and especially large corporations whose influence on national life he did not approve of.

"A lot of professors tell me not to worry about politics and just go for the training," Mike said, "but how do you help U.S. Steel hold up a pollution abatement order during the day, then go home and read your mail from the Sierra Club and tell yourself that you're one human being?"

There are alternatives to big-firm practice—"corporate law," students usually call it—but there are difficulties with each of them. Advancement in government practice is limited by the fact that top-echelon positions are usually political appointments. The "White Knight" jobs—working for the ACLU, or NAACP, or public-interest law firms which support themselves by suing on behalf of all citizens, as in consumer and pollution suits—are extremely difficult to get when coming straight out of law school. And the idea of hanging out your own shingle is increasingly unrealistic in these days of lawyer glut and of "firm practice" (which means that as an individual lawyer you can find yourself opposed by a seventy-member law firm that is capable of quickly exhausting you with a series of work-creating tactics). Additionally, all of those alternatives suffer considerably when compared to corporate practice in one area of indisputable attraction to job seekers: money.

Firm practice is lucrative, and right from the start. Mike Wald, for instance, finally split his summer—six weeks in a Legal Aid office on an Indian reservation, six weeks with a Chicago firm. Legal Aid paid him $80 a week; the firm $325. Money was a topic always in the air during interview season, and my mind was sometimes boggled by the numbers I heard. I was accustomed to teachers' salaries. At Stanford, in the English department, a full professor, well respected, after a lifetime of successful teaching and scholarship might have been earning $22,000. That is the starting salary for Harvard graduates at many firms in New York. Moreover, the figure rises rapidly as time passes, especially after a lawyer becomes a partner. The law-school newspaper reported that an informal survey of alumni attending a fifteenth reunion revealed that for those working as attorneys, the average annual income was $70,000.

Considering where I'd been, the talk of all that money sometimes made me self-conscious, even embarrassed. That attitude was not always shared. One day in early October, Aubrey and Stephen and I bumped into Peter Geocaris. Peter was in a suit, fresh from a day of interviewing, and he talked readily about the whole process. Peter wanted to do firm work in New York, where salaries are traditionally highest. When I asked if the amount of money he'd be making ever left him uncomfortable, he told me no.

"I'm worth it," he said. "I've gone to school for a long time, I've developed a skill, and people are willing to pay me for it. I'm not stealing from anybody. I'll work like hell for what I make. I probably like law enough to work like hell for a lot less than what they'll give me, but I'm gonna get it, and I don't mind. The truth is that I'm the kind of person who knows how to enjoy the things that you can do with a lot of money—and dammit, I'm gonna enjoy them."

As first-year students, most of my classmates did not have well-developed feelings on these subjects—corporate practice and money. For most of us the interview season served only to raise those questions in a muted way for the first time. I had a few classmates who expressed a guiltless avarice when they looked ahead. "I came for the bucks," one man named Jack Weiss had told me early in the year when I asked what brought him to law school. But most 1Ls did not see dollar signs whenever they looked into a casebook. A poll taken during interview season and published in the law-school newspaper showed that the 1Ls responding hoped for an average income of $28,000 in their twentieth year out of law school and a starting salary of $13,000. Some were eager for corporate practice, but about eighty percent said they would ideally prefer to do something else—public-interest work, political work, work on behalf of the poor. But many who did not want to do corporate work—about twenty-five percent—expected they would ultimately do it anyway.

That was realistic, because that was where the great majority of us were going to end up. Over three fourths of the members of each HLS class practice with private firms at one time or another. Things just seem to push that way. Some students—many more, probably, than the newspaper poll showed—arrive with a strong interest in business law, and others develop it while in school. And there is a still larger number who come to feel over time that their obligations as attorneys are simply to represent the clients who call on them, without making an extensive ethical scrutiny of either the clients or themselves. For those students, the money, the power, the training, the quality of practice all make joining the big firms inevitable.

But while I watched the interview season from the sidelines, I knew that if I was going to make that kind of conversion, it would not be painless or quick. Like Mike Wald, I'd spent much of my life involved in activist politics—the civil-rights and the antiwar movements, the McGovern campaign in '72. In mellower form, my activist convictions had stayed with me; corporate practice seemed to embrace a regime of power to which I'd long objected.

When we left Peter that afternoon, Stephen said he would never take a job in a corporate firm, that he was heading back to the academy without detours. Aubrey, with his M.B.A., a believer in the proposition that business could be conducted with decency, teasingly told Stephen that he lived in an ivory tower. Stephen called Aubrey a fat cat. They asked me what I felt and I answered that I thought it would be difficult for me to take a corporate job.

"But I don't know," I quickly added. "I feel so damned uncertain about everything I'm doing anyway. Who can tell?"

Later, I thought about what I'd said. I realized that was only the truth. Forced by interview season to look at the future, I was not sure that when my turn came I would be able to sacrifice all the advantages of work in one of the big law firms. But it irked and pained and surprised me that I was already feeling that kind of temptation, that kind of doubt.

10/9/75
(Thursday)

Another crowded week. In Legal Methods we "filed" Jack Katz's lawsuit. Each of us drafted a version of the complaint, and we'll also have to represent the other side—Grueman's— next week and prepare an answer, though God knows where I'll find the time to do it.

Time remains a scarce commodity, and I'm still dragging through the week on five or six hours of sleep each night. The work itself is a lot easier. I can read a case with concentration and need only go over it once, if very slowly, to absorb the outstanding points. But with the increased skill which my classmates and I feel, come new liabilities. The professors are all assigning more work and much of it seems more difficult. In the casebooks, as we go on, it seems as if more crucial material has been edited out of the reports. The other day, in Contracts, we had a case where it was just impossible to tell which party was the plaintiff.

Whatever the burdens, my condition remains good, even outstanding. I am still awfully excited by the law. Increasingly, I can see patterns in what I'm learning, rather than just a series of abstruse doctrines. There are a lot of perpetual paradoxes—such as the fact that the law claims absolute authority, a ceaseless obedience, from citizens, even while it is in a constant process of change. I also see repetitive philosophical dilemmas such as the one Nicky has talked about often: the struggle to design rules which can be easily and equally applied, but which can also be adjusted to allow for what's unique in each case. How can the law be efficient and certain without resorting to flat declarations such as "Death to all thieves"?

The stuff is still in my head all the time, although at moments I wonder if that absorption isn't a little dangerous or crazy. The other day I ordered a hamburger and sat a few minutes earnestly puzzling over whether a contract had been formed and what the damages would be if I reneged. Would the restaurant be entitled to the reasonable value of the hamburger, or their full profit?

A lot of my classmates continue to feel a greater remove from the law and a lot more unhappiness in it than I do. Many more people are enthusiastic about law school than were, for instance, at the end of the first week. But there's also a hard core—at least a third of the section—who can't seem to find a way to enjoy it. Karen Sondergard is still crying almost daily and there are plenty of people who talk about how frightened, uncertain, overwhelmed they constantly feel. Some classmates complain about boredom. Many still bemoan the competition and the hard-driving atmosphere. On those matters, I continue to feel people should be looking a little more honestly—and charitably—at themselves. There are not many of us around there who like to run at only half speed, even though we probably end up pushing each other.

However, whatever their reasons, I know that people are sincere when they talk about how unhappy they are. I've heard more than one person describe the past month as the worst in his life. It's some sign of the crazy intensity of the experience that from my own perspective, I'd have to call it one of the best.

Over the Columbus Day weekend, Annette and I went with David and his wife, Lynne, to upstate New York, where David's family owns a cabin on a lake in the Catskills. He and Lynne had invited us up there to see the fall colors for the first time after our years in California and to take a rest, which we all needed. It was the first weekend off I'd had since I'd started law school, six weeks before.

As we drove out of town, I sat in the front seat with David, talking law. We arrived at the cabin after dark and did not see the hills until the next morning, but as Lynne and David promised, they were magnificent. Maybe nothing but that kind of grandeur would have been enough to remove me from my legal trance. Even so, it worked. We hiked and fished, drank and talked by the fire. We looked around the small, pretty upstate towns and often simply stood dazed by the splendid spread of color across the small mountains.

I had a chance for the first time in weeks to spend some time with my wife. For Annette, it had not been an easy month and a half. She'd started a new job as an art teacher in a grade-school district in one of the northern suburbs. It was an excellent job and she felt lucky to have it, but the work was physically taxing and it left her exhausted. She saw 700 children a week and carried her materials with her from room to room. And I was in no state to help her with the adjustments to a new environment. I was barely there, distracted at all moments and usually studying. Toward me Annette had maintained a generous good humor. She told me she considered this year a period when we were "living on our savings," the fund of love, regard, good feeling accumulated through five years of a good marriage. But despite her tolerance, I knew it was no fun. She was alone and tired, and also stuck with most of the housework.

For us it was important and exceedingly pleasant to have time together again when my head was not boiling over with law.

"You're relaxed," Annette told me on Sunday morning. "I wasn't sure I'd ever see you this way again."

She was right. I was somewhat amazed, just by the changes in my physical state. I felt slower, stronger, more substantial. I had slept. My stomach was not perpetually clenched. My pulse seemed less violent. I did not feel always on the verge of a light sweat. I realized for the first time how great the pressure was which I'd been under. I was a different person here, the man I'd been six weeks ago. I thought about different things. I was not trying to keep my language precise, or analyzing every spoken proposition to find its converse. I could look at mountains as well as words and books. I could live with nothing but the dull gray buzz of tranquillity passing through my head.

"I've stolen away from the brain thieves," I told Annette.

With Lynne and David, we had a late breakfast, then read the Sunday *Times*. In the afternoon, the four of us began a climb of the hill behind the cabin. We passed through a stand of small trees and Annette and Lynne, who'd come out in loafers, didn't think they could go on without something to grasp for support. They headed back to the cabin and David and I continued on toward the crest of the hill.

From the top you could see the whole valley: the lake under clouds, a rich gray like slate; the hills brilliant with color. We sat quiet, watching. I thought again how peculiar the demands I'd made on myself all these weeks seemed from here. Achieve, succeed, do and be excellent. It was a kind of madness. What was going on? What the hell was I doing to myself?

I asked David how he'd describe his state of mind during his first year of law school.

"Looking back," he said solemnly, "I think I was crazy."

"I think I am too," I said.

"Well, don't worry about it," he answered, "it always seems to pass, and around the law school, no one will ever notice. People there would all tell you the same thing." David hoarsened his voice in imitation of an unknown elder and clapped me once soundly on the back. "'My boy,'" he said, "'you're just learning to love the law.'"

OCTOBER AND NOVEMBER
Disgrace

10/18/75
(Saturday)

Law school seems now to be entering its second phase. The zing of the first few weeks, the exhilaration at the mammoth complexness of the law, and the brilliance of classmates have started to dissipate. The dimmer aspects of law-school life begin to make themselves apparent. Which is not to say that school has become boring—only that there is a balance emerging, albeit one I still find greatly favorable.

Within the section, relations seem to have regularized, much as do those in any large group. Having been in class, having recognized mutual ignorance and fallibility, has made us all a little less awed by each other and consequently a little less attracted. For the most part, an atmosphere of modesty and bonhomie has taken over. We no longer see one another as the unknown objects on which all the splashy accolades and achievements were displayed like the tour decals on luggage. Dealings are more personal, and we feel for each other the normal range of attractions and aversions. There are a few in-section romances, many growing friendships. I've become increasingly close to Steve Litowitz. We spend a good deal of time with one another during the day, walk together to the Harvard Square bus station in the late afternoon, even hang on the phone like high-schoolers in the evening. I admire his wit; and being almost from the same pod, we seem to react to most things the same way.

The work is still there, crushing in amount and far from easy. In Legal Methods, the assignments continue to pile on. Soon we will face our big project in there: drafting a brief in support of a motion for summary judgment in the Jack Katz case. In the regular courses, I feel a growing resistance to a number of things. There is only one class about which I have no complaints. Incredibly, that's Torts. For two or three weeks now, my affection for William Zechman and the subject he teaches has been growing. It started while we were studying consent, the defense in which the defendant maintains there was no wrong because the plaintiff agreed to the activity which caused his injury. Befuddlement in the class had hit such a high level that it had been transformed into a kind of hopeless boredom. The woman who sits beside me was discreetly reading a newspaper. The man on the other side was groaning for diversion: "If he'd just move," he'd whisper, looking down at Zechman, frozen behind the podium. "*Move.*"

I was not much happier. Him and his goddamn questions, I thought, his crazy hypos: If battery is a mere offensive touching, is it battery to kiss a woman good night, if she demurely says no? To push a man off a bridge that's about to collapse? Or does consent somehow cure those wrongs?

I wondered when he would cut it out. There was no answer to these questions. There never would be.

I sat still for a second. Then I repeated what I'd just thought to myself: There were no answers. That was the point, the one Zechman—and some of the other professors, less tirelessly— had been trying to make for weeks. Rules are declared. But the theoretical dispute is never settled. If you start out in Torts with a moral system that fixes blame on the deliberately wicked—the guy who wants to run somebody over—what do you do when that running down is only an accident? How do you parcel out blame when A hopes to hurt B in one way— frighten him by shooting a gun—and ends up injuring him in another freakishly comic manner—clobbered on the head with a falling duck? How far do basic moral notions carry you? At what point do you have to say, It's nobody's fault, life is tough?

With the realization that I was not missing some clear solution to all of the problems, Zechman's class suddenly has begun to make sense. I now see him as a sort of jeweler of ideas. He uses his questions like a goldsmith's hammer, working the concepts down to an incredible fineness and shine.

Not all of the people in the section yet share my enthusiasm. The man and woman on either side are still groaning and reading respectively. Nazzario is also displeased. "The dude's on some philosophical trip I can't handle," Terry told me last week. But I think there's now a majority of us who relish the class. I'm often so excited that I literally cannot sit still. We're back there in the second-to-the-last row, the woman reading, the man groaning, and me bouncing up and down in my seat.

The other classes, unfortunately, are not going as well. In Criminal, Mann is near to intolerable. He plods straight ahead like some kind of bewildered plow horse, each class a trudging comparison of the case law and the code. And when my objections are not to bad teaching, they seem to be to the professors personally. Like my classmates, the teachers are becoming known quantities—people now, and not deities—and I have developing feelings about each. Perini is still brilliant in class. He picks students' minds like a clairvoyant and I give him the prize as the best lecturer I've ever heard. We've started the "basic triad" of contract law—offer, acceptance, and consideration, the three elements required to form a binding obligation—and Perini has shown a wonderful finesse in presenting those hard ideas. But the atmosphere he creates in the classroom strikes me as more and more objectionable.

"Monday, Tuesday, Wednesday, the mornings we have Contracts, I got on the bus in Watertown and I'm nearly sick to my stomach," Stephen confessed to me on the phone last week. "I can't believe it, but I think about that class and I get ill. And when I walk out of there on Wednesday, I feel as if the week is already over."

The same sort of thing can be said for almost everyone in the section. What bothers me most is that Perini seems to recognize our discomfort, and takes it with something only a little short of glee.

Even Nicky Morris has started to get on my nerves. I'm grateful for his easygoing manner in the classroom, but there are moments when that gentleness seems less friendship than condescension. We're still doing jurisdiction over the person, a topic which has mushroomed in complexity as we've gone along. Historically, courts could assert their power only over persons found inside the state where the court sat. These days a precarious weighing of subtle factors takes place to determine how far that power can extend. Sometimes in explaining that process, it seems that Nicky is trying to be deliberately confusing. When the class does not understand, he can then address us in that increasingly familiar tone which suggests that not only are we people far less knowledgeable than he, but also substantially less intelligent. The thought has crossed my mind that Nicky, the famous football competitor, came to teaching seeking a field on which he could always win.

Reading all of this over, it sounds as if I am totally bummed out. That is not so. I still feel plenty of that thirsty pleasure in school. I've just begun to recognize the bad with the good—a balance, as I said at the start. I suppose the task of the next few weeks will be to adjust to those small disappointments I'm starting to feel.

Sooner or later, I had to touch down. For six weeks, I had been swooning and careening like some sky-dazed hawk, and my Columbus Day weekend away from the law had shown me how perilous and crazy that flight sometimes had been. I couldn't go on asking that much of myself. I had to ease off. Settling back in on the following Tuesday, concentrating, scrutinizing, pressed at again by that atmosphere of tense precision, I'd actually become dizzy and a little bit ill.

As I moved through those middle weeks in October, a lot of things were serving to sober my mood. That gray cap which hovers over Cambridge at least six months a year had begun to appear. The squirrels were burrowing, storing nuts. Winter, cold and slushy and despised—the first this temporary Californian had been through in five years—was nearing. And in retrospect, to a far greater extent than I then recognized, I see that the warnings I gave myself when we were in the mountains came too late. I had simply burnt myself out. The initial strength and enthusiasm I'd brought to law school had been spent and I had no reserves left. I was exhausted, still under the same pressures, and, in consequence, occasionally gloomy.

I was also increasingly vulnerable to a lot of things I'd suppressed. In the first weeks I'd recognized many troubles without allowing them to alter my prevailing high mood—the sacrificial demands of the achievement ethic, the personal changes forced by the education which Gina had pointed to, the self-doubt I felt during interview season. Now all of those things, and a series of new but similar realizations, began to have an impact. I also had to deal with the plain fact that the new shine had worn off. For my classmates and myself, there'd been a stunning gain in knowledge and competence, but in the process, the thrilling mystery of the law had started to dissolve.

All in all, my expectations were changing, but the sane and prudent tone I struck in my journal—saying that I would have to "adjust" to "small disappointments"—masked a wildness and bitterness and lack of control in my feelings which would intensify in the coming weeks, and had to an extent already set in.

Many of the things I felt during that period were unique to me, the result of my personal lunacies, but a sense of spirits stepping down seemed widespread. Most of us in Section 2 appeared to take on a sort of sullen grimness about what we were doing. A few people seemed to develop strength from the emerging routine and ground ahead remorselessly, but the more common reaction was the beginning of an active resistance to law school and its demands. No one quit, of course. In the first weeks of the term, one man, always gently complaining about how perplexed he felt, had withdrawn. That is not unprecedented. Each year, two to three percent of the entering class leaves. The reasons vary: marriage, illness, determinations by students that they're simply not cut out for the law. Some persons in each of those categories eventually return.

But in Section 2, virtually everyone decided to stick it through. They all wanted to be lawyers, I guess; and besides, almost all of us had arrived prepared for exactly the kind of emotional letdown we felt by the middle of October. We all had friends who'd gone to Harvard Law School and who'd issued grim reports. We'd chosen to come anyway. Perhaps the expectation of difficulties hastened trouble's arrival.

Whatever the source, many were displeased enough to become slightly uncooperative. Attendance, though nominally required, began to fall off in each of the courses, especially Mann's, where it was frequently down as much as fifteen or twenty percent for each session. Except in Perini's Contracts, where it was not permitted, backbenching had also become common. Every time a class met, between six and a dozen people were located in the rear seats—that lost world not mapped on the seating chart.

Terry was one of those who began to show up irregularly and to backbench when he did come.

"I just can't sit still, man," he told me. "I'm tired of those guys talkin' at me, tellin' me how to think. I've gotta do it my own way."

To me the most dramatic sign of the changing attitude among students came one day in Torts in mid-October. Zechman was talking about conversion, one of the tort remedies for theft. If a car thief makes off with your Chevy, you can sue him civilly for conversion, even if he's criminally tried for joyriding. Zechman described the tort as a "judicially-enforced sale," meaning that the thief would keep the car and you would get what it was worth—a valuable option if the joyrider had, for instance, cracked up your Chevy on his tour through the neighborhood. It was a point many of us had missed.

From the center of the classroom, one man called out, a little belligerently, "Where do you get that from?"

Zechman was normally inordinately polite to us, but I guess that remark struck him as a breach of decorum. He looked icily at the student and said, "When you get a chance sometime, read the cases."

It was quick and snide. Some people laughed, but after a few seconds a rattling hiss spread from various parts of the room. Hissing the speaker for a disagreeable comment is an old Harvard habit, practiced throughout much of the university.

It's imported to the law school each year by those 1Ls who were undergraduates at Harvard College and it had been quickly picked up in my section. Until that day in the middle of October, hissing had been reserved for fellow students, usually when the speaker's remarks were politically conservative. (Most of the hissers seemed to be leftwing.) But after that day when Zechman was treated to it, hissing became a piece of student weaponry frequently used against the faculty, most commonly when a professor dismissed a student's comments unfairly or said something hardhearted. Usually, the teachers accepted the hissing with a dim frown or a weak attempt to justify their remarks.

There was more and more of that mood of open confrontation. In the first few weeks many of the students who were uncomfortable or unhappy had assumed that it was their fault, that they were somehow incompetent. Now they seemed to stop blaming themselves and were pointing the finger at the institution and the educational style. The Socratic method, they said, was unfair and intimidating. In class we learned too much raw technique with too little attention to the ethical duties lawyers owed the society. And the atmosphere around HLS was often bitterly deplored—a robot factory, people began to call it; a legal pressure cooker.

As often as not, the most vigorous in their criticisms were the members of the Harvard Law Guild, a student organization dedicated to progressive reform in the structure and educational format of the law school. The Guild had held an organizational meeting early in the year, and many of the men and women of the section had joined. Kyle, the fuzzy-haired Harvard grad in my study group, was a member. So was Helen Kirchner, the woman who'd complained about the aggressiveness of our classmates. There were quite a few other Guild members in Section 2. Most of them, during the first weeks, had been somewhat circumspect, usually sharing their complaints only with each other. But as the mid-term mood of displeasure made itself more apparent, the Guild members, sensing a more hospitable environment, tended to speak up frequently. Occasionally they challenged the professors in class, especially Mann, who often assumed moderate or conservative positions on loaded subjects such as sentencing, bail reform, white-collar crime.

The most outspoken of the Guild members was Wade Strunk. Wade was from Alabama and he made a paradoxical radical. He was mannerly, precise. He wore his hair short and he was usually very well dressed. He often had on expensive foulards and designer shirts, and his accent sounded of all the luxury and graciousness of a bygone southern age. But he was unstinting in his criticism of the law school.

My first brush with Wade came late in September. On Thursday and Friday, Torts and Civil Procedure met in the same room in Langdell and there was a half-hour break between classes. After Torts, one man who sat near me asked if I thought it would be safe to leave his books. I said I was sure it was, that none of our classmates struck me as the thieving kind.

Wade, standing nearby, overheard.

"These people here?" he asked at once. "Why, half of them are thieves already and don't know it. Three years from now they'll be working for these big corporate law firms whose fees are paid by nothing much better than thieving. Plenty of them are stealing right now. My teaching fellow's briefcase was ripped off right out of his office."

I wasn't sure Wade was serious. I said to him that this was a large school and that there were probably a few people here capable of anything. And there was no question that in the future some good people might become trapped in bad institutions.

"But you don't really think everybody here is a bad guy, do you?" I asked.

"Absolutely," Wade answered. "Most of them. Most of them are quite corrupt."

Many of Wade's classmates held an equally charitable view of him. By the middle of October, there were a number who snickered out loud every time Wade spoke in class. We all knew it was going to be the same dime-store Marxism, a description of how the particular doctrine we were studying had been laid down for the protection of the upper classes and their wealth. After one of Wade's more unreasoned outbursts, one of the wryer members of the section approached me at the end of class. He nodded toward Wade, expensively dressed as ever, and said, closely imitating Wade's accent, "Aftuh the revolution, ever'one will wear Yves St. Laurent."

Yet by the middle of October, I'd begun to pay more attention to all of the Guild members, even to Wade, who I knew was made silly only by passion and real concern. I felt some caution toward the people in the Guild. They were kids from Harvard and Yale, Park Avenue and Beverly Hills, who would lecture you freely on the plight of the poor. But I admired their forthrightness, and as time went on, I'd become less certain that whatever else could be said of them, I'd call them entirely wrong.

10/21/75
(Tuesday)

A difficult day. A disturbing incident at lunch.

For a while, I've felt that there's a cohesion lacking in my studying and it has seemed to me that the study group could help provide some focusing. In talking it over, I found that everyone else felt the same way. It seemed time for a meeting, to see if we could hash over the problems with the study group and consolidate purposes, and so, with the exception of

Stephen, who had a date for lunch, we all got together at noon.

The complaints about the group came out at once: too disorganized, too uncommitted, rudderless, overaggressive in discussion (Aubrey's point, aimed at me, I think), and too many people.

That last was Kyle's complaint, and he kept hammering at it.

"We've got too many people. We can't have effective discussions. We can't concentrate on anything. We're going to keep BS'ing." Finally, Kyle said, "We've got to narrow the group to four people, five at the most."

The suggestion pretty plainly was that we throw somebody out, and it offended me. I was telling Kyle exactly that when Sandy Stern, guileless or guilty, suddenly spoke up.

"You're not going to throw me out, are you?" Sandy asked. "Not just because I'm in two groups?"

Two? we all asked. Sandy quickly admitted that he was part of another group which had been busy all term outlining courses and preparing review notes. He had joined our group too, he said, because we seemed more interested in high-minded, speculative talk about the law, which he felt was missing in the other.

"Hey," Terry told him, "we don't wanna do that kind of jiving around anymore. We wanna start putting it all together now."

Sandy refused to take the hint. He sat there pulling at his big scraggly moustache and proposing compromises: One day, with him present, we could speculate. On a second, without him, we could review. As a last hope, he even offered to make copies for us of the outline he was preparing for the other group.

It did no good. Kyle, pointedly, kept repeating. "Somebody's gotta go, someone *has* to."

I told Sandy that it should be his decision. I said that I was against his sudden exclusion and that if he wanted to stay it would be okay with me, but I also told him that I felt it had been deceptive to conceal his membership in the other group, and that so far as I knew, everyone always assumed study groups were exclusive.

Sandy debated my points but finally said that he would do whatever we preferred. Aubrey seemed to hold the crucial weight and he shook his head no. He had wanted a smaller group from the start.

With apologies issued all around, Sandy gathered his books and departed. We stayed to plan further activities for the group. But the whole event stayed with me all day. I felt a frustrated pity, angered by Sandy's obtuseness but ashamed that we had been so hard-nosed as to boot him. What difference is it to us really if he thinks he can handle being in two groups? I was disturbed by what had emerged in each of us. Kyle had been ruthless and Aubrey a little matter-of-fact. Terry all along was bothered by Sandy's mincing way and was visibly anxious to have him gone. I had hardly been stalwart in defending Sandy's right to stay.

When I told the story to Stephen tonight on the phone, he was dismayed.

"That goddamn Kyle," he said.

I admitted that none of us had been shown to much advantage this afternoon. I'm beginning to get some idea of what might be involved in meeting my enemy.

"Yes, Mr. Turow?" Professor Mann said, looking down at his seating chart to be certain of my name.

It was the fourth week in October, and we were discussing inchoate crimes—crimes attempted or solicited, but never completed. The case concerned a man who'd come into a bar, drunk and obviously disturbed. He'd brandished a gun, threat-

ened a number of patrons, and finally, with the gun at the bar-
tender's head, had pulled the trigger. The gun had not gone
off. Mann had asked us how the case would be classified under
the Model Penal Code. The members of the section had paged
through the code and come up with various suggestions: assault, attempted murder. Mann himself had asked if this were
possibly attempted manslaughter. I had the answer to that, a
very clever one, I thought, and raised my hand.

"It can't possibly be attempted manslaughter," I said. "Attempted crimes have to be intended and manslaughter's an un-
intentional offense."

People smiled around me. I heard somebody say, "Ah!" I'd
got it. A good point.

Mann glanced down from the ceiling and looked at me
kindly.

"Don't you hear the wind whistling behind you?" he asked.
I froze.

"I'm afraid you've gone through the trapdoor," he said, and
as I sank lower in my seat, he explained that an intended attempt at murder, given mitigating circumstances like drunkenness or insanity, could be classed as attempted manslaughter
under the code.

I'd made a mistake. It wasn't the blunder of the year, but I
felt horribly embarrassed—worse than that, corrosively
ashamed. This seemed to be happening to me a lot recently—
raising my hand to say things which were somehow inappropriate or flatly wrong. And none of us found it easy to endure
our classroom errors, let alone on a regular basis.

"Isn't it awful?" Stephen asked me one day after he'd muffed
an answer in Civil Procedure. "I haven't felt that bad in years."
Gina said she brooded on her mistakes for hours.

As the year had worn on, classroom performance had assumed an increasing importance. We now engaged in close as-
sessments daily of how well people had done in class, especially

when they'd been called on, almost as if it had been an athletic event. "Jack was terrific today." "Yeah, but I felt bad for him when Perini nailed him on that question. McTerney really saw that all the way. She *is* smart."

The reasons we all put that kind of stock in what happened in class were complex. Superficially, I suppose it was no more than a further sign of how competitive we were with each other. But there were a number of environmental effects which had recently begun to exaggerate the drive and ambition within each of us. For two months now we had all been doing exactly the same things day in and day out, listening to the same professors, doing the same reading, making the same discoveries. Moreover, there was little time to find more personal outlets outside of school. For many of us, then, the feeling had grown pronounced of being faceless, lost in the mob—and the only kind of distinction available was to be known as good, bright, quick, adept with the law. Thus a striving for a sense of identity began to be mixed in with our hopes for success.

That, in turn, led to another problem. As students became more desirous of doing well, they could only grow more conscious of the fact that there was now no sure indication of how much or how well they were learning. Though we'd all been working like Trojans for a couple of months, none of us could even be sure that we'd pass each course. Obviously, odds were in our favor. There are few Fs given at Harvard Law School. Forty years ago a third of the entering class would flunk out, but these days almost no one leaves for academic reasons. Nevertheless, considering the difficulty of the material, the possibility of something close to failure, however remote, sometimes invited contemplation. Though I wanted to do well, for me, and I imagine for others, the less clear my standing became the more my fantasy cycle intensified at the darker end—a few thoughts of wild success obliterated by panicked visions of being thrown out in the street.

The only end to that fear of failure would come when we were examined in January. There would be no grades until then, and the single test would be the sole basis for determining marks in each course. Longing perhaps for the assurance exams would provide—and also hoping to lay the ground for good results—many people, even at the end of October, had begun pointing toward the tests. In the meanwhile we looked wherever we could for signs that we were holding our own. People who had high LSAT scores often speculated about whether the correlation between the test and law-school grades would hold true for them. On a number of occasions I was told that because I was older and married, I was certain to rank high in the section and there were many moments when I half-heartedly repeated that wisdom to myself.

But it was in the classroom, with the 140 of us together facing the professor, that exam competition was most closely simulated; and it was to what happened there that we gave the greatest weight. The more people tended to see classroom performance as an index of standing, the more pressed we all felt to do well. The unofficial ban on outside research had been inadvertently lifted one day early in October when Sandy Stern had raised his hand in Contracts. We were studying a case about a Pennsylvanian who had volunteered for service in the Civil War. He promised he would send his wife a living allowance of $20 a month while he was away, but he had never paid it. The wife sued for breach of contract and lost. Perini used the case to illustrate the differing ways in which courts treat agreements between family members compared to agreements between persons in business—a theme he returned to often during the year. Sandy, however, had gone far afield.

"I have an interesting note on this case," Sandy said. "I thought that since the husband had served in the Union army, he would have a Civil War pension, and that if he had died his wife might have received something anyway. So I went to

Widener and found the official roll of U.S. Civil War pension-
ers and sure enough, in 1877 Mrs. Tish, as survivor, began to
receive eight dollars a month."

The reaction from the class to Sandy's historical probing was
a mixture of outraged laughter and the inevitable hissing.
Perini, who'd already found that Sandy's straightfaced dogged-
ness made him the perfect foil, said that he was disappointed—that he'd have expected Sandy, being Sandy, to make
a trip to Harrisburg to see if Mrs. Tish's aggrieved ghost wasn't
still stalking the graveyards.

Yet despite the humor with which Sandy's efforts were received, it became clear within a few days that they'd served to
declare open season on outside work, a month ahead of schedule. A number of people now admitted delving into Perini's
hornbook, and most reported that much of Perini's classroom
commentary seemed to come from there directly. Many men
and women began to treat the hornbook as part of the required
reading, in hopes of doing well when called on. Even more dis-
concerting, I suddenly heard that a number of classmates had
been observed in the library reading law-review articles, sections of the treatises, the illustrative cases noted in the casebooks.

"I don't know what those guys think they're proving," Tony
Dawes, a classmate, told me one day when I saw him in the
library. Tony had regularly studied near the reserve section
where the treatises were located and he was telling me about
the sudden rush of people from Section 2 who'd begun to appear there. "These professors aren't dumb. They know what
those people are up to. It'll all come clear at the end of the
year. None of 'em are gonna get any better grades than the rest
of us."

Not everyone was convinced that what Tony said was true.
Many people felt a new pressure to consult sources other than
the casebook, and to put even more time into study. Often I

heard tales of students who appeared to those who knew them well to be doing nothing but law 20 hours a day, 140 hours a week—types who were in the library the moment it opened, or who broke their study in their dorm rooms only for half an hour of dinner each night, people who went over their class notes at the end of each day and typed all of them up over the weekend. Those stories were frightening. A standard was being set that not all of us could match. People were getting ahead, it seemed. People were falling behind.

Certainly in class it was beginning to appear that in spite of all initial impressions of parity, there really were some people who had an edge. We had all heard stories about students magically able in the law who appeared on rare occasions like a showing of the northern lights, the kind who would make straight A-pluses on their exams. Some of our professors were said to have been students like that, and we often shared speculations on whether there was anyone similarly gifted within the section. Lately it had started to look as if there were some likely candidates. In recent weeks, two or three people had begun to speak up in class who showed something more than what had been demonstrated by Clarissa and Wally Karlin and some of the others who had talked regularly from the start of the year. Clarissa and Wally were on again and off. Many of their remarks were things the rest of us had merely felt too abashed to say. But the people now emerging, armed with native talent, and often with intelligence gathered in the library, seemed to make frighteningly penetrating comments every time. And unlike the kind of humorous distaste with which Wally and Clarissa and the others were treated, these people—"the stars," they were sometimes called, bitterly—occasioned feelings close to loathing, and often for no other reason than the kind of fear many of us felt in comparing ourselves to them.

Ned Cauley, for instance, a lanky man with a strong Maine

accent, had by October become the star of Perini's class. He was exceedingly quick and he also loved contract law. Perini obviously admired him. The extent to which he'd become convinced of Ned's talent was dramatized one day when he'd gone on another of his treasure hunts across the room, waiting for a student to come up with the exact answer to a question. Suddenly, without looking behind, Perini whirled, pointed, and called out Ned's name. Cauley gave the response half a dozen others had missed.

Ned performed remarkably every day. And most people in the section made faces whenever his name was mentioned. They groaned. Some told me that Ned was unintelligent, that his success was some kind of academic illusion, and that he did it all by burying himself in Contracts treatises. To an extent which shames me, I often agreed. Somehow, it seemed obvious that anyone who had the right answer that often had to be a con man and an SOB.

When I finally got to know Ned, late in the fall, I found that he was one of the best-humored and most diverse persons in the section. He taught a course in Chinese cooking in the free university—the sort of swapshop of skills run by student government—he knew the theatre, politics, music. If he did well in Contracts, it was because his interest and talents were genuine.

There were of course one or two of the stars who, even with allowances for envy, seemed to merit some of the enmity they generated. Harold Hochschild was a small man with a raspy voice and a head of rusty curls pasted to his scalp. Harold appeared quite arrogant. He had gone to Swarthmore and he often delivered himself of the opinion that everyone else in the section had had a second-rate education. In class, Harold loved to drone on, dropping his head emphatically at certain instants like an orchestra leader on the downbeat. By spring term he had mellowed a good deal, but in late October, Harold was the unrivaled leader in classmate contempt. About that time, I had some contact with him, which allowed me to make up my mind on my own.

In the last week of the month, when we were studying the law of trespass, Zechman had provoked a vigorous class debate. He had given us a complicated hypo about two railroads with adjoining rights of way. Should one railroad's representatives be allowed to trespass on the other's property in order to lay there, on a piece of waste land, a drainpipe which would carry away water obstructing the first railroad's track? For forty-five minutes the argument went on. People who believed in absolute property rights earnestly claimed that the trespass should not be permitted and that the pipe should be removed. Others, with equal force, said that the social utility of a running railroad meant the trespass should be overlooked. It was a fine class. When the session was over, Zechman revealed that his hypo was actually the fact situation of an old Iowa case.

"Who won?" a number of people called out.

Zechman, as usual, gave away ice in the wintertime. "The railroad," he answered, then wrote the case citation on the board.

After a late meeting of the study group, Aubrey and I went to the library to look the case over. The report volume was missing from the shelf. I saw Harold Hochschild sitting nearby. Suspicious, I went to his carrel. Sure enough, the report volume was lying there unread while Harold studied.

It is, needless to mention, considered bad form around the law school to hoard a book that 140 others might be looking for. I ignored that, and asked Harold if we could look at the case for a second. He fluttered the back of his hand at me to take the book.

Aubrey and I read the report together. The trespassing railroad had to pay for the use of the land, but the court refused to order the drainpipe removed. Given what we knew, the outcome seemed peculiar, although a good compromise of the positions struck by the class. (Later we learned that the Iowa case had begun the first formulation of the contemporary law of nuisance.)

I took the book back to Harold.

"That's really a strange result, isn't it?" I said to Harold.

He was reading and he didn't look up.

"I'm not sure which way it went," I said.

Harold still did not reply. I looked at him for a moment, then replaced the book.

"Thanks again," I said. Still no answer.

Repeating the story in the next couple of days, I was informed by classmates that Harold had a policy of talking to no one when he studied. No one. He would not be interrupted in the midst of the glorious task. Getting the back of his hand when I picked up the book was miraculous, people said, more than could have been expected had I announced the second coming.

Stephen had a dark, grisly sense of humor and when I told him all of this he began cackling. "You know what's great?" he asked, laughing. "You know what I love about this place? Hochschild's going to be number one. *He's* the one who'll get A-pluses. *That's* the meritocracy."

I agreed with what Stephen said, but I had a hard time finding any humor in it. That notion simply depressed me. The word Stephen used, "meritocracy," kept popping up more and more often. It meant that Harvard Law School was a place where only merit, only raw intelligence and perseverance, both of extraordinary degree, were the sole means of success. Increasingly, I'd become certain that I was short on both counts. I was too exhausted to become a twenty-hour-a-day person, and too slow with the rest of my work to get to outside sources in the twelve to fourteen hours I studied each day. And compared to people like Harold and Ned, I had nothing worth saying in class. I made *mistakes*—in fact, silly blunders. If lucky, I was mediocre. And my conviction of my mediocrity was sour and unhappy. I had given up a good career, some security and distinction, to be swallowed in the horde, to confront intelligence which overshadowed my own. The shame at what I'd lost and was incapable of doing had become acute; and the day I embarrassed myself by making that mistake in Mann's class, I was low enough that my feelings worsened into something harrowing.

Walking out of that session, I was as close to tears as I had been in a decade. I wanted to explain to Mann, to all my classmates, that I really wasn't dumb or indiscreet, that I was able to accomplish many things worth doing. But there was no way to prove that, to them or even to myself.

When I had recovered somewhat, I vowed that I wouldn't let that feeling overcome me again. But that didn't mean taking a more balanced view of my feelings or a broader perspective on what was going on in general. I was too caught up in all of it by then. I promised instead that I would not talk in class. That meant feeling distant and frustrated while I sat in each meeting; it meant that I was giving in to fear. But I suffered it all, rather than face that horrible shame again, and for weeks I did not let myself be heard.

10/30/75
(Thursday)

Primarily a down week, with a couple of lighter spots—specifically, the lunches with two of our professors. The five of us in the study group went out with Perini yesterday and Zechman today. Both proved mildly interesting events, though I hardly felt I'd achieved anything profound with either man.

Having lunch with faculty members is something of an institution at HLS. It is one of the least painful ways that teachers can try to ease one of the most persistent criticisms of the place—that there is not enough contact between professors and students. Most of the professors seem freely available to those who ask for lunch appointments and there are a number who openly encourage small groups of students to join them for a drink or a meal. Peter Geocaris reports that last year Professor Mann went so far as to pick up the tabs.

In Perini's case, an invitation was issued with typical panache. Earlier in the month he started class by peering up sternly at the tiers of students around him.

"I have an announcement to make," he said. Then he brightened and turned both palms up. "I am free for lunch," he told us. "Dutch."

Since then he's gone out almost every noon with a group of students. With him we went to Ferdinand's, a smooth French place near Harvard Square. He remained much the man behind the lectern—probably the most practiced human being I've ever met, the person who most desires to have his world in perfect order. He had to turn his lobster salad at the proper angle before he could eat. I watched him rotate the bowl.

Nonetheless, he was engaging, charming in an arid way. He was careful to look each of us square in the eye as he talked; mainly the conversation was about some of the projects Perini takes on outside of school. He does a good deal of consulting with various Republicans in Congress, and a lot of Washington names got dropped throughout the meal: Percy, Rhodes, Fred Graham, various senators. I was surprised to hear that Perini treats senators the way he treats students and takes the same delight in it. He described an argument he had in a restaurant with one politician, the chairman of a subcommittee he's worked for. "I had him pinned on a point, absolutely pinned. I was standing right over him and he was getting red up to the neck. It was wonderful."

On the whole, he proved a lot more reasonable on certain matters than I'd expected—affirmative action in law-school admissions for women and minorities, for example. I did have one brush with him unintentionally, when I said, almost casually, that there is a deliberate emphasis at the law school on corporate law.

"I deny that," he told me heatedly, "I deny that completely. Students and not the faculty are the ones who emphasize corporate law. You're the consumers here. *We* are not lining up to take Corporations and Advanced Business Planning. You should compare the enrollment in those courses with Family Law or Criminal Procedure."

I suppose it's a point. He was fair in general—candid, if not loose. Seeing him up close enhanced my understanding of him personally. I think he's free only when he's teaching, behind the podium, on stage. He seems to have that kind of showman's personality.

As for Zechman, he proved much the shy, formal man he is in the classroom. With him, we went to a far less imposing place, a small Italian restaurant where we could sit and talk. He spoke a lot about practice. For the past few years he was with one of the big Washington firms, appearing often before the Supreme Court. He passed a little tepid Supreme Court gossip, especially about Justice Douglas, for whom he clerked in the '50s, still sees socially, and greatly admires. For the most part Zechman seemed to be glad to be back in the academy. "He's a bright guy, quite a scholar" was a comment he repeated a few times about various people—his idea, I think, of high praise. When he asked how the class was going, we all told him how much we like it, a reaction that is now close to universal.

As I mentioned in the journal, faculty lunch is a traditional, and often very sincere, attempt to make some personal contact in a situation that does not much favor it. With 140 in a class there is little chance for professors or students to get to know one another well. The situation hardly improves in the second and third years, when classes are often even larger. To an extent the problem of class size is unique to Harvard, where there are more students to be accommodated than anywhere else; but at all American law schools the ratio of students to faculty is notoriously high, probably rivaled among American educational institutions only by the business schools. It is another of the institutional difficulties often laid at the door of Dean Langdell.

"One of Dean Langdell's great contributions to legal education," I heard one professor say later in the year, in addressing a group of students, "was to make it cheap. By establishing the Socratic method, he found a way to educate 140 people at the same time, a form of educational mass production. He proved to the presidents of universities all over America that they too could make money by opening a law school and hiring just a few people to teach."

Some professors deny that the reason for large classes is economic. A faculty adviser named Thomas Heinrich, a teacher of business and tax courses, was appointed for our Legal Methods group. Heinrich invited all of us to his house one evening, and in the course of conversation he defended the large classes as producing a better educational environment.

"You have Smith over here and Johnson over there and they both want to make the same point. And there's Green there who has something to say to each of them. With 140 people in the same class you get a greater diversity of response and sharper answers." Heinrich also reminded us that the pressures of speaking in a large class may offer good training for people soon to be making their careers in court.

Whatever the reason for large classes, it is a safe bet that many students would prefer a more intimate setting. During the first term, the Law School Council, the student governing body, proposed that in the future, for 1Ls, one course in each section should be taught in small classes of thirty-five. That compromise, one smaller first-year class, has been adopted at many other law schools—Yale, California (Boalt), Minnesota. At our lunch with him, Perini surprised me by saying that he favored the proposal and believed that all classes in all years should ideally have enrollments no higher than forty. But the majority of the HLS faculty judged the proposal too expensive and impracticable and it was never seriously taken up.

To me, though, the proposal had made good sense. When I was deciding between law schools, a number of friends had encouraged me to go to Yale, because it has the lowest student/faculty ratio of any law school in the country. I had tended to dismiss the point, but now I could see how valuable an opportunity for more regular contact with the professors would have been for us all.

For one thing, much of that gnawing, maddening sense of not knowing how you are doing could have been eased with smaller classes. Most of the professors were loath to grant us any kind of praise in the large classes, no matter how extraordinary was a student's performance. Their thinking, I guess, was that to do so would only increase the resentments in an environment that was already emotionally taut. On occasion, Nicky Morris could compliment students quite skillfully—a quick, casual, "That's very good," after a person had spoken—but much of that ability might have been a function of Nicky's ease in the classroom, hard for many on the faculty to duplicate. In smaller courses, however, professors could easily give individuals the small amounts of personal attention which would allow them to feel reassured about their progress, not to mention the additional benefit of providing students with a sense of recognition as persons apart from the mob.

The other point I felt in favor of the smaller classes was that in subtle ways the teaching would be better and more complete. A lot of snags in learning law, like any other subject, are idiosyncratic—little mental wrinkles that seem to crease every brain in the room but yours. Sometimes peers, who are just getting acquainted with the point themselves, can't help; but the professors can straighten you out in a minute. Yet it was frequently impossible to get to the faculty. After class there was that cattle show, fifteen or twenty people clustered about the teachers, the brownnosers and the shouters and a few people who'd resolved not to miss a single faculty word no matter when uttered, as well as a number of students who had sincere questions that had seemed too minor or personal to disturb the whole section with during class. To visit professors in their offices was even trickier. Frequently they were out, and if your problem was small, you were reluctant to make an appointment. Some teachers—Morris, Zechman—were actually exceedingly generous with their time. But too often, students got the clear impression that most professors would much prefer not to be disturbed in their offices. It was seven weeks before Mann announced the number of his faculty office in class and when he did, he said, "Don't come yet—you won't find me there."

I am sympathetic to a degree to the faculty wish to be left alone sometimes. Students, especially those as tense and eager for knowledge as we were, can devour a professor. Yet at HLS, by the middle of the fall I'd already begun to feel that the distance between faculty and students—not just in terms of the classroom, but even on a more personal level—was extreme. Part of the problem was one of personalities.

"I'm not sure you'd enjoy getting to know some of my colleagues in a smaller setting," Heinrich told us that night at his house when we discussed the Law School Council's small-class proposal. "Many of them wouldn't *come out* well," he put it, trying to be delicate about the fact that there are some stuffy and arrogant people who teach at Harvard Law School. Many on the HLS faculty are accustomed to thinking of themselves as the best of the best, the finest minds for miles, and there are a number who appear reluctant to waste too much of their brilliance on students.

And beyond that, the sheer numbers often spell great distance and formality in relations. At HLS, it is rare to be called anything but "Mr." or "Ms." by a professor and even rarer to address faculty members by their first names. Seldom do students and teachers pass more than a nod or a smile when they see each other out of the classroom. You are business acquaintances rather than friends, persons bound only by the slenderest connection: the fact that they know and you don't.

A few of the students in my section more or less assaulted the faculty into closer contacts. One simply presented himself at a professor's house and invited himself in. Another employed one of our teachers to work on a specialized legal problem. But less exceptional means of making contact are few. I can count on the finger of one hand the number of professors I saw in the student dining hall during the year. The rest stuck to the faculty eating place. And not many of the teachers seemed to walk through the underground tunnels that connect all the law-school buildings and through which, during the winter, the students usually travel. Most faculty members seemed to prefer slush, snow, and cold to dealing with 1Ls, 2Ls, and 3Ls.

I remember how amused Peter Geocaris was the day I stopped him to ask why I never saw a professor in the library.

"Because," he said, smiling, "they have their own." It had never occurred to me that with the biggest law-school library in the world only a hundred yards away, the professors would build another on the fifth floor of the faculty office building, one from which students are normally excluded.

The fact that professors were so remote naturally tended to increase the kind of awe in which we held them. As it was, the faculty to us were figures of great power. They could intimidate. They could clarify. They could ruin our weekends and evenings with assignments. They could fill our heads with the ideas with which we struggled night and day. Most important, they were world-renowned masters in the game of law—the learning of which now had our full attention. In many ways they were the people we most wanted to be, and at moments we seemed to regard them as if they were half mythological. When we were not engrossed in actual discussion of the law, we seemed to spend all our time talking about professors, exchanging rumors—about the famous cases Mann had prosecuted or the Washington figures who'd had this or that to say about Perini. About Morris, our talk was especially reverential, because he had so recently been through the law school himself and had left such an astonishing record. The most amazing tale of his prowess was a story, perhaps apocryphal, that in a single four-hour exam period he had written not only the test in the course, but also a term paper which he'd forgotten to do in the crush of Law Review duties. On both, he'd received the highest grade in the class.

For me, dealings with the faculty were complicated by the fact that only the year before, I had been a teacher myself, up there in front of the classroom, listened to, obeyed. Now I was in the seats, unheeded—in an assigned seat, in fact—with many details of my life suddenly controlled by other people. I began to sense that I'd been turned into a child again, an adolescent. With its murky corridors tiled in linoleum and lined with the lockers used by students who live off campus, the law school has much of the look and smell of a high school, and there were an increasing number of moments when I really felt like a teenager, angry and adolescently rebellious. That was not a unique reaction. In many of the Guild members, I saw a similar pattern of response, a return to teenaged rages. It was the source, I think, of some of the vehemence of our criticisms.

But there were also times when that feeling of having re-treated was more passive and more quietly painful. Our ab-sorption with the faculty frequently reminded me of children's concern with their parents. By late October I had to confess that the hot feeling which came over me when I raised my hand in class was very much a child's wish for commendation, and recognizing that bothered me a great deal. I thought I'd grown beyond emotions of that kind. Now I learned that my childishness had disappeared only because there'd been a pe-riod when I had not been treated like a child. Thus there were episodes, like the one in Mann's class, when I blundered and felt not only the horrible shame of the child in disappointing grown-ups but also a grown-up's shame in having lost all that ground as a human being.

An incident with a friend, Tom Blaustein, is illustrative of how grimly confused all my feelings about teachers were be-coming. Tom was a young law professor from another school who was visiting at Harvard for the year. Annette and I had met Tom and his wife a couple of years before at the home of a mu-tual friend in California; and when we'd found ourselves here to-gether, we'd all gotten to know each other much better. Tom was open and generous with me and our friendship was conducted not as law professor and student, but on the personal plane on which we'd first met. On occasion the four of us would get to-gether; now and then I'd see Tom alone for lunch. When we spent time together, we were usually away from the law school.

One day, I ran into Tom in the law-school gym. I was with Terry and we had just left class. I guess the setting overcame me. Somehow when I saw Tom, the first thing that went through my head was that he was a law-school teacher. Nor-mally, I would never have thought of calling him by anything other than his first name, but when he said, warmly, "Hi, Scott," I couldn't quite keep the words "Hello, Professor" from coming out of my mouth.

11/1/75
(Saturday)

November arrives with drizzle and depression. Lord, but I feel bum. It seems as if I'm living in a tunnel. It's dark when I get up; it's dark when I go home. I keep moving straight ahead but there's no sign of light.

At home, things are in a trough. Annette's patience with the law-school wife bit appears to have worn thin, and we are bickering often. For A., I guess it is hard not to feel cheated. She's been dragged across the country and stuck in an exhausting job, while I am treated to the glories of Harvard Law. It does not help that in the little time we get together, I am frequently too preoccupied to be fully attentive. And since we are in a new place there is not an established circle of friends who might bolster her spirits. The law school has not provided a community with which we're eager to get involved. It's not a social place. On the weekends we're all just as happy not to see each other. And with good reason. On the few evenings we've had law-school friends here, as we did last night, the conversation has centered obsessively on HLS.

For Annette, there is no easy solution, and she's often left frustrated and alone. During the daytime on weekends she has taken to heading off for outings in the city by herself—to museums, to exhibits, on shopping expeditions. But there are instants when it is plain that she is bitter at how unavailable I am. Last week she told me that I am more intimate with the law than with her, a not-so-subtle reference to the fact that we have been getting together in the bedroom infrequently. (From the drift of conversations around school, I take it that the problem is not unique to us.) All of it leaves me feeling toweringly guilty at moments, and also helpless, since I cannot make the law school and its demands dissolve.

The wearying routine continues there, the work load, the

confusion, the relentless, small-minded concentration required to learn the law. And the worse week yet is coming. Legal Methods has hit full tilt, with motions for summary judgment, reports on negotiating sessions, and a research project all due sometime in the next few weeks for each group in the section. In our group the brief must be handed in on Monday and we'll have oral argument Wednesday. I've spent much of the weekend with my partner, Willie Hewitt. In addition, the two semester courses, Torts and Criminal Law, are beginning to move at a panic rate now that we're into the second half of the term—sixty-page to eighty-page assignments each week—and the pace is picking up in Procedure as well.

The work cannot be done thoroughly or precisely. I'll have to give up briefing for the week and I'm not sure I can get through it all anyway. And I'm not sure how much I care. Nearly everybody feels almost as bad as me. Too much pressure and no sleep. Three hours. Four. A lot of all-nighters. And the air in the place almost seems to smell of the very effluvium of people's bad feelings about themselves and the rigors of what they're going through. Heavy times.

The gray season is upon us.

It was a year of frequent ups and downs, but in those first two weeks of November, I touched bottom. Things for me were never worse. Thank God.

The Legal Methods assignments had worked the section into a general frenzy that would not be duplicated until exams. It was a surprising development, since many of my classmates had seemed bored by Legal Methods through much of the term. In my group, Chris Henley taught well and the skills in which he had instructed us were obviously fundamental. One week we had seen a videotape of a classmate (Aubrey, in fact, who was strikingly good) conducting a fictionalized client interview. We'd learned something about taking depositions—a

form of pretrial testimony—and how to draft interrogatories
(the written questions and answers exchanged by parties to a
lawsuit). Just the week earlier we'd been assigned to run
through a mock negotiating session, attempting to settle the
Katz case.

I'd found much of the work worthwhile, but most of the 1Ls
seemed to feel that Methods required an unfair sacrifice of time
that could have been put into the larger courses. Being graded,
they were regarded as more important.

Yet the brief-writing assignment—which would be the end
of the Methods course—had cut through that disinterest. Most
everyone had thrown themselves into the project furiously. A
brief is a lawyer's written argument to a judge. In it he cites
and describes previously decided cases which he believes support his position on a point. At the same time he tries to "distinguish" the cases his opponent will rely on, attempting to
show why those decisions are inapplicable to the situation at
hand. In Methods we had been reading through the opinions
again and again, searching out the smallest points. And although we'd been told to use no other cases, many of the
women and men in the section had gone to the library to consult outside sources, like the legal encyclopedias. People were
proud of how hard they were working. I remember the day in
the library that Aubrey and his partner, Phil Pollack, displayed
to me the nearly forty pages they'd written for a brief that was
supposed to run ten pages at most.

At the time, I couldn't understand why everyone was going
to such extremes. The only person I heard make a half-credible
excuse was Ilene Trevka, a witty, outgoing woman from the
section. One day during those weeks we got into the elevator
in Langdell together on our way to the fourth-floor library.
Ilene canted back against the wall and made one of the familiar
complaints about how little she'd slept in the last week while
she was working on her brief.

"Why are you taking this thing so seriously?" I asked her as I had many others.

"Because I couldn't stand to lose and then have to listen to our opponent gloat." Then she smiled. "We're arguing against Harry Hochschild," she told me.

But in most other cases, I saw the fury generated by the methods project as more of the success/achievement/competition hysteria. People just wanted to beat each other. In retrospect, though, I recognize that the summary-judgment motion satisfied impulses that had been frustrated all term. A job well done would let students feel that they were actually on the way to being able to handle lawyer's work—it would prove they were learning something. Even more significant, I think, was the fact that the briefs and the arguments could answer some of that longing for evaluation and provide a sense of relative standing. A motion for summary judgment is an attempt to have a decision rendered on a lawsuit without a trial. The judge examines the briefs and the attached affidavits, listens to argument, and decides whether the law and the facts of the case favor one side so heavily that a trial would be a worthless exercise. If the court decides in favor of the party moving for summary judgment, he wins the suit; a decision against the movant means there will be a trial.

In the *Katz* case, both sides were moving for summary judgment. Although the odds were that neither motion would be granted, the issues in the case were delicate enough that a particularly persuasive brief and argument might allow one side to win. The prospect of real victory, clean and conclusive, seemed to tantalize many of my classmates. It would be an authoritative way to prove a superior gift for the law. Toward that end, they labored tirelessly. But I, in the face of all this competitive heat, chose withdrawal. I was feeling too glum for a total effort. I told myself the brief was unimportant. Although we would have an oral argument—a kind of spoken defense in which you repeat the brief's main points and answer any of the judge's questions about them—I assured myself that I had always been pretty good at slinging it when on my feet. I encouraged Willie to take it easy and I hardly had to repeat the suggestion. In my section, there was a handful of people—five of them, ten at the most—who had come to Harvard Law School wanting no more than the degree. They had no desire even to stand equal to their classmates. Willie was one of those persons, and he was virtually immune to competitive pressures. He had, for instance, told me that we would have to tailor our work around his Thursday-evening drunk and his Friday-morning hangover.

Willie and I promised that we'd spend no more than ten to twelve hours each on the brief. I gave it Friday night and most of Saturday. Willie did the same. That was probably a third of the time the majority of our classmates had spent, and the brief showed it. It opened (as I later recognized) by quoting our opponent's most persuasive case and claiming it as our own—a gruesome error—and went downhill from there. Handing the brief in to Henley on Monday, I felt a little uncomfortable, but I suppressed my worries. I figured I'd made off like a bandit.

Having taken the brief so lightly, I should have had far more time on my hands. But I'd elected the previous week to do a voluntary library research project which Henley had given us in Methods. The assignment involved searching out the statute and case law on a complicated tort problem, and the task had occupied twenty-five or thirty hours. Only a few people in my group chose to do the assignment. I had done it because I knew I was going to back off from the brief and, already guilty, I did not want to feel lazy or unoccupied while everybody else was working so hard. In that, I succeeded. I was now as pressed as anybody in the section, a hundred pages behind in Torts and falling off the pace in each of the other courses.

That work load did not, however, keep me from going to see

Ralph Nader when he came to speak at the law school on Tuesday night. Annette did not feel well, so I toted my Torts book along and went by myself.

I am a Nader admirer. I take him for a zealot, but I also think he is a person of uncommon imagination, somebody who sees beyond the flak and baloney most of us buy in thinking about social institutions. The institutions Nader was going to speak about that evening were Harvard Law School and legal education in general. Nader is an HLS grad, but he is hardly an enamored alumnus. In a biography, he's quoted as describing the law school as a place where students were "taught the freedom to roam in their cages." In my funk, I was eager to hear his criticisms. I was ready to believe that there was more causing my bleak feelings than my own neuroses.

Nader gave a great speech. He spoke for well over an hour, without a note. He leaned on the podium, but he talked with a preacher's fervor—a lean, dark man, somewhat better-looking than he is on TV.

"Legal education," Nader said, "assumes its chief purpose to be the development within a refined ethical framework of the analytical and empirical skills necessary to further justice." But Harvard, he claimed, and most other law schools largely failed in those aims because they limited the uses for which those skills were cultivated.

He talked about the style of close analysis we were being urged to make a part of our mental reflexes. As Gina had pointed out to me, he reminded us of the habitual wariness and hesitancy that comes from that kind of thinking, and asked if we were becoming cut off from our common sense and our basic intuitions of justice.

He talked about the shortcomings of the case-study method. He asked us *whose* law those cases taught. Who else but the well-to-do could afford the huge legal fees of prosecuting an appeal, of bringing a case to the stage where it was likely to be reprinted in our casebooks? There were wrongs, he said—violations of law, legal problems throughout the society—which were never the subject of courtroom battles and case reports. "How many share-croppers," he asked, "do you think sue Minute Maid?"

He talked about the model of a lawyer's work that the steady stream of appellate cases suggests. Weren't we really training to be lawyers who only interview clients and write briefs and argue before courts—the kind of lawyers Legal Methods was teaching us to be? Where were we shown images of lawyers as organizers, determined advocates, rather than the disinterested hired hands of whoever could throw the price? Did we honestly believe, as was sometimes suggested, that the most intriguing legal problems were those presented in cases? Was it really more absorbing to fuss over the details of some company's tax shelters than to face (as our education so seldom asked us to do) the gravest legal problems confronting the society—corporate and government corruption, the bilking of consumers, the dilemma of bringing adequate legal services to the poor?

"Ask yourself," Nader said near the end, "shouldn't the best, the brightest, the people who think of themselves as more self-confident, better qualified—shouldn't they be the ones to take on those impossible problems? You don't have to lend your power to those huge drug companies that don't care about the public they deal with or to the big law firms that defend them. They can get other people to do that. If you say, 'I will be a narrow professional, finding pleasure where I can,' then you are demeaning yourself."

I left Nader's speech feeling high. There were some weaknesses, as usual, to what he had said. I wasn't sure I'd favor an education as acutely political as the one he'd advocated. But on many points he'd been convincing and he left me feeling better than I had for a while that I was becoming an attorney.

Yet as I drove home that evening, full of hot purpose and

temporarily out of my depression, I was not sure where those feelings could rightly be aimed. My enemy, in this form, was a collection of attitudes, nothing tangible. There was no obvious place to apply pressure for change.

I did not know that within twenty-four hours such a prominent target would emerge.

On Wednesday morning, Annette did not feel any better. She had one of the viruses she was perpetually catching from the children, and she was far too hoarse to teach. Her plans were to rest in the morning, and then, if she felt better, to join me at school. She wanted to take advantage of her day out to see the professors I'd talked so much about, Perini and Zechman, and to watch the oral argument I'd give at two.

When she arrived at noon, the whole section was in unusually good humor. We'd just had the most engaging criminal class of the term. Some student criticism had reached Mann and he now seemed to be making an earnest effort to invigorate the course. He'd set aside statute reading and we were studying Criminal Procedure, far livelier material, which centers on a long line of controversial U.S. Supreme Court cases, like the *Miranda* and *Escobedo* decisions, that deal with the rights of the accused. Today Mann had asked a local policeman to visit the class to demonstrate the stop-and-frisk procedure approved by the Warren court in *Terry* v. *Ohio*. The cop frisked a student volunteer, Charley Maier, whom Mann had set up in advance with a concealed cap gun. When the cop did a light pat-down of Maier's clothes and missed the gun, Charley had pulled it from his pocket and pointed it straight at the policeman. There was a lot of giggling, but the cop had the last laugh. He backed Charley up against the wall and demonstrated the frisk he used on "smart guys." It included a quick poke between the legs to make sure there was nothing else Charley had concealed.

The episode was carried off with a lot of hamming and joviality on all sides, and the discussion afterwards, trying to reconcile court decisions and the realities of police conduct, had been pragmatic but searching. When we came into Contracts, everyone was quite chipper, perhaps with the sense of better things ahead. I introduced Annette to a number of people whom she hadn't met yet—Gina and Kyle and Karen Sondergard—and together we steered her to a seat on the back benches, suggesting a number of half-obscene responses in case Perini called on her or commented on her presence.

When class started, it was apparent that Perini did not share our high mood. Attendance had been lagging throughout the period while the Methods briefs were being written. Now, with oral arguments at hand, attendance had dropped substantially. Many people were preparing for the argument even more doggedly than for the brief. Perhaps a quarter of the seats were empty and Perini had stared for a long time at the sparsely occupied tiers before beginning.

Perini's normal pattern was to treat a single case each day. I don't know whether it was his upset over attendance or just the nature of the material that caused Perini to press so far ahead in that session. Whatever the reason, by forty minutes into the period he had finished two cases, and there was a lot of uneasy shifting about among the students as Perini headed back to the seating chart. My guess was that a number of people had not read the last of the prescribed three cases very carefully. Yesterday, I had read nothing at all; but I took the precaution of leaving Perini a note. "Overburdened," it read. "Barely breathing. Unprepared." Some of the men and women in the section would not hand Perini a note except in the event of typhoon or leukemia. At HLS exams are graded anonymously, with a private identifying number affixed to the test instead of the name. The registrar matches numbers and grades with names, and professors often never know who got what. But many of my classmates, overawed by Perini, were convinced he filed our notes and would find some way to use them to detract from our marks. I didn't believe Perini would go that far.

"Mr. Mooney!" Perini cried out. He was still calling our names in that sharply rising, stabbing voice every time a student was selected for the case.

Mooney was a long, thin, mild man, extremely quiet and barely expressive. He glanced up with his usual serious look, but when he spoke my heart turned solid.

"I am sorry, sir," Mooney said, "I'm not prepared."

Perini froze over the seating chart, stock-still, one elbow hooked in the air as he held his pencil. His jaw rotated once or twice before he spoke.

"You mean, you didn't think we'd get that far," he said. He was looking up at Mooney with horrible hatred in his face and his voice was icy with contempt. This was betrayal. That was it. Mooney had betrayed him.

Mooney tried once, weakly, to explain. "I have this oral argument today in Legal Methods. I—"

"There are other people in this room who have an argument today, *aren't* there? Do I have a note from you? The rules of the road were laid down on the first day, Mr. Mooney. If there is *any* excuse, I want a note about it." Perini stepped away from the podium for an instant, his face still wrought with anger. I'd heard that this had happened once several years before and that Perini had stood over the student and made him read the case right there, answering questions line by line as he went through it, a torture of exposure which had lasted nearly forty minutes. But Perini seemed to have no punishment as immediate in mind for Mooney.

He touched the podium.

"I hope you are *very* well prepared on Monday, Mr. Mooney." Again that voice and look, brewed hatred. What would he do to Mooney on Monday? Something unpleasant. Something terrible. Right now Perini looked mad enough for murder. And Mooney would have to carry that worry for the next five days.

The class sat stunned, absolutely still. Perini leaned over the seating chart and made a furious mark on it; then he called on the man who sat on Mooney's left. Calling on the person beside an unprepared student is a familiar device, used by law professors to increase the pressure on those who fail to respond. Mann, despite the gentleness of his rhetoric on the first day, often did the same thing. Pass, and you served up the head of your nearest classmate, thus adding peer contempt to your disgrace. It was the Socratic classroom's answer to the thumbscrew.

The man, Zimmerman, started slowly, softly—breathless, like the rest of us.

"What did he say?" a few people murmured.

"Nothing worth listening to," Perini snapped. Then he went back to the seating chart and, while Zimmerman recited, made a ceremony of marking off the absences around the room.

When the hour had expired, Perini packed the seating chart beneath his arm. He glared about.

"I had hoped to get further," he said, "but the level of preparation was so *poor*." Then he stalked out, awkward in his fury.

Slowly, quietly, we followed him from the classroom. I didn't know what to think. Annette and I walked down the corridor toward Torts with Greg Dawson beside us—the man who sat next to me in class. I introduced him to Annette.

"How did you feel about that?" I asked.

He shrugged. "I thought Perini lost his cool."

"Did it bother you?"

"Not really," he said. "Mooney knew what would be coming if he got caught."

"You're used to it," I said, smiling, "you just got out of the marines." But the incident did not sit right with me as humor. I knew what I thought now. "It was wrong," I said suddenly, "really wrong. A teacher shouldn't treat a student that way. Not in front of a hundred and forty people. Not anywhere."

I was not the only one disturbed. In the minute before Torts began, Lindsey Steiner got to her feet. She is a thin, dark woman in her mid-twenties, one of the people most active in the Guild and the Women's Law Association.

"I hope anyone who was upset by what happened in Contracts will stay around for a few minutes after class so we can have some kind of discussion," she said.

When Torts was over and Zechman gone, Kyle—from my study group—and Wade Strunk joined Lindsey at the front of the room. Well over three quarters of the men and women in the section had remained. Most were angry. As they spoke up, people said repeatedly that they didn't like being treated as children, that they had had it with subscribing to Perini's terror and his iron rules. There was broad agreement that some kind of protest should be made.

A few students stuck up for Perini. Ned Cauley said it was a single error on the part of a great teacher and that it should be overlooked. A number of people said it was a matter between Mooney and Perini. Mooney himself was of that opinion.

"I'd prefer if nobody did anything," he said several times. "I made a mistake. I'll settle it with the man myself."

But most of the people present would not be dissuaded. Kyle said that it was a matter which touched all of us. We were all threatened with similar treatment.

For a while those present debated an appropriate response. Someone suggested we boycott class on Monday. Somebody else said that we should all turn in notes saying we were unprepared. Finally, it was agreed that a letter of protest would be written. Kyle and Lindsey and Wade and anyone else who was interested would join in writing it, and it would be presented to the section for approval the following day.

Before the meeting broke, I slipped out with Annette. My

oral argument would begin in a few minutes and we headed toward Pound, where it was to be held. I was quiet, thinking about the entire incident, including my classmates' reaction. We had watched the meeting from the back of the room. I was still not sure how caught up with all of it I should get.

Annette suddenly spoke up. "You know, it wasn't *that* bad," she said, "Perini was rude and he shouldn't have talked to Mooney that way. But it wasn't *so* awful."

I was surprised at her. "Babe," I said, "did you see the *hatred* when he looked at that kid?"

"But you've been saying all year how terrible he is. That's all I hear every night—Perini's so tough. Perini's so mean. And now you're having mass meetings."

I thought for a second about what Annette had said. Maybe she was right. I could see how the whole episode might appear trifling to an outside observer. But there was so much wrapped up in it: the pressures, and the uncertainty, and the personal humblings, and the rules of the road—all the crap we had put up with. It was a frightening prospect to joust with Perini, but we were ready to fight back now and it seemed important not to let that moment pass.

"I'm not sure you can understand, babe," I told her.

She agreed. She agreed that was quite possible.

The oral argument was a disaster.

I saw the moment we arrived outside the classroom in Pound where we'd argue that Willie and I were in trouble. Our opponents, Jim DeMarco and Jody May, had shown up in their best, he in an expensive three-piece suit, Jody wearing a smart tailored outfit. Willie and I were in old sports coats.

Far more disturbing was the identity of the judges. An authentic summary-judgment motion is a trial-level procedure, argued to a single judge. But the more judges, the sharper the questioning, and for that reason the Methods arguments were conducted before a court of two, a teaching fellow and a member of BSA. In all other regards, we'd be observing courtroom formalities, calling the judges "Your Honor," and being addressed as "Counsel." Because of that, I'd assumed the judges would be people whom we didn't know well; that would make all the pretending easier. As I expected, the chief judge was a Methods teacher from another section, somebody named Quinley whom I'd never laid eyes on. But there'd been a mix-up in the BSA office and the student judge was Peter Geocaris. When I saw him, my heart sank. I knew how seriously Peter, with all his standard-of-excellence ideas, would take this business. I hated the notion of disappointing him.

We all filed into the room together. Quinley and Peter sat behind the professor's podium. Willie and I, Jody and Jim took the first row of desks, the two sides being separated by the aisle. Annette sat in back.

Willie got to his feet and commenced the argument with the traditional opening line, "May it please the court." That was probably the last correct thing either of us said. Willie made it plain how little interest he had in being here. He spoke rapidly and his tone was casual, even flip. He seemed to give the back of his hand to the judges' questions. "That's what *you* think, Judge," he told Quinley at one point. He turned aside one of Peter's inquiries, saying, "Maybe that's so, but I don't want to talk about it."

When he sat down, it was apparent that Quinley was displeased. Nor did Peter look happy. And I only made things worse. Oral advocacy, this process of arguing aloud to a court, is one of the most highly respected elements of the lawyer's craft. The great oral advocates—Daniel Webster, John W. Davis—are legends in the legal world. To be an advocate of that quality, it is usually said that two things are required. First, you must be extraordinarily well-spoken and quick-witted. The judge is liable to interrupt with questions regarding *any* aspect of the case, no matter how trivial, which seems to him a hindrance in accepting your argument or dismissing your opponent's. You have to be ready to address any point. And to do that, a second thing is needed: You must be consummately prepared, acquainted with the minutest details of the case.

I was not ready in that way. I'd glossed the sheaf of cases we'd been given when I'd picked out the series of slick quotations I'd stuck into my brief. I'd figured that no more would be necessary—I'd just stand up there and mumble for a while. When, a minute or two after I'd started, Quinley and Peter began to drill me with sharp questions about cases I could barely recall, I knew I was in deep. I resorted to any device to get through the fifteen minutes. I haggled the smallest points. I tried to make every question semantic. I even smiled warmly at Peter now and then, trying, I guess, to remind him that we were students, allies, friends, which was a quiet but unscrupulous breach of the formalities we were supposedly observing.

The Jack Katz case ultimately turned on a typically slender legal question. In order to fire Katz, could Elliot Grueman, the raincoat-factory owner, merely claim to have been personally dissatisfied with Katz's performance, or did he have to offer reasons which a reasonable person would regard as valid? Representing Grueman, Willie and I were arguing that the law required no more than Elliot's subjective dissatisfaction. There was a lot of material in the cases which supported that position, but I had missed most of it, and Quinley, for at least ten minutes, tried gently to lead me onto that track. By then, however, I had assumed a battlefront mentality and just fought back blindly. Thus, for half the time I was on my feet, I was fiercely trying to punch holes in my own best arguments. Near the end, Quinley gave up hope.

"Counsel," he said, "we seem to be going in circles."

"Indeed we do, your honor," I answered, and soon after that

I sat down. I caught Peter's eyes for a second. He looked incredulous and somewhat pained.

In a real courtroom, the judge might have ruled against us
then, but here Jim and Jody were required to speak and in turn
they got to their feet. Jody was the M.D. in the section, a tall,
handsome, genial woman. Jim was a Chinese scholar from Cor-
nell. They had been fine people to work against. Many of the
opponent pairs had actually become quite heated with each
other. Stephen and Kyle, for instance, had ended up on opposite sides and Kyle was still loudly complaining about
Stephen's negotiating tactics. But with Jim and Jody there had
been no strain, no sense that they were out for any kind of
ruthless victory. They'd merely done a good job, written a
thorough brief, and come ready for the argument. Watching
them, I realized suddenly how reasonably the whole project
could have been handled. I was not surprised when, in the moment after they'd finished, Quinley announced they had won.
It was one of the few out-and-out victories I heard of during
those weeks.

"I'd like to comment on the argument," Quinley said
soberly before he let us go. He was a gentle, patient teacher
and he mentioned no names, but it was obvious how angered
he'd been by Willie's performance and mine. Some of the counsel, he said, didn't seem to care what they were saying. Some of
the counsel had been too argumentative to listen to questions.
Some of the counsel had slumped, had gestured too much,
hadn't bothered to button their sports coats, had looked almost
insolent.

Outside in the lobby, we had a piece of a coffee cake which
Jody had baked. We all talked about how nice it was to be
done with the work of Legal Methods. All that was left of the
course now was the mock trial of the Katz suit, which we were
not required to attend.

I congratulated Jim and Jody again; then Annette and I

went home. I had two quick drinks, unusual for me, and waited for the alcohol to work. Now and then, as I sat bleakly in the kitchen, Annette would pat me on the shoulder and say in a hoarse, ironical voice that she still loved me. I did not laugh much.

I see now that during that period last fall, I was learning all about disgrace. I was suffering a broad variety of shames and embarrassments—over failure, at feeling a child, over losing control. Kyle, at one point, said that much of the section's anger with Perini earlier that day arose from a shamed sense of having continually submitted to things we did not admire.

In looking back at all those shamed feelings, I see much of the pain as crazy and exaggerated and unnecessary. But I think even now I would feel a little of what hit me after that argument. I had finally realized that there had been a worthwhile job to do and that I had done it badly. I had mocked what I should have cared about, and in the process I had strained a friendship, even embarrassed my wife a bit. I felt like the bottom of somebody's shoe. And there was no way out. No professors to blame, no institutions. This time I'd been the entire source of my own humiliation and there was nothing to do but drink, and wait until I could forget it.

On Thursday, the movement to rebuke Perini began to divide. In the half hour between Torts and Civil Procedure, Kyle read the letter he and Wade and Lindsey had written overnight, and it was apparent at once that much of the support for the protest had dissolved. Only sixty or seventy persons stayed to listen and many of them quibbled with the letter's language.

In twenty-four hours, tempers had cooled. Many people were ready now to heed what Ned Cauley had said—that a single misstep by a great teacher should be forgiven—or to honor Mooney's request that he be allowed to deal with the matter

himself. In addition, a number of people had become frightened. Rumors—probably baseless ones—were now circulating
that Perini had instructed his student research assistants to
make it clear that he would retaliate for any gestures on our
parts which he found embarrassing. Once more people feared
that their grades would suffer, or that Perini would somehow
take out his anger in class in the long period between now and
June.

Many of the Guild members who continued to favor the letter spoke out angrily. They disparaged their classmates'
courage and moral sense. There were a few hot-tempered
speeches, a little name-calling. Finally, Kyle cut off the argument by saying that those who wanted to sign the letter could
do so. He was the first, writing his name on the sheet with a
dramatic flourish.

Watching, again from the back, I was not sure what to do.
Gina came up to me.

"Are you going to sign?" she asked. She looked troubled.

"I don't know," I said, "I don't know." I was in the grip of
more of that painful confusion. Perini *was* a great teacher, I
thought, and God only knew, I had learned for myself the previous afternoon the value of being prepared. I could see why
Perini had impressed its importance on his students.

But still, it seemed to me that he had been rude and unfair,
that he had been cruel. In considering excuses and counter-
weights I thought I might be doing what Nader had described
the other night: hesitating where months ago common sense
would have made things clear. Something ugly had happened
the day before and there was nothing wrong in trying to make
certain that it did not happen again. I just wanted to speak my
mind. I dismissed the rumors of retaliation. If they proved to
be true, that would in itself justify protest.

I walked to the front and read the letter once. It was really a
moderate document. It praised Perini's teaching; it acknowl-

edged the value of preparing for class. Its only critical note was struck in one carefully worded paragraph, in which the hope was expressed that in the event of a similar occurrence Perini's response would be more restrained. I put my name on it.

In the end, there were only 29 of us, in a section of 140, who signed the letter. Aubrey and Terry did. Stephen and Gina did not. I understood everybody's point of view. I still feel I did the thing which was right for me.

The signing of the letter was hardly the end of what was quickly becoming known to everyone as "the Incident." Organized rebellion by a first-year section was virtually unheard of at Harvard Law School, and word of the letter had passed quickly. By Monday Kyle had led a number of the Guild members in formation of an organization called Section 100, whose purpose was to spread the protest throughout the first-year class. They had decided to direct to all 1Ls a mimeographed statement in which they would describe their dissatisfactions with their entire experience at HLS and ask those who felt as they did to join in a mass meeting where some collective action could be planned.

Kyle had urged me to become part of Section 100. I looked in on one or two of their meetings but I was reluctant to get caught up in something in which Kyle was so prominent a force. There was a wonderful, attractive energy to Kyle, and he was highly intelligent; but I knew the kind of unyielding seriousness with which he regarded himself. All his class notes, for example, were inscribed in leather-bound notebooks purchased at the Law Coop for four bucks apiece. No one ever dared to kid him about his ostentation: There was little doubt that he considered his remarks on the law well worth preservation. In study group, he liked to have silence while he more or less lectured on the topic at hand. Early in the year he had admitted that he hoped to become a law professor, and I suspected that he saw himself right here, on the faculty at HLS. It was a high ambition. He would need to make straight As, Law Review, and a deep impression on his teachers, but Kyle had already left behind a string of achievements. He had been *summa cum laude* at Harvard, and in his junior year he had established some kind of college-wide note-taking service which was still operating. The service, as I heard it, had made Kyle a campus celebrity and also a great deal of money. On rainy days, he arrived at school in a taxi. Now that Kyle had emerged as an activist, I was not sure where that combination of self-seriousness and raw ambition would lead. I admired him for taking a stand, but I preferred to move aside.

Perini, for his part, seemed to be trying to put the whole thing behind us. When we faced him on Monday for the first time since the Incident, the class was more tense than we'd been since the opening day. There was a lot of nervous gossip and I stole a glance at Mooney, who wore his usual implacable expression but who looked pale. The room fell silent as soon as Perini appeared.

"I was out of town over the weekend," Perini said as he set his books on the podium, "and I have to admit that I nearly came to class unprepared."

It was as close as the man could come to an apology. The members of the section laughed and applauded. A great swell of relief passed back through the room. My classmates were delighted to be on good terms again with their stern Uncle Rudolph and class proceeded as normal, Perini commanding the room with wit and show and verbal force. He left Mooney alone.

Kyle and the Guild members, however, were not mollified. They felt Perini owed the section a genuine apology, and they also had complaints that went beyond any one episode. On Thursday, Section 100's statement to the first-year class appeared in our mailboxes in the basement of Langdell.

"What is happening to us at Harvard Law School?" the

statement demanded in its opening line. It mentioned no professors by name, but it contained complaints about the irrelevance of our Criminal Law class, the intimidation we all felt in Contracts, the model of the lawyer's role taught in Legal Methods. I was told that a paragraph indirectly criticizing Nicky Morris's condescension had been omitted on a close vote. The statement asked all who felt similar reservations about what had gone on in their sections to join for a meeting the following Wednesday.

On the same day that Section 100's statement appeared, a new alarm spread through Section 2. But it had nothing to do with "Incidents" or protest. Nicky Morris had announced that the following morning he was going to give us an exam.

"It will not count," Nicky said, with his hands raised to hush the tumult which followed his announcement. "It will have nothing to do with your final grade. I *will* mark these tests, but I just want to give you some experience in taking exams and I'd like to check on how much of what I've been saying has been getting across. You can take the test anonymously or you can just skip it. It's your choice. I'd advise you to take it. But, please, don't study for it longer than an hour or two."

Aside from the purposes he mentioned, I think Nicky also wanted to provide us with some of the feedback and reassurance which we'd needed for weeks. But coming when it did, his announcement fed into the mood of stress and competition created by the Methods arguments. Nicky had said it would be a real exam question, given under authentic conditions, and for that reason most people figured the test and its results would be an indubitable indication of future standing. Many in the section lapsed at once back into the kind of panic which had prevailed for the past weeks.

Stephen grabbed me immediately after class. He was obviously in a heat.

"We'll meet, right? The group? Talk about Procedure?"

Here we were again, back at the familiar emotional crossing between panic or withdrawal. Terry had already chosen the latter course. He sat behind me in Procedure and when I had asked him if he'd take the test, he shook his head.

"No way," he said, "I'm not working myself up for nothing. Man, I don't put my bucks down when they're just joggin' around the track. I'm not taking any tests when I'm not *all* prepared."

I was looking for some more moderate response. I told Stephen I wanted to write the exam but that I saw no need for a study-group cram session. I reminded him that Morris had said only an hour's preparation would be needed.

"Don't be naive," Stephen told me. "Everybody's crawling the walls already. They'll study all night. We've got to get together just to have a chance."

Aubrey, even Kyle busy with Section 100, agreed. So the four of us met late that afternoon. I was not happy to be there and after an hour I left. I studied my Procedure notes briefly at home, then put them away. Moderation, I told myself. Moderation. I was still collected when I arrived at school on Friday morning. Near my locker, a group of men and women from my section were quizzing each other on Procedure. It was obvious that as Stephen had predicted, they'd studied hard. They were glib about cases I couldn't even recall. I tried to ignore them and hustled away.

In Langdell, in my mail slot, I found a copy of our motion brief. It was the one Peter Geocaris had been given at the argument to read and comment on. I hadn't spoken with Peter about the argument. He'd had to leave for a class as soon as we finished, and I'd avoided him since. But to the brief Peter had appended a long personal note.

"Your brief was not as bad as your argument," Peter wrote, "but I would be lying if I told you to be proud of either of them.

I have seen worse briefs and heard worse arguments, but I know what you are capable of. Frankly, I expected a lot more."

The note was blunt and I was not prepared to deal again with the way I'd felt last week. My first reaction was anger. I threw the brief on the floor. I think I may have kicked it. All that snotty excellence crap, I thought. Then I counseled myself: Whose fault, really? Who are you angry at? I recovered the brief, removed Peter's note, and left the paper for Willie. Suddenly dreary again, I headed back to the hallway, where I ran into Stephen.

"Have you heard?" he asked me.

"Heard what?"

"You won't believe it." He took me with him to his locker and removed a copy of one of the morning papers. He opened it to an inside page. There was a small, single-column article. The headline read "Harvard Law Students Protest" and in four or five inches of type the Incident and the birth of Section 100 were described. Perini's name was mentioned a number of times, but the only direct criticism of him was contained in the article's conclusion—a verbatim quote of the one critical paragraph from the letter which Perini had been sent by the twenty-nine of us from the class. I was mortified.

"Why would they *print* that?" I asked Stephen. "Where'd they get the letter?"

"Maybe they think we're going to sit in," Stephen said. He explained that a man in the section lived with a woman who was a reporter. She'd seen Section 100's statement and had followed things from there. According to rumor, she'd called Wade Strunk, who had provided her with all the information, including the quote from the letter we had sent Perini. That was the part which bothered me. I had signed that letter and I felt responsible for what happened with it. I'd thought it was a private matter. I never intended the letter to become an element in any sort of public humiliation for Perini.

Stephen knew no more and I headed for the Torts classroom, where there would be fresher information. I got hold of Lindsey Steiner, the woman who'd asked everyone to stay after class the day of the Incident. I'd been told she'd seen Perini this morning.

"He's angry," she said to me, "very angry. I went to apologize to him, but he could barely speak. A lot of people he has contact with are going to see that. It's a real embarrassment for him. And he was *very* unhappy about that letter being printed. He said it was a breach of confidence. He said he's holding everyone who signed it responsible."

"Great," I said.

Lindsey shrugged gently.

"He'll cool off," she told me.

"And Wade was the one?" I asked.

Lindsey looked around to see who was listening before she answered.

"Everybody's talked to him, but he doesn't even understand what he did wrong. He's so innocent."

Innocent, I thought. Christ. I went to my seat and stewed. I could pay no attention to Zechman that morning. Were it not for the use of the letter, I'd have felt Perini had made his own bed. But he was right—there had been a breach there. He'd been bad-mouthed through an inappropriate source. I felt guilty and increasingly depressed. Now and then, my mind wandered to Peter and my spirits declined further.

In the interim between Torts and Procedure, the study group met again to discuss the exam. I still couldn't concentrate. When we returned to Langdell, the addition of nervousness about the test left me feeling disoriented. Nicky passed around the blue books. I shook my head sadly as I considered mine. I clearly remembered the day a few years before when I'd finished my graduate course work in English and had exulted in having written my last exam. Nicky recited the question:

"Discuss the case of *Pennoyer* v. *Neff*." The answer would require a brief essay on some of the prominent ideas in the subject of jurisdiction, which we'd studied for the first two months. It did not seem all that hard.

But when I opened my blue book some kind of emotional sluice opened in me as well. Everything accumulating the past few weeks arrived as a grand swell of pain and dread and confusion. How, *how*, I thought, with a quick and stricken wonder, could I have returned to this low point of having to *prove* myself? Suddenly all I could feel was the kind of miserable dishonor and failure which had followed on everything I had done the past few weeks, and I was sure, desperately certain, that it would happen again right now. I *knew* it. I could not shake that certainty of failure from my mind. And so within a few minutes that prophecy had fulfilled itself.

Three quarters of the way through the brief exam period I tore up what I'd scribbled and tried to get down something coherent. There was no way to make up the lost ground. When Nicky called time I knew I had failed—literally, absolutely flunked. I'd done it, and now the gathered shame and grief were overpowering. Much of my pain was in seeing the kind of downward spiral I seemed to be on, these worsening screw-ups, this deepening hurt and fright. I knew I had to do something about it.

As soon as class was over, I went to the basement of Pound, where the Law School Health Center is located. There is a psychiatrist housed there, as handy as a fire extinguisher on the wall in case of emergencies.

I was trying gaily to hold my act together when I arrived.

"How loud," I asked, gesturing toward the psychiatrist's door, "do you have to moan to get in to see her?"

Pretty loudly, it turned out. The nurse asked quietly if I was suicidal. No, of course not, I answered, just aching. There were plenty of people around HLS in that category. I would have to wait until after Thanksgiving to see the doctor. I glumly accepted my appointment and went home.

Over the weekend I remained in agony and disarray. I had never before failed an exam. That it would have no bearing on my grade did not matter. I had been confirmed in my suspicion that I was a ludicrous, miserable, unworthy failure. The disgrace turned inside me like a fierce, fiery wheel. The world as I saw it was peopled only by those whom I'd disappointed and hurt: Mann, Perini, Blaustein, Peter, my friends, my parents, my wife. And all of those feelings only worsened when on Monday I walked back into school, the scene of the crime. I went up to Harkness to have a cup of cocoa—my nerves were too shot for coffee. I was bad off. I took out my notebook and wrote the passage which appears at the front of this book.

———

Somehow I dragged myself through the next week and a half. I didn't feel much better, but I felt no worse. There were no further crises.

On Monday, Perini became reconciled with the section again. He was slightly bitter this time. He made a comment about the kinds of things one reads in the newspaper. Then he called on Mooney. He was no gentler, nor any harder, on him than on his predecessors. It seemed an effective way to put the whole business to an end.

Section 100's meeting went forward. Only thirty people showed up, though, and the group promptly dissolved. Kyle, I was told, had written a letter of apology to Perini.

At the end of the week, Nicky gave us another test. This one was a short multiple-choice exam to be worked on at home. I was more comfortable in my own study and I tried to do the test carefully.

When Thanksgiving arrived, I was desperately grateful for the rest. Sleep alone seemed to go a long way toward healing me. Marsha, a dear friend from California, was visiting. We had Thanksgiving with her, then she and Annette went down to Connecticut to spend time there with Marsha's family.

I stayed in Arlington alone. I had to study. Despite all the resolutions earlier in the term, the study group was now busy assembling an outline of Mann's Criminal class in preparation for the exam. His casebook was new and none of the commercial guides was yet available. And the course had been so disorganized that we had all been forced to agree that a collective effort was required to put it together. I knew that with only three weeks left in the semester, I'd better get my share done now.

Over the weekend, I worked at the outline listlessly. I spent most of my time walking through the empty apartment, trying to figure out exactly what had happened to me the past month. I recognized many of the things I've repeated here about the demands of the student life and of Harvard Law School. I saw that yet another cost of HLS's size is the depletion of trust, the fact that there are too many people there to maintain the kind of close bonds that could forestall some of the rumor mongering and mass paranoia that had lately been driving me nuts.

And I'd seen some more of "my enemy," that funny, indefinite collection of shadowy and unnerving recognitions about myself and what was around me to which I more and more willingly gave that name. The latest sighting had come in the oral argument and in Nicky's test, where wisely or unwisely I had tried to slow down in a stampede. Now I had to admit that I did not have the strength yet to stand up on my own. Looking forward to exams in January, I saw that I should more or less abandon hope of maintaining my perspective. Health, in that circumstance, might well be in excusing myself for giving in.

It was that kind of charity toward myself that characterized

the weekend. I decided that by and large I was a sound creature. By Monday, I felt well enough collected to cancel my appointment with the psychiatrist. I'd been a little whacked out,
I decided, but that was as much a reflection of the experience as
of any personal crisis. I began to read in the extensive psychological literature about law school and was reassured to learn
that my bad spell was hardly unique. "I have never seen more
manifest anxieties in a group of persons under 'normal' circumstances than is visible in first-year law students," one psychiatrist had written. As the year went on, I learned that there
were many 1Ls who felt they'd tilted a little, many of them in
more severe and more painful ways than I had. I know of at
least one suicide attempt in my class, and there were more people than I can count who confided that they'd been driven
through the door of the psychiatrist's office for the first time in
their lives by the experience of being a Harvard 1L. The fact
that the psychiatrist is down there at all is indicative of something.

No doubt, some of us who've had our hard times during the
first year of law school are carrying around a lot of delicate psychological china that's bound to be damaged somewhat with
any abnormal shaking and strain. But I resist, in general, the
suggestion that the many HLS students who sink into prolonged bouts of panic, anxiety, and despair should bear all the
blame on their own.

Late in the year, I heard Nicky Morris address a crowd of
students on the topic of legal education at Harvard. He said
something worth repeating:

"I keep running into Harvard Law School graduates, people
of all ages, who tell me that 'court held no fear' for them. A lot
of them are men who fought in World War II or Korea or Vietnam, and most say that even having had those experiences,
they never felt as scared or oppressed as they did when they
were law students at Harvard; and that afterwards, by compar-

ison, their anxiety about going into a courtroom for the first time was nothing.

"Well, I'm glad if we can prepare our students so that they feel self-confident about performing their professional tasks. But it doesn't fill me with pride to be part of an institution that has provided so many people with the worst times of their lives. I don't think that's an affirmative thing to say about this law school. I think there has to be something wrong with a place like that."

Nicky nodded his head as he looked at us all.

"Something," he repeated.

DECEMBER AND JANUARY
Exams (First Act)

*12/4/75
(Friday)*

For the first time in a month, I felt some peace and pleasure this week at HLS. A moment ago I was laughing at myself. Thinking over the day, I felt simultaneously elated, depressed, and confused. I knew I could only have been at law school.

Today Nicky Morris returned the two tests he gave us. He had the blue books spread out on the broad podium when we entered and people were instantly clustered wildly in front. Then, immediately, the comparing of grades took place, remarkably rapid and willing.

As I've long recognized, I potted the discuss-the-case essay. Nicky invented an especially generous curve, nothing like the stingy thing which will be used for exams next month, and I

149

had a C—far better than I expected. But there were only twenty grades below B in the section and Nicky said bluntly that those of us who had low marks should be "concerned." My dismay was lessened by my previous suffering over that test and the fact that I received one of the highest grades in the section on the multiple-choice exam. When I spoke with Morris later in his office, he told me not to worry about the essay, and I've decided to take him at his word.

For most everybody, though, the tests set the mood of the day. Superachievers in an era of grade inflation, many people—Stephen among them—were despondent about Bs—especially on the essay, which Nicky obviously gave greater weight. Hearing of my C seemed to make none of them any brighter. The majority, I guess, just walked away convinced that I am a dummy.

The students with As—Aubrey was one—tried to be self-effacing but could not fully conceal their delight. Kyle was particularly pleased, and with good reason. Nicky had written a long note on his exam saying it was the finest he'd read.

To observe the powerful hold the grades and tests exerted on all of us was a little disturbing. I can't help wondering what kind of month it'll be between now and January 9, when we have our first exam.

Final exams play on a law student's world like some weirdly orbiting moon. They are always in sight; but while they're at a distance, they serve merely to create the tensions which swell daily like tides—to read, to keep pace, to understand. As exams draw close, however, in December and May, their gravitational force starts to shake the whole place to pieces.

When we came back after Thanksgiving, I could sense the exam mood taking hold. Many of the upperclassmen, the people who'd been through exams before, seemed to have returned from the holiday with a pale, grim look. When they greeted each other in the hallways, most made jokes about how much better they'd feel in a month and a half. To a 1L, that was not a good sign.

I was also struck by the appearance of the red books. Each year, late in the fall, the law school publishes the text of the previous year's finals. A professor's former tests are considered by students a good index to the topics in a course which the teacher deems most important and to the approach to legal problems to which he or she is most receptive. Students in all years pore over past exams, sometimes to an extent unrecognized by the faculty. This year, one professor repeated a test he'd used three or four years earlier and had to award a classful of As and A-pluses.

The tests are published in two bound volumes, 1L and upper-year courses separate, their covers a shade of red so vibrant that the books themselves look a little alarming. They are left in boxes in the tunnels from which almost all were grabbed off within a day. What was most significant to me about the books was that they were published at all. That the law school would go to that trouble and expense indicated how seriously everybody, teachers and administrators, took exams; it was an official stamp, confirming their gravity.

So the results of Nicky Morris's tests only served to accentuate a tension which was already becoming pronounced. We were all stopping each other now at lunch, in the hallways, to ask questions about cases and concepts we'd covered at the beginning of the term. And the study groups were growing more active. Some people preferred to work alone, either because they did not want to rely on others, or simply because they felt they learned better independently. But by now, most of the members of the section had found their way into groups, almost all of which were meeting a number of times every week to swap information and outlines and to work out past tests.

My group was especially earnest, in large part a result of the efforts of Stephen, who was growing more nervous daily in the face of exams. A year or so before he'd started law school, Stephen had been divorced. He was still upset about his marriage. He talked often about his wife, in tones alternately wistful and bitter. He lived by himself now in a small apartment in Watertown and I think that law school was one of the first things he'd found that took his mind off his loneliness. Increasingly, he had become involved in school, always full of law-school gossip, his susceptibility to the law school's demands growing, the more so because he had an obvious gift for the law.

Gradually, Stephen had emerged as one of the persons, like Hochschild and Stern and Cauley, although far better liked, who could be counted on always to say something penetrating. The others had a talent for paring away at an idea, peeling it down like an onion until there was nothing left; but Stephen was an intellectual builder, somebody who could take a bare notion and turn it into something fuller—a concept, a policy. He rarely volunteered in class—he was too shy for that—but when Stephen was called on or made one of his infrequent remarks, his answers were precise and deeply reasoned, and the professors often praised the power of the points he'd brought up. Aubrey and Terry and I would meet after class, shaking our heads at Stephen's fluency and intelligence. "He's so damn smart," Aubrey often said, "he's so damn smart." We admired him sincerely.

Despite all of that manifest talent, Stephen was no less frightened than any of us at the prospect of the tests. I suppose he's a nervous person by disposition. One afternoon late in November he asked the study group to gather so we could discuss our plans for exam preparation.

"We're all doing well," he said as he looked around the table. "We're really on top of this stuff compared to everybody else in the section. We're in much better shape."

We all murmured denials, and I suspect that Stephen's opinion too was actually the opposite. Like a lot of people, he was apt to say the precise reverse of what he felt about those subjects which made him most uncomfortable. He would, for example, often tell me how much he hated law and law school, even as he poured himself into it. In this instance, there was no point in arguing, for Stephen immediately held up a hand.

"We're doing well," he said, "but we can do better." At that point, Stephen set out his plan for the Criminal Law outline. It would require us to boil down class notes and case briefs, to describe and reference the relevant portions of the Model Penal Code, and then to integrate all of that information. It would be a long, laborious effort and we all briefly resisted, but Stephen's logic seemed inevitable when we considered the disorganization of the course. Reluctantly, we each pledged responsibility for a different portion of the semester's work and agreed to have certain segments of the outline complete by various deadlines. We also promised to meet each day in the weeks after Thanksgiving to discuss what we'd outlined thus far.

The initial review sessions were fruitful. We worked together until six or so, probing at each other, trying to clarify, then we'd often sit and gossip for another half an hour, usually about who was going to make Law Review. As exams neared, Law Review somehow seemed to dominate our conversations. Regularly we'd exchange speculations about who the top candidates were—Hochschild, Sandy Stern. After Nicky's exam, Stephen decided that Kyle was a shoo-in. Often we would tell Stephen that he too was a hot prospect, but he would hear none of it. We were sitting in one of the Pound lounges early one evening at the end of a study-group session, draped in various poses on the butcher-block furniture, when someone accused me of being a possibility.

I shook my head and said I did not have that kind of mind.

"And I'll tell you something else," I said. "I wouldn't take it."

Terry didn't believe me. He had been making good use of the time he was not in class and lately had been spending hours in the library reading law-review articles on whatever he found interesting. In the process, he'd become quite enthusiastic about legal scholarship. He was even talking about teaching law when he finished school and we'd all been told a number of times that Review membership was an invaluable aid to an academic career. But Terry did not like to think that he alone had succumbed to the Law Review mystique.

"You mean you wouldn't even *try* it? I mean, come on, I would *try* it. I admit that."

"I still don't see it," I said. "Fifty hours a week extra. Buried in the library? What do I need that for?" I asked Stephen if he'd do it.

"Never," he said. "It's crazy."

"Hey, man," Terry cut in. "But you'd like to *make* it, right, even if you were gonna turn it down. Right? Admit it. It'd be nice to do that good."

"I'm not sure," I answered. "I hope it won't break my heart if I don't do well." I had been concentrating on developing that kind of attitude since I'd emerged from my depression in November. I'd realized how much I had taken the achievement ethic to heart—I had been so hard on my mistakes and middling performances. A sincere effort was all I owed myself. "I mean, I think that's kind of an ugly desire to feel that you have to do better than everyone else."

Aubrey came in then. "Why is it ugly?" he asked. "There's nothing wrong with that. That's what makes the world go round. Frankly, I'd *love* to be on the Review. It opens every door. I'll jump if I have the chance."

Terry nodded. I said again that I wouldn't want to do it. Stephen did too. But I knew I was being a little disingenuous.

There was another side to my feelings. I had no desire to do the Review work. And I had resolved to be satisfied with less. But there had been moments when I envisioned my best efforts as somehow being good enough that I would have the opportunity to turn the Review down. I still had no conclusive idea on how far I could reach with the law, and like many first-year students I had heard about the Review so often that it had finally been digested as the emblem of a success which was otherwise hard to define. I liked to think of that kind of status and prestige accruing to me. And God knows, I, like most of my classmates, had worked hard enough to feel that I deserved some extraordinary reward.

The next day I was talking with Terry in the library and the Review came up again, as it so often did now. Terry's a hard man to resist, especially when he thinks he's hit on the truth, and today I had to give in.

"Admit it, right. You'd like to make it, at least."

"All right," I said, "I admit it. In some ways, I'd sort of like to make it."

Terry laughed and socked me in the arm.

"Right," he said.

"Right," I agreed. But I felt I'd done something precarious, something quite dangerous, the minute the words were out of my mouth.

As we entered the last week of the term, right before Christmas, most of the students at the law school seemed to abandon any effort to maintain a brave front in the face of exams. The evidence of great apprehension was widespread. Whenever I visited the library, there were long lines before each of the Xerox machines, as people waited to copy earlier editions of the red books or Law Review articles which were said to offer particularly trenchant digests of the material in various courses. Everybody around the school seemed to be fretting aloud that they would never catch up in their classwork in time to make a thorough review. Karen Sondergard was now crying four or five times a day. And the students who lived in the on-campus dorms reported that people were running up and down the hallways, shouting questions to each other, at all hours, night and day.

For me, the anxieties showed in a spending spree on horn-books, outlines, and prepared briefs. The purchase of study aids by all students was proceeding so briskly that one person had set up a sales counter outside the dining hall; I was a par-ticularly willing customer. By the last week, I knew I had gathered more aids than I could possibly examine between then and the second week of January, but I could not resist my insecurities. Both the Torts and Criminal exams would be "open book," meaning that we could consult any printed source during the test. I was convinced that if I skipped the purchase of any one item it would prove to be crucial. With Stephen, I made a number of trips to a Harvard Square book-store where legal study aids were stocked in shelf-high abun-dance, and on each occasion I bought something else. My own doubts and Stephen's rationale would persuade me each time.

"After three thousand for tuition," Stephen would say, "how can you worry about six bucks for the Criminal Procedure *Nut-shell?*"

I would agree. After all, I could sell it next year in the law-book thrift shop. I must have spent close to $100 that way.

The faculty did what little they could to lessen our obvious uneasiness. Both Mann and Zechman described in some detail the tests they were planning to give. Mann's would be an eight-hour affair which could be taken at home; it would re-quire us to relate a fact situation to the Model Penal Code and to delineate the procedural issues. In Torts, the test would last only four hours but we'd have to take it in school, together, with proctors. Each professor tried to give us some advice on approach. Mann passed out a model answer to the previous year's exam. Zechman put off the start of one of the final classes for nearly twenty minutes while he offered suggestions on how to review.

Yet no matter how well-meaning the advice, we still had to live through the exam process ourselves. In the meantime there would be strain, and the evidence of it was increasingly visible to me, most noticeably in the study group, where relations were rapidly deteriorating. Aubrey was upset with the disorganization of the afternoon discussion sessions and had ceased attending, believing that his time could be more profitably spent alone. Stephen was miffed with Terry, who he felt was doing a shoddy job on his portions of the Criminal outline, and Terry, devoted to doing things his own way, was angered by the criticism. I was generally aggravated with the outline, and especially by the stiff standards Stephen seemed to have set for it. Racing to finish my portions before the end of classes, I felt as if I was little more than Stephen's employee. "Beef up the case summaries," he had snapped when he saw my first section. I considered the outline itself an albatross, not worth nearly the energy that had gone into its preparation. What we were doing for the most part, it seemed, was soothing Stephen's nerves. With exams approaching, I could see better uses for my time.

Whatever the tension between the four of us, it was mild in contrast to what we were feeling toward Kyle. From the start Kyle had been somewhat isolated from all of us because he was younger and straight out of college. He resented the distance. On occasion he would complain to me about being treated as "the kid." I think the rise of Section 100, which none of us had joined, had convinced him that there were more sympathetic personalities among the Guild membership.

In consequence, he had become personally remote, and after the start of December he also withdrew from most of the activities of the group. He announced first that he would attend none of the study-group sessions because he'd fallen too far behind in his work during the course of the Incident. We knew that was true and the four of us took his absence without much complaint. But as it became apparent that Kyle was not going to finish his work on the outline on time, we became less generous, particularly since Kyle had already happily accepted what the rest of us had produced.

We drew straws and I was dispatched to find out whether he was going to do the work at all. In his desperation to catch up, Kyle was barely in school and I had to reach him by phone. He assured me that the outline would be done. By the middle of the last week, however, he had to concede that he'd never finish before we all left for the Christmas break. He said he'd have to mail the portions to us.

When I brought that word back, the four of us shared our bad feelings. Terry said aloud what we all were thinking, that the outline would never arrive; and Aubrey, though milder, was also displeased. Kyle, he said, had gotten a little impressed with himself, had stopped caring as much as he normally would have about his responsibilities. Stephen was angriest of all.

"Next time you talk to him," Stephen told me, "you tell him to kiss my crack."

Yet within a day or so, Stephen too had announced that he was not going to be able to complete the final portion of his outline before we left. He had set a standard of detail in the work too elaborate for even him to match in limited time. At that word, Terry had fumed. He'd taken off the last three weeks of Criminal class in order to scour the commentaries and review articles on the Model Penal Code and he'd presented the research to the group. In return, he'd expected the last few days before vacation to be spent on some mutual effort to clarify Torts, a subject which still mystified Terry. Now that he realized that we were all too busy with Criminal for anything like that to occur, he felt badly outdone and held Stephen to blame, since he'd designed the study project in the first place.

"He sure expects a lot, I'll say that," Terry said to me. "Sometimes, I wonder, man, where he gets off."

With Terry I agreed that Stephen was terribly demanding. To Aubrey I complained that Terry had not done all he'd promised. I can only imagine what they said about me.

It was late December at Harvard Law School. Fa la la la la, la la la la.

12/21/75
(Sunday)

Classes are finished and everybody's headed away for home and vacation. At HLS they'll soon turn off the heat. Wednesday Annette and I fly to Chicago, where we'll spend the holidays with our families.

Despite the atmosphere of rancor and tension, the final events of the term came off neatly. Last Thursday, Legal Methods concluded with the "trial" of *Katz* v. *Grueman.* Jack finally got justice. All quite authentic. The proceedings were conducted in the Ames Courtroom on the second floor of Austin, a huge chamber with oak paneling and flying buttresses and banks of judicial benches. A real judge from the Middlesex County Superior Court presided over the trial, and two Boston lawyers went through the case step by step. Katz was played by a gruff, hefty tax attorney from the city who fenced questions nimbly on cross-examination and who won not only loud applause from the assembled 1Ls who've been rooting for him so long, but also a verdict for $231,000, when the jury composed of Harvard undergraduates returned long after midnight. The trial was sparsely attended, most 1Ls being too burdened by the work of approaching finals, but the reaction of those who did come was instructive. Most were bored. Many of my class-mates have never been inside a courtroom and couldn't believe that a real trial would move so slowly. In a way, that's the prob-lem the Methods course has faced all term, convincing us that the lawyer's job is usually more drudgery than Perry Mason.

The two classes which ended this week also closed nicely. Mann managed real grace as he left. This term, for the first time at HLS, student course evaluations were circulated. Mann was bitter when he saw the results. Graham Heller had lunch with him last week and reported that Mann had reminded the students of how much he could be making practicing corpo-rate law. By today, he'd cooled. He admitted the course had gone badly, said that he'd tried to cover too much, that he was disturbed that he hadn't made clear how much he cared about the issues in criminal law.

"But I want you to know that I respect you," he said to the section at large. He praised our intelligence, even "the fierce mutual protectiveness you show to each other," an apologetic reference, I guess, to the many occasions on which he'd been hissed for smart remarks or short replies to sincere questions. When he made the traditional exit ahead of his students, he re-ceived a rousing hand.

But the greatest warmth was reserved for Zechman on Fri-day. Almost all of us have moved beyond the point of mere in-terest in the course and have become engrossed, fascinated. The middle of the term was absorbed with the study of what Zechman called "the heartland of Tort"—the concepts of neg-ligence and fault, and the kinds of recompense available for un-intentional injuries. Zechman taught fault as an idea of utility combining philosophy and economics. If precautions against injury are less costly than the likely toll of possible losses, then we say that the person who failed to take those precautions was negligent and must pay for the harms suffered. For weeks Zechman persuaded us to endorse that idea and all its ramifications, then in the final nine or ten classes he engaged in extensive criticism of the fault concept. At the end he was asking why we don't hold people responsible for whatever losses their actions cause, precautions or no. As usual, there was no way to read him, to figure which set of ideas he himself subscribed to. For each he offered the same unencumbered advocacy. Yet with that kind of poker-faced rationality he managed to show us the exciting breadth and play that exists in legal ideas.

Yesterday was an uninhibited showing of the class's gratitude and goodwill. As Zechman was about to begin, a student stood and announced, "Professor Zechman, Section 2 presents 'A Tort.'" There followed an enactment, with ten or twelve players, of one of Zechman's crazy hypotheticals, replete with rifles and hunters and meteors and other strange things falling from the sky. Zechman was then presented with a series of gifts, including a frozen duck. But what was probably the warmest moment came when Zechman's relentless formality finally eroded. After the skit, he started his lecture. Suddenly he paced away from the podium, turned fully about, and spread his arms.

"I'm just lost," he declared. The class applauded wildly. When he left at the end he went out to a roaring ovation with all of us on our feet.

12/28/75
(Sunday)

Christmas vacation at home. A few days of eating, drinking, seeing friends. A chance to be the fair-haired boy from Harvard.

Today I began to study for exams. I'll do it five, six hours a day while we're here, leave the mornings for sleep, the evenings for friends and family. I feel only mild and occasional pressure. For the most part, I'm relaxed and whole.

Away from the law school, I marvel at the frenzy of pressure and learning and intellectual stimulation in which I've been embroiled. The law, the law. I've probably not been as thoroughly taken by something since I hit puberty. Still, listening to the conversations of friends, it is hard to believe all I've missed while so absorbed: the football season, television shows, political doings, many recent movies. When people ask how we like the Boston area, I tell them to speak with Annette. I have seen only the two-mile stretch which runs from the law school to our apartment.

I've also found it difficult to describe HLS to others. They regard it as talismanic and often seem disappointed or confused when I tell them that some things are wrong there. Frequently, I find myself hard-pressed to describe quite what the problem is. My inclination is to say that it's not a human place, and yet I know that what's difficult there is that everyone is so full of feeling, all of us tortured by our little agonies of doubt and incomprehension and concern.

1/2/76

Happy New Year.

Late this afternoon, we head back to Massachusetts. I felt the first threads of exam anxiety weaving through me last night and did not get much sleep. I'm trying now to study Torts, but I'm really too bleary to do much. I will be grateful if in the next couple weeks, I can keep myself under control.

Reviewing for law-school exams proved to be some of the most arduous study I've done in my life. Many of the 2Ls and 3Ls who returned in January faced four or even five exams. The 1Ls had only the two, but the job of getting ready still seemed staggering to me. Between the two courses, we'd covered about 1,800 pages of cases, all of it dense reading and much of it worth remembering. I also had taken over 500 pages of class notes, not to mention the hornbooks, outlines, and briefs, many of which I was actively consulting. Even on second encounter, none of that material was instantly comprehensible. There were many things I'd passed over or missed the first time which I felt I had to wrestle through now.

So I spent a lot of time—between 200 and 250 hours—preparing for those tests. When we got back to Massachusetts I put myself on a sixteen-hour-a-day schedule. There seemed no other way to cram all that material in. And after all the work I'd done throughout the term, this hardly seemed the time to cut corners. Annette did her best to ignore me. I sat in my study, making notes, poring over case books, or hornbooks, or notebooks, or Gilbert's.

As taxing as the volume of work, sometimes, was its nature. The typical law-school test is what's usually referred to as an "issue spotter." A long narrative is presented, involving a complicated series of events and a number of actors. The exam generally instructs the student to put himself in the position of a law-firm associate who has been asked by a senior partner for a memo describing the legal issues raised.

Inevitably, the narrative has been constructed in such a way that its facts straddle the boundaries of dozens of legal categories. A varying interpretation of a single detail can produce a Merlin-like change in the issues, and often the outcome of the case. For the student, the job is to sort quickly through the situation to try to name the endless skein of applicable rules and also to describe the implications of using one rule rather than another. Like a good lawyer, the student is expected to be able to argue both sides of each choice.

Issue spotters obviously place considerable weight on detailed mastery of the predominant common-law rules—the ones followed by the courts of most states and sometimes referred to as "black-letter law"—and the students at HLS object to them for just that reason. Little of what goes on in classes aims at developing intricate knowledge of rules. In my course, it was important to be able to work with the rules, to deduce them from cases, to compare and distinguish them; but as the semester went on, more and more class discussion had focused on those philosophical, political, economic, and other pragmatic concerns which justify the rules and usually pass under the name of "policy." Issue spotters, then, do not seem to test what was learned.

A number of professors are responsive to that criticism. The issue spotter has been a fixture for decades—sixty-year-old and thirty-year-old lawyers were both put through the same kinds of exams—and many teachers admit that the approach may no longer be fully suited to an education which has become more frankly speculative and intellectual. The "discuss the case" essay which Nicky gave us on the practice exam is an example of more open-ended and policy-oriented questions that are now sometimes included on law-school tests. Zechman, too, told us not to trouble ourselves with too much learning of dry detail. He wanted us to concentrate on seeing patterns in the material—"the forest," he said, "and not the trees." Nevertheless, the Torts test, like every other exam I took last year, would contain an issue spotter. It remains the staple. Professors believe that the most gifted students will discuss the facts thoroughly in terms of both abstract theory and doctrine.

In consequence, I spent much of my time in early January bent over various commercial outlines doing a lot of straight memorization of rules. It was dull, unrewarding work and there was no way around it. Although I would have all the books beside me when I took the exams, time would be far too short to be looking things up then.

After I'd more or less learned by heart the rules in a subject area, I'd go back to my class notes and try to digest the specific policy rationales for the rules. Then, as Zechman had advised,

I'd see if I could relate those ideas to the broadest thematic concerns of each course. Holding all of it together in my mind was something of a feat. When I was a kid I saw a TV show about some U.S. soldier who kept himself sane in a Korean prison by designing a house in his head. Learning a law course is much the same kind of process: putting up the struts, the walls, the roof; rule/policy/theory; trying to remember exactly how each of the layers joins and fits. Some students prefer to outline each course themselves, believing that is the best way to capture the flow and organization of the material. Others like to read and memorize prepared aids. A third school says you can sharpen your hold of the course by doing past exams. I've tried a little of each method and never found much difference between them. It's always the same slow accumulation of knowledge, the methodical job of putting that house up nail by nail. And when you get to the roof raising, when the course has really begun to fall together, with the term-long mysteries dissolving and the basic patterns becoming clearer and clearer, the study can seem as gratifying as it was boring in the rule-storing phase.

In all stages, it was largely a personal project. When we got back from Christmas, it became apparent that Stephen and Terry and Aubrey and I were all thinking about the courses in slightly different ways. For that reason, study-group sessions were of limited use. We tried on a couple of occasions to get together, but the variations in the way we were preparing and in the progress each of us had made seemed mostly to disquiet us all. We each seemed to leave those meetings with the sensation that we were doing something wrong.

Instead, we resorted to the telephone for sporadic consultations. Whenever there was an area I couldn't quite grasp or a line of reasoning I couldn't follow, I would call Stephen or Aubrey or Terry for advice, and they called me. I was on the phone with one of them between eight and a dozen times each day during the reading period. Inevitably, I got solid instruction from each of them, and some of the comforting I also needed on occasion.

As the exams grew closer we were all becoming tense. My sleep was fitful and a nervous sensation was constantly in my gut. Looking back to the first of Nicky's practice tests, I could not help remembering that I had proven a capacity for screwing these things up.

But the most emotionally telling factor was that persistent double bind which I still couldn't get away from: I badly wanted to succeed and I sorely feared failing. These abstract ideas raised far more powerful feelings in me than the mere prospect of getting As or Fs. Exams represented a kind of opening (or closing) world of opportunity—Law Review, clerkships, jobs, honor, prestige—and I both dearly hoped for and dreaded losing the chance at all of those things. There is a native desire, I guess, to avoid limitations.

By the day before the Torts exam I was too keyed up to study much anymore. In the afternoon, I looked over a past exam. In the evening I called Stephen. He sounded as tense as me, though he was not willing to admit it.

"Listen," he told me, "we've got a floor under ourselves. You've really got hold of the policy in this course, and the doctrine, and I have too. We're going to do okay. Other people just don't understand this stuff as well as we do. I was over in the Ed School library and for Chrissake, Ellie Winship is still trying to figure out what assumption of risk is. I feel really composed," he concluded, "I feel very calm."

I did not. I paced and muttered and stared frozen at my notes until about ten o'clock, when I decided I should go to bed. The most important thing, I knew, was to get a good night's sleep. The exam would be at nine the next morning.

During my first year of law school, my wife put up with a lot of excessive behavior from me. I worked too hard, slept too little. I was always up or down, at extremes. But Annette still thinks the night before the Torts exam was my least collected moment and I won't disagree.

When I went to bed I took a sleeping pill, and after some thought about how nervous I was, a few milligrams of Valium. I was certain that would do the trick. At midnight, I was still awake. I got up and had a drink. It didn't seem to do much. A half hour later, I rose again to have more wine. This time Annette pulled herself out of bed to beg me not to drink again. I was going to kill myself with the pills and liquor, she said. I was going to be crazy with drugs in the morning. I went back to bed. We made love another time. Still no peace. At one-thirty, wild now with drugs and frustration, I rolled out and began to flail at the mattress: I was *trying* to destroy myself, I shouted; I was *insuring* failure. Annette quieted me and went to the living-room sofa so I could have the bed to myself. At two-thirty I got up to tell her to come back. She instructed me to go to sleep. Sometime after three, I finally did.

At around six-thirty Annette came in to dress for school and I woke to her stirrings. She kissed me good-bye and wished me good luck and then I got up. I felt horrible. I'd had about three hours' sleep and now the sedatives had taken hold. I was cloudy and numb. My eyes ached and itched as if I'd tucked brambles under each lid. I poured five or six cups of coffee into myself, then, at eight, set off for school. I took my backpack full of books, a thermos of coffee, and my electric typewriter. I was still dizzy and spaced out as I rode down Massachusetts Avenue on the bus, and I thought vaguely that I was doomed.

At HLS students can either handwrite or type their exams. There are separate rooms set aside for each method. I chose to type, because I do all my writing on the machine and feel comfortable in front of it. But the typing room was one of the old classrooms in Langdell, and I realized when I got there that the clatter from thirty or forty machines in a room without carpet was going to be something terrific. I was still too bleary to be overly concerned, but I was grateful when Terry showed up with earplugs for both of us. It was real generosity on his part, not only because he'd thought of me, but also because the tests were being distributed as he arrived and he'd still taken the time to bring the plugs over.

I thanked him and asked how he was.

"Scared," he answered. "I was on the can all night, man. No sleep."

"Me neither," I said. I wished him good luck, then turned to the exam pamphlet which the proctor had just handed me. I read the questions. The first was a straight issue spotter. An M.D. had given a patient a drug still in experimental stages and the series of disasters you come to expect in a Torts course had followed: blindness, car crashes, paralysis—the world, in general, falling apart. We were asked what torts had occurred. The second question was wide open. It was another kind of issue-spotting narrative about a gardener and a tree falling on a neighbor's house, but we were instructed to emphasize theory and policy in our answer. The final question cited three well-known cases of nuisance law and asked for an essay about them.

We had four hours.

What had never quite struck home with me about a law exam was the importance of time. I had realized that we would be tested over a few hours on a knowledge which had taken months to acquire. And I'd looked at past exams. But I'd never really tried to write out an answer. It was only now that I saw that there was not a quarter of the time I'd need to frame a reasonably thorough response. The questions themselves covered four single-spaced pages and even after reading them twice I knew I hadn't recognized half of what was there. As it was, I couldn't figure out how I'd ever write down all of what I had seen. It was all split-second reaction, instantaneous stuff; there'd be no deep contemplation.

I was hit at once with a powerful jolt of adrenaline. It made little difference that I'd felt detached from my body when I'd entered that room. By the time I'd finished reading the questions, I was hopping. My heart started when I heard the first key strike on somebody else's typewriter, but after that, the incredible clatter of forty machines became as vague to me as Muzak. For the most part, I was lost those four hours in the oblivion of the adrenal rush. The promise of an "open book" test proved illusory, as I'd expected. I looked at my casebook for an instant, but that was mostly for comfort; I barely flipped the cover open and shut. There was no time. Proverbial wisdom is to spend at least a third of the exam period planning your answers and I tried to do that. But with my body jumping, I tended to just empty my head. I spent too long on the first question, as it was, and was typing after that in a mad fury.

When time was called, I had written nearly twelve pages. Even as I stapled the sheets and handed them to the proctor, I knew I had made some gruesome errors. But I was exhilarated. I was sure I had passed. The first law-school exam. I was going to make it.

Terry took me out to lunch in celebration, then drove me home. I slept the afternoon. At five, I got up to begin studying criminal law.

I could not pump myself up the same way for the Criminal test two days off. By the next morning I was a little depressed about the mistakes I'd made on the Torts exam, more of which seemed to occur to me on the hour. It was not that I felt that I'd done poorly; I just realized that I'd missed the chance to do very well. Nor did I feel any of the sharpening effects of first-time apprehensions. I'd seen the monster now.

"They'll never have us that way again," Stephen said when I spoke to him. Aubrey and Terry expressed similar sentiments. We were all more relaxed, even a little somber. There were fewer of those brainstorms by phone.

Finally, the procedure for the Criminal test made it seem less forbidding. It would be taken in the more comfortable setting of home, and although it would cover no more material than the Torts exam, the test would last eight hours, not four. The eight-hour exam is a relative innovation at HLS. It's designed to ease some of the overwhelming time pressure of the traditional exam. Many professors are sniffish about take-homes. They feel that they do not provide the same stiff trial of mental agility as tests in the classroom. On the other side, there are more than a few students who feel that having twice the time just means doubling the agony. But I found it gratifying to know that I'd have a while to think.

I studied almost lethargically, sifting through the huge outline—it was over 400 pages—which we'd put together. Most of the pre-Christmas work seemed now to have been purposeless. Time and Torts had pushed almost all of it out of my head and I made a note to myself to avoid getting enmeshed in that kind of project in the spring. I had to cram everything back in again.

On Sunday night, I had no trouble sleeping. Annette, who'd been snowed out of school, drove me home after I'd picked up the exam Monday morning. I looked the test through while in the car. Because of the nature of the material, the narratives in Crim tests are often burlesques. They frequently read like parodies of the last act of *Hamlet*, with people being murdered all over the stage. But this one was down-to-earth, realistic, about a prostitution and theft ring of the kind of which there must be a dozen in every large city. The exam described the apprehension of the ring's members through the use of police decoys and a bugging. We were instructed to act as assistant district attorneys assigned to write a memo listing possible charges against those arrested and evaluating the admissibility of each piece of evidence which had been gathered.

At home I worked the first few hours in the same kind of listless way I'd studied. I paged through the Model Penal Code, looking up crimes—waiting, I guess, for things to fall into place. They didn't; and at about 11:30, I panicked. I'd wasted more than a quarter of the time and I was sure—positive—that now I really would fail. The adrenaline came then, but for some reason it was too much. My body overdid it. I turned white, and crazy things seemed to go on inside my chest. I had a peculiar kind of arthritic reaction, maybe just because the rush lasted so long, and the joints throughout my body became too painful for me to work sitting down. I had to write on my feet, but I finished in time, getting back to school through the snow and the rush-hour traffic on schedule.

Afterwards, we tried to celebrate. Annette and I went out with Terry and Aubrey and their wives, Donna and Arlene. Aubrey drank a vodka Gibson, then a bottle of Beaujolais and three or four beers. I also got roaring. But exams and that amazing wash of panic had left me limp.

When I got home I made a note in my journal:

I feel rotten. I feel wasted. I have finished my first term at the law.

In the aftermath of exams, I felt bitter and cheated. After the long buildup, some kind of letdown was probably inevitable. And in part, my disappointment really had little to do with the tests themselves. In reviewing, I'd seen how much of my elaborate daily preparation for classes had not been worthwhile. The finest points of the cases, which I'd stayed up to all hours struggling to comprehend, were not merely irrelevant to the exams, but had also proved to be beyond the grasp of my memory. I promised myself not to be as relentless in the term ahead.

Yet even granting that I was victim of my own excesses, there were other aspects of exams which for me took a relish out of law school that was never quite restored. All along, 2Ls and 3Ls had told me that I'd never been through anything like a law exam, and they were right. But that did nothing to enhance my respect for the tests. I felt insulted by them—there's no other way to put it. Finals were regarded with an institutional earnestness which had left my classmates and me believing for months that the tests would offer some consummate evaluation, not simply of how well we'd learned, but—almost mystically—of the depths of our capacity in the law. Exams were something to point to, a proving ground for all the hard and sincere labor. And instead they had been intellectual quick-draw contests, frantic exercises that seemed to place no premium on the sustained insight and imagination which I most admired in others, and when they occurred, felt proudest of in myself.

When I returned to school, I found that most of my classmates seemed to share my feelings. People were incredulous now that these peculiar, limited instruments would be the sole basis for our grades. Reports of the haphazard way professors marked finals—comparing the papers against a checklist of salient points, giving no more than a few minutes to each test—only heightened the sense of injustice and frustration. And there was another group who continued grieving over errors. We'd all made mistakes, grand-style blunders and omissions. It's natural in the midst of that furious rushing. There is no such thing as a perfect law exam. Chris Henley told me later that touching on about sixty percent of the possible issues is often enough for an A. But some people could not be convinced that lapses were expected, and walked around for weeks making wan jokes about having their bags packed.

Distress over law exams is nothing new. The student outcry for reform, for the opportunity to be evaluated through papers as well as tests, or by way of more frequent and less charged examinations, has been heard for years, and has in large part been rebuffed. Some faculty members frankly admit that they prefer not to spend the additional time that the alternative systems would require. Students sometimes suspect there are other reasons for the faculty's resistance to change. The professors are persons who did quite well on exams; in fact, they all owe much of their present position to that success. It is difficult at moments not to see them as merely perpetuating the regime on which they base their sense of authority and self-esteem.

Tom Blaustein offered a limited defense of exams when I told him how angered I had been by the whole process. He admitted that he preferred to get papers from his students and that traditional law exams hardly measured the full range of qualities important in a good attorney.

"But over the long haul," Tom said, "they do give you some reading on the way your mind works in certain situations—one skill. And if you're making a career choice—or if someone is making decisions about you—it's better to know that than nothing at all."

Maybe. Even conceding Tom's point, I'm still not sure that that one quality should be allowed to determine so much of who gets what jobs, who teaches, who clerks, who gets the Law Review's training in legal scholarship. But the truth is that exams have so dominated my year as a law student that I have no objectivity about them. We'll all end up as lawyers anyway, entering a world of fine opportunities, and in the end I've tried to write off exams as a quaint professional custom, another rite of passage for a novice.

But one thing nags which does not bear directly on me anymore, but is worth mention. Right now admissions at most American law schools are based on predictions of how well applicants will do in school, which is to say how high they will rank on exams. Those forecasts, based on statistical formulae that combine LSAT scores and college grades, are often quite accurate. But that amounts only to saying that American law schools admit people who will be good test-takers rather than good attorneys. Correlations between exam success and worthwhile achievements in the practice of law are speculative at best. Until that connection is better established, the narrow and arbitrary nature of exams will continue to dictate a narrow and arbitrary means of selection for training for the bar. And that is a peculiar state of affairs for a profession and an education which claim to concern themselves with rationality and fairness.

FEBRUARY AND MARCH
Getting By

1/19/76
(Monday)

At 1½ L now. The second term begins. Boredom where there once was trepidation. Devices where there once was energy. I have resolved to brief no cases this term. I want to conserve time to read a newspaper now and then, and even on occasion, a novel.

Around Harvard Law School it is just so damn hard to keep a sense of perspective from slipping into exhausted cynicism. In the wake of exams, I still feel the impulse to give the whole joint the finger. Last night, in trying to figure out what elective I should take, I found myself concentrating on profound pedagogical questions. How easy was the course? How hard did the final look in the red book? Could I slide by without much daily preparation?

Before I came to law school, there were even times when I thought of myself as an intellectual.

Archibald Cox, the former Watergate prosecutor, is about as close as one gets these days to being an authentic American hero. A prim embodiment of Yankee virtue, it was Cox, then Watergate prosecutor, who first confronted Nixon over the White House tapes, and in the process, reminded the American people that public men can still be decent.

In a different environment, Cox would be an object of constant worship. About the time I started law school, two friends visited me from Chicago and stood in hushed awe just at the sight of Cox's nameplate beside his office door. But at Harvard Law School, where Cox for years has been a member of the faculty, students are not subject to the same kind of wonder. This year there was a bum rap out on Cox. It was said that he was soporific in the class and—far more repellent at HLS—a notoriously low grader. Given the opportunity to take a course with Cox, most of the first-year class moved stalwartly in the other direction.

In 1972 the first-year curriculum at HLS was reformed. Among many changes, 1Ls, in the second term, were given the new liberty of selecting a course to go with the prescribed regimen of Contracts, Civil Procedure, and Property. The elective courses were to be "relevant," concentrating less on common law and case reading, and more on subjects and policy matters with greater intrinsic appeal to students. This year, for example, elective offerings included courses on Chinese law, contract theory, broadcasting law, legal ethics, environmental law, and comparative law (which examines the legal systems of other countries), and a course entitled "Law and Public Policy," normally taught at Harvard's John F. Kennedy School of Government.

It all sounds like a great idea, but the classes have turned out to be watered-down versions of advanced courses, boring to the faculty who teach them and also to 1Ls. As a result, I—like nearly half of the first-year class—opted for the most traditional selection: Constitutional Law, another basic course. Con Law, which concerns the major pronouncements of the U.S. Supreme Court about the Constitution, was offered in two classes this year. One was taught by a young professor who'd established a glowing reputation with 1Ls as instructor of one of the first-term courses in another section. The other class was to be taught by Archibald Cox.

The rumors bruited among 1Ls about Cox's grading and classroom style were not true, but elective registration took place during that hysterical period in late December before exams when all of us were somehow ready to believe the worst about everything. Enrollment for the young professor's class outran Cox's six to one, and when the dean and the registrar tried to even out the class sizes there was a confrontation with angry students and a lot of fur flying—lotteries, mass meetings, open letters to the class.

As the second term began, seventy students were still assigned to Professor Cox's course—many of them, like me, involuntarily. I tried to keep an open mind in the first two days, but Cox did seem dry; and more important, I realized how little I wanted to take another heavy law course. I was too weary of the stuff. When the Public Policy class opened for the additional registrants, I dashed for freedom.

Law and Public Policy amounted to a crash course in the working skills needed in upper-level positions in government: analytic knowledge (economics, statistics, decision theory), methods of planning, management techniques. The course was taught by the "problem method" developed at Harvard Business School. For each meeting we were assigned a "case study," a lengthy description of the setting and difficulties facing some potential decision maker. In class, we'd talk through possible solutions. The material and much of what was said about it had a fuzziness typical of social science, a far cry from the hard-edged principles enunciated in the usual law-school classroom. Many of my classmates felt they were being outdone somehow. "All of this is crap," Kyle told me the day before he dropped the course.

I didn't agree. I valued the relief of a less tortured approach, as compared with that of the rest of our courses. The class was smaller—70 students—and like all the electives, it contained students from other sections. That was welcome leavening after looking at the same 140 people every day for months. I also liked the professor. Guy Sternlieb was a member of the faculties of both the law and government schools, and a former high official with the Department of Health, Education, and Welfare. He was tall, fortyish, quiet-spoken—and a remarkably decent guy, generous to his students and down-to-earth. In Guy's class you were not called on. If you had something to say, you raised your hand. You were addressed by your first name, and you spoke to Guy the same way. Despite the size of the class, it had the feel of a seminar.

Karen Sondergard was also taking the course, and during the second week she said to me, "You know what's amazing about this class? I realized the other day that it's the only one where I walk in and I'm not terrified. I'm actually *happy* to be here."

Few of the students in my section would have made a similar statement about Property, our other new course. Property law concerns the rules and devices relating to the ownership of things. Gifts, wills, trusts, zoning, the many sides of real-estate law—these form most of the general subject matter. It is a peculiar and often extremely difficult course. The ownership of property is a first principle of Western societies and the rules regulating that ownership are not easily altered without upsetting the entire social scheme. Many elements of property law have not changed since the Middle Ages. Much real-estate law, for instance, still shows the influence of feudalism, the doc-

trines shaped by the needs of the lord of the manor. A lot of
those rules no longer make sense and simply have to be absorbed by rote.

But other aspects of the course were fascinating. Despite
having been jaded by exams, I felt a good deal of excitement as
I read the initial cases and considered the questions they presented. What, really, does it mean to say somebody "owns"
something? That that person can use a thing? Or control it
somehow? Or just that he is recognized as the owner? Why are
certain kinds of use or control legitimate, and others the stuff
of thievery and fraud? But as in Criminal Law, I soon discovered that some of my natural enthusiasm was being dampened
by my reactions to the professor.

Like most of the people in the section, I had heard all year
about Isaac Fowler. Each story made him sound less appealing.
One 3L claimed to have taken a total of twelve pages of notes
in a term with Fowler. I'd also been told several tales about the
snubs and indifference Fowler had routinely shown students.

He was a strange person, small, spare, always in the same
tweed sport coat, a moody middle-aged man who seemed to
have thought everything over and decided that nothing was
worth much. He was, of course, a noted legal scholar, an expert
on international law and the UN; but as a teacher he appeared
to have burned out years before. For each class he would arrive
with a weathered sheaf of notes which he would read as enthusiastically as the instructions off a soup can. In his questioning
of students he was gentle at some moments, but far more often
he was abrupt and dismissive. "No, no," he'd say, "that's
ridiculous," cutting off whomever he'd called on. At the start
of the term, Fowler had been particularly harsh.

"I'm going to see if these rumors are true that you learned
something last semester," he told us in the first session. The
initial cases were all mid-nineteenth-century English reports.
With his questions, Fowler tried to befuddle the class, asking

for definitions of terms and procedural maneuvers we'd never seen before, trying to drive us into the inferential chasms created by the absence of material which Fowler, editor of the casebook, had cut from the opinions himself. Section 2 was not buying any. We'd seen this routine the first day with Perini; and besides, the class was already indisposed to Fowler by reputation. When somebody could not answer a question, no other hands appeared. By the end of the first class, it looked as if the term was going to be a long, slow contest, one against one hundred and forty.

On the second day Fowler called on Wade Strunk.

"I pass," Wade answered in his soft accent. Fowler ran his class in the old-fashioned way, in which students were always expected to respond. When Wade spoke my heart clutched and I thought to myself, the Incident, Part II.

"I didn't hear you," Fowler said.

"I pass."

"I'm sorry?"

"I pass," Wade said again, louder, looking straight at Fowler.

"Are we playing bridge or something?" Fowler asked. He stared at Wade, then, of course, called on the person beside him.

Wade afterwards said he had been quite prepared, he was merely trying to establish his classmates' right to remain silent when they chose to. A number of people expressed the opinion that were it not for the Incident, Fowler would have been far harsher, an observation which may have been true. Whatever else, though, that moment with Wade served to make overt the mood of quiet opposition and the determination of some in the class to resist any heavy-handed techniques. In the aftermath, Fowler softened somewhat. But he could not make himself less painfully dull. By the end of the first week, attendance had begun to drop and continued downward the rest of the term. Terry looked in on the first few classes and never came back. Willie Hewitt went out the door in the middle of a session, muttering loudly that he could sleep just as well at home. The man beside me explained that his loud sucking of mentholated cough drops was an effort to keep himself awake during class.

I did not really enjoy Fowler, either. I wished that he would bring more out of the material. I wished, in fact, that I had another teacher. But every now and then something brilliant would escape him. He was obviously a learned man, and he regularly made refreshing little departures, relating classroom problems to literature, anthropology, economics, history. He also had a pleasing, light wit. In midsentence he was liable to interrupt himself with observations such as "Here in Property we study the Golden Rule—he who has the gold rules." The asides seemed enough to warrant attendance.

On the whole, I shared Stephen's sentiments. At the end of the first week of the second term, as we were heading out of class, I asked what he thought of Fowler.

"I figure it might have been a lot worse," Stephen told me. "We could have had him first term, and then we wouldn't have known enough to ignore him."

———

Late in January, the moot court competition began. At Harvard, the competition is an annual memorial to James Barr Ames, a renowned law professor who died early in the century; and in all its phases, the competition is usually known simply as "Ames."

Moot court competitions are yet another of the universals of first-year education at most American law schools. Like the Legal Methods program, of which Ames is technically an extension, moot court seeks to acquaint the beginning law student with some of the practical aspects of being a lawyer. Students prepare and argue appellate cases—cases on which there is already a trial decision—against one another, and at HLS all arguments supposedly take place in the mythical state of Ames. Every 1L is required to take part in the program. Those who enjoy their initial experience in moot court can, at Harvard and most other law schools, go on in their second and third years to what is called "upper-round competition," where there are money prizes and considerable honor to the winners.

First-year Ames features nothing so glamorous. There is only a single argument, in which it makes little practical difference who wins. Anyone with the inclination can go on to the upper rounds. In many regards, Ames is just a grander version of the summary-judgment motion we prepared for Legal Methods, which was, in fact, partly intended to ready us for moot court. Again, students work in pairs. Once more we would have to write a brief—although for Ames the formalities of legal citation were to be observed—and again we would argue to a mock court, though there would be three judges this time instead of two, and one of them would be a member of the law-school faculty.

The great distinction, however, between Ames and what we'd done in the fall was that for moot court no one was going to hand us the case law as they had in Methods. Now we would be in a position more like the one in which practicing attorneys often find themselves. We'd be presented with an abbreviated version of a trial record and assigned to argue on appeal either for or against the trial court's decision. From that point forward, we'd be on our own. We would have to analyze the case, figure out the matters in issue, and then retreat to the library and find the best law to support our side. The period from the time the record is first received to the date of the argument is about six weeks, so the work on Ames is expected to be extensive. We'd be closely supervised by 2Ls and 3Ls, usually from BSA, which presides over first-year Ames. Prior to the argument we'd have to prepare a research memo and a draft of our brief as well as the final brief itself. I'd been told that for many 1Ls Ames became the primary event of the winter, with more time invested in it than in any of the classes, which usually lolled into doldrums during the period.

In the kinds of cases 1Ls could argue, we had considerable choice. BSA offered thirteen cases, all fictionalized, but each relating to an area of law touched on by the first-year subjects. In addition, there were a number of "alternative" cases, sponsored by many of the upper-year extracurricular groups like the Environmental Law Society or the Civil Rights–Civil Liberties Research Committee.

I had asked Terry to be my partner and together we decided to request assignment to a BSA case on defamation. It was a subject Zechman had not reached in Torts and we were both interested in learning something about it.

On January 30, we went to the BSA office to pick up our trial report. It was a lulu. The Reverend Edward Gantry was minister of a church in Pound City. Previously, he had been the pastor of a congregation in a nearby town, but he had been dismissed in reproof for his antiwar activities. Now, Ralph Wilson, one of Gantry's former congregants, writes the reverend, irate that Gantry is still disgracing the ministry. He threatens to make public a distorted version of the events surrounding Gantry's discharge unless the Reverend Mr. Gantry resigns his current pastorate. Rather than allow the story to reach his congregation as pernicious gossip, Gantry reads Wilson's letter to the Pound City church members and explains his point of view. Nonetheless, he is fired again. He sues Wilson for the defamation contained in the letter and wins.

On the appeal, Terry and I were assigned to the side of Wilson, the letter writer. It made no difference that he sounded like a clod. The principle of advocacy we had been taught all year was that he deserved full and unbiased representation. We would have two lines of attack. Defamation occurs when someone publicly makes remarks, in print or by word of mouth, which are untrue and damaging to another's reputation. In *Gantry* v. *Wilson*, it was the minister himself who had chosen to allow the letter's content to be known. One issue on appeal would be Gantry's role in making the defamatory material public. The other was a Constitutional matter. On the face of it, there is some conflict between the law of defamation, which restricts what people can say about each other, and the First Amendment's guarantee of freedom of speech. For many years the U.S. Supreme Court has been seeking to reconcile the two principles, and the most recent doctrine is that short of reckless disregard for the truth, you can say what you want about somebody who is considered a public figure. Therefore on appeal, we would also argue that the minister was a public figure within the meaning of the law.

On Saturday morning I met Terry at the library to begin the research. The night before I had gone through Gilbert's on Torts and the Prosser hornbook and absorbed the outlines of the law on defamation. Now I was interested in more specific points of the law, which meant reading cases. In arguing to the Supreme Court of Ames, we would be contending that the trial judge had followed the wrong law, the wrong precedents. We would have to present the court with cases decided on similar facts which came to results more favorable to our client.

Normally, an attorney doing that kind of research would not look far beyond cases which arose in his own state. Cases from other jurisdictions do not have the same precedential effect in court. But the moot court competition was set up in such a way that the common law of the state of Ames was comprised of all the reported cases of every state in the nation. Those volumes occupy a good part of the enormous vaulted top floor of the huge Harvard Law School library and much of the lower stories.

Nevertheless, the job was not quite as forbidding as it

sounds. The private company which publishes most of those reports analyzes each opinion in an elaborate code. By resorting to huge digests, and sometimes the treatises and legal encyclopedias, it is possible to follow the code and to find cases from all around the country on the point which concerns you. Problems remain. To avoid misleading the court, before you cite a case—call it *Black* v. *White*—you must be certain that it has not been overruled, as sometimes happens, or that other judges have not criticized the opinion as badly reasoned. Therefore it is wise to check, at least cursorily, every subsequent case in which there has been a reference to *Black* v. *White*. That means resort to another index, which lists those references, and then, usually, going over each one. Finally, if you are new to all of this, like most first-year law students, you'll find that the cases you read tend to expose smaller weaknesses in your argument which you hadn't noticed, each one of which must be shored up by more cases and citations. It's like unpacking a molecule, only to find that the molecule contains atoms, the atoms contain parts, and the parts particles.

The research can be needless but Terry and I had sworn to do a creditable job without going crazy. By the end of Saturday, I thought we'd made a good start. I had more or less appropriated the Constitutional issue and been through a few Supreme Court opinions. Working on the publication question, Terry had already located material all over the library—cases, law-review articles, even copies of briefs. In the hours he'd spent up here while he was skipping class, he'd acquired phenomenal research skills.

During the week we each handed in a memo describing our research and initial analysis of the case. Friday we met for the first time with the advisor we had been assigned by BSA to discuss what we had found. Her name was Margo Sakarian. She was small and dark and extremely pretty. Like Terry, she was from New Jersey. Ames is probably the bane of the BSA Advisors' year. They must supervise half a dozen Ames teams, all working on the same case, and read through reams of memos and draft briefs, checking each to be certain that the various legal formalities which Ames serves to introduce have been observed.

Margo was harried and a little short with us in our first encounter.

"You guys forgot the facts," she told us at once. Each of us was to summarize the facts of the case in the memo. We'd both overlooked it. Terry was nonchalant.

"Look," he told her, "if we can't get the facts out, we don't deserve to be at Harvard Law School."

She didn't like that response.

"They're supposed to be here. You guys have a draft brief due in two weeks. Don't forget the facts in there."

She made a few more comments about our memos, mostly mild complaints, then left. I could see she had not made a big hit with Terry. HLS had managed to accentuate everybody's eccentricities. Stephen had become more nervous. I'd gotten louder and more insecure. Terry seemed increasingly sensitive to criticism. That made sense. He had pulled himself a long distance doing things his own way and in this highly regimented atmosphere he felt a threat to the independence he valued. He resented anything which felt like control. Right after the Torts exam, when we'd had lunch, he'd sworn that he would mend his ways and start going to classes again—he had been too frightened facing that test. But in the first week of the new term, while we were on our way to Civil Procedure, he had suddenly done a little dance and sung out, "Ooo, ooo, I'm gettin' that itchy feelin', just can't sit." He'd laughed and socked me in the arm and headed off for the library. If anything, his attendance was worse now. He was learning law his own way, reading through the biggest law-school library in the world.

As we watched Margo leave, he said to me, "Hey, that girl's a little snooty, don't you think?"

I told him not to worry about it. We had two weeks to research and write a brief. That seemed like a lot to do.

———————

Contracts and Civil Procedure continued in the second term. As time went on, however, I found my attitude toward each course different than it had been in the first semester. In Contracts a single event had worked a remarkable change in my perspective.

Perini had finally called on me to state the case.

It had happened in the final week of the first term. In a way, I had brought the trouble on myself. Perini apparently teaches Contracts at the same pace each year and with the end of the first semester imminent he seemed anxious to hit some sort of benchmark. I was unwise enough to delay him with a question at the opening of class.

"What about the effect of the contracts clause of the Constitution," I asked, "in yesterday's case?"

"What about *Bard* v. *Kent*?" Perini replied. "Today's case. Why don't you tell us about that?"

The class laughed vigorously, as we all usually did when Perini had somehow taken advantage of one of us. I smiled as I opened the casebook, but I knew this could have come at a more welcome time. I'd been so well prepared in so many instances in the past. That day, I didn't even have a brief. With all the work in the face of exams, I'd skipped the case abstract as well as the morning cram session. And the case was hard. We were deep in the murk of the "consideration doctrine," one of the law's perpetual mysteries, a concept as elusive as transubstantiation. No contract is complete unless both sides have proved consideration. In general, it is some evidence that the transaction is intended to be a positive exchange, a bargain and not the giving of a gift. Consideration can be the payment of money, or something as slender as a promise. Perini had called consideration "the conceptual analytical core of the course, our most challenging topic." My luck.

"The case is in the California Court of Appeals in 1942," I said, my voice quailing a bit as I started.

"Court of *Appeals?*" Perini cried.

Lord, already, I thought. I couldn't see the mistake. "California Supreme Court," Don beside me whispered. I was so nervous I thought I'd said that.

I corrected myself and went on, more or less reading the facts out of the casebook. The suit involved a fairly shady-looking operation in which a lawyer who represented an elderly widow had made use of his power of attorney to lease himself some of her real estate. He'd then sublet the property at a handsome profit. When the widow died, new and more virtuous lawyers, hired by her estate, sued, hoping to bust the first attorney's lease. The only way out was a lot of fancy foot-work with the consideration doctrine, and the opinion, which held for the estate, was closely reasoned.

I was fairly nimble with Perini's questions about the case, but had more difficulty when he asked me to compare it with others we'd read in recent weeks. Most of the time I sat there with a look of profound concentration or made weak re-sponses—"weasling," Perini called one of them—before he went on to someone else, Clarissa or Hochschild or Cauley, for answers. I'd done well enough, though, that he returned to me throughout the period with more questions.

In the next twenty-four hours, I was the object of the kind of assessment I'd practiced on everyone else. Terry, forever gen-erous, told me it was the toughest case of the year. It wasn't. Stephen also praised me lavishly. Aubrey, on the other hand, seemed to think I could have done better—he asked if I had read Perini's hornbook, in which, apparently, all the answers to the questions I'd missed were contained. A number of persons made it a point to tell me I had looked relaxed at those moments when Perini had come to stand directly over me.

To all of them I gave the same response: I was satisfied. I had not been great, but I fell into no swoon over an imperfect performance. In December that had seemed evidence that I was developing some perspective on the HLS achievement ethic, resisting that impulse to write off as worthless or a disgrace all things not done superbly.

But in the second term, I found that being called on had even greater significance. I was suddenly no longer a member of that legion who half swallowed their hearts every time they entered the room with Perini. He would not call on me again, and in class each day I suddenly felt almost like an outside observer. Most of my classmates still brought to Contracts the same rapt intensity they had from the start of the year. The effects of the Incident had been more or less expunged. Reportedly, Perini was still bitter about the affair and his public embarrassment. Letters and articles, most of them defending Perini, appeared on a couple of occasions in various law-school publications, but, within the classroom it was all but forgotten. Perini displayed the same domineering charm, and the great majority of the members of Section 2 still thought of him as an inspired teacher and of Contracts as the best class we had.

But not me. My sense of release had a strong effect on the way I regarded the man and the course he taught. Standing next to Perini one day late in January, I was stunned to discover that he was two or three inches shorter than I had thought at the beginning of the year. Truly, he was diminished in my estimate. No longer afraid, I felt my resentments of him more clearly, particularly of his pretensions. In class we were paying a good deal of attention to Article 2 of the Uniform Commercial Code, a statutory scheme devised like the Model Penal Code by a national group of legal scholars and since adopted as the law of every state. Article 2 covers "sales," and has supplanted much of what was once dealt with in traditional common-law contract doctrine. When you buy something in any store in America, the UCC now regulates many aspects of your purchase. As we had done with the Penal Code in Criminal Law, Perini would compare the holdings of the Contracts cases we were studying with the analogous stipulations of the UCC.

Perini loved to show off with the UCC. Article 2 is a hundred pages of intricate provisions, but Perini seemed to have it memorized down to the commas. Even when he touched on points inadvertently, in an aside, he would press his fingers to his forehead like a sideshow clairvoyant and come up with the precise portions of the code in which an issue was discussed. "You'll find that, I believe, in 2-617, paren 'a,' sub 1." He was always right, and the class was in awe of his grasp of detail. The first semester he'd made similar citations to his hornbook or to treatises.

There were some among the small group of students who shared my quiet hostility to Perini, who believed those episodes were phonics, scripted events carefully acted out in order to intimidate the section. I did not go that far, although I was increasingly aware that Perini did make errors, albeit trivial ones, often contradicting his own hornbook. What disturbed me in those instances and others like them was the way Perini played on our lack of knowledge and power. He had had twenty years to learn the UCC; we were new to it, vulnerable—and captive. If you came to class, you had no choice but to watch those flamboyant demonstrations, possessing no real standard by which to know if they deserved the kind of open admiration Perini seemed to expect. On the whole, I had the sense that Perini was using the classroom to live out some strange vision of himself and that struck me as a misappropriation of a teacher's power.

As my esteem for Perini declined, I tended to shirk the work of the course. That was an adolescent reaction, but the only tangible rebellion I could make. On Monday mornings, I found myself running contests with myself to see if I could read through a week's Contracts assignments in three hours or less.

For me, the compensating time and interest went into Civil Pro. As the second term began, Nicky Morris had stopped talking down to the class. We'd absorbed a groundwork of legal concepts and terminology and Morris had now started on the kind of wide-ranging philosophical tour which Peter Geocaris had said at the beginning of the year was in the offing.

Ostensibly, the second term in Nicky's course was devoted to close examination of the Federal Rules of Civil Procedure. The federal rules regulate most aspects of how a federal court runs: how actions are initiated, how information can be gathered by each side, the handling of many details relating to trial and appeal. Not only are the rules central in federal courts, but they are also the model for the procedural schemes of many of the states and study of them is an indispensable if unexciting part of most first-year educations at the law.

But Nicky's teaching of the rules was anything but dull. In late December we had spent a number of days studying *Erie Railroad Company* v. *Tompkins*, a 1938 decision of the U.S. Supreme Court, which had proved the intellectual watershed of the course. In *Erie*, the Supreme Court instructed the lower federal judges to apply state law rather than federal law to many of the cases which came before them. Thus federal courts in different states would often be using differing rules in evaluating the same legal questions.

"By recognizing variation in the law," Nicky told us, "the Supreme Court is accepting the idea that no one rule can be thought of as somehow 'natural.' We see the law after *Erie* only as an imposed order, a response to political and social tradition and not something sent from heaven. The law can change; the law can vary from place to place. And in those changes and variations, the law, like any other social product, reflects the persistent conflicts and contradictions within the society."

In teaching the cases we read to illustrate the federal rules, Nicky returned to those themes. He demonstrated how each rule, despite a neutral appearance, reflected those "persistent societal contradictions" which he had first mentioned in *Erie*. He continued to talk about the tension between our common desire that the law be uniform and certain, and our wish that it somehow meet the needs of justice in the individual case. He described the conflicting roles of judges, members of a decision-making elite in a democratic society. Should judges conform to popular sentiments? Nicky asked us. Should judges somehow watch out for the welfare of those who come before them? Should they assist the ignorant, or just apply disinterestedly the machinery of the law? Nicky talked about differing concepts of the duties of the parties to a lawsuit. Should they be forced to aid each other in some kind of higher service to the truth, or were the plaintiff and defendant independent gladiators, going at each other with no holds barred? What is the community's stake in the just resolution of disputes? How much does the idea of a right require an individual to enforce it on his own?

The questions, the conflicts, were elaborate and Nicky began to work them out in increasing complexity as the term wore on. Some members of the section were infuriated by Morris's approach. They found it abstruse, confusing, and—worst—impractical.

"He's in outer space," Ned Cauley told me one day. "We're not learning Civil Procedure; we're learning Nicky Morris's theory of rules. What's going to happen to all of us when we go into a courtroom and make a motion under Rule Twelve E? Do you think the judge is going to give a damn whether it's a model of legal informalism?"

But the majority of the section were enthusiasts and I was among them. Like Ned, I had come to law school for professional training, but I was also looking for something more, something which was lost when teachers concentrated more directly on the kind of professionalizing Ned desired. In those classes, law study was treated primarily as the means for learning the circumscribed skills and customs of a sort of elevated priesthood. The uniqueness of legal thought was emphasized. In consequence, I and many other classmates were often left with the sense of a gap between legal ideas and those we had known in other areas of study. Nicky was out to efface that boundary.

"The law," Nicky said at one point in the second term, "is a humanistic discipline. It is so broad a reflection of the society, the culture, that it is ripe for the questions posed by any field of inquiry: linguistics, philosophy, history, literary studies, sociology, economics, mathematics."

Nicky did not touch on all those subjects, but his teaching was always animated by a sense of the law's search as unlimited and profound. In Morris's class I found myself launched once again on that kind of scrutiny of the most fundamental assumptions regarding the way we lived each day—the manner in which we treated each other—which had seemed so important when I had come to school. Each time I walked into Morris's classroom all that rapturous discovery of the first six weeks returned. And I knew I would leave after each meeting with the same crazy feeling, half heat, half thirst—the sensation of being nearly sucked dry by excitement.

2/11/76
(Wednesday)

Life around the law school at the moment is consumed by the Ames competition, politics, and flu. It seems as though everybody has been bitten by the same bug. Annette was sick three days last week. I was out on Thursday. The classes all resound with coughs and sniffles.

The Massachusetts primary is drawing near and many of the candidates seem to feel obligated to touch base at that august American institution, the Harvard Law School. It's not the students' votes they're after—most of those belong to Udall, as mine does, or to Fred Harris. Some candidates, I guess, come to meet with HLS profs, many of whom are advisors to the various campaigns. More of the pols, I think, just want to latch hold of the law-school name so it can be boosted throughout the campaign. "Well, when I spoke to that question at Harvard Law School . . ." I've tried to see them all. First through was Jimmy Carter, the Georgia peanut farmer, way back in September when most people didn't know who he was. Many of his lines sounded like bumper-strip slogans, and he was incredibly, even disturbingly, neat about his person. Friday, Scoop Jackson proved dull and unimpressive before a crowd in Austin. Shapp, Mo, and Harris will be by before the end of the month.

I feel more relaxed in school now than I have all year. The promises the 2Ls and 3Ls made me—that someday it would be easier to read a case—have finally come true. Something fell into place after Christmas. It's still not like the funny papers, of course, but comprehension is fluid, line by line. Even with Ames, I have more free time than in the worst moments last term, and after the draft brief, I should be able to knock off weekends for a while. I can be with Annette more often now. A few days ago, we actually got out for a movie in the middle of the week, and I've also reorganized my schedule somewhat, getting up with A. in the mornings so we can have coffee together before she heads off to teach.

As for classes, I am still enjoying the elective, Law and Public Policy. Sternlieb has spent the first weeks trying to acquaint us with the social-science skills he considers invaluable to policy planners. Right now we're doing statistics and the Bayes theorem. Last week it was game theory. Before that, we had another heavy dose of economics, going over marginalism, Pareto optimality, and cost/benefit analysis.

Along that line, I have some advice for anybody considering law school: take some econ before you come. The policy course is the fourth of the year to place considerable emphasis on economics. The free market in Contracts; allocation theory in Torts. In Property, Fowler has introduced us to something called Coase's theorem, an economic approach to the distribution of property rights. Even Nicky on occasion has talked about rules in terms of their costs and benefits. In all instances, econ has been introduced as a rationalizing principle, a way to make more sense of the many hard choices in the law.

For those of us without any background in the subject it is sometimes heavy sledding. Nothing is surer to turn on Sondergard's tears than prolonged talk of economics. Another section has been in a state of muted rebellion all year against their young Contracts professor who follows an unyielding economic analysis, which, for a lot of students, is like not being allowed to come up for air.

I am still not certain how seriously I should take this stuff. Much of what we're taught about economics seems to disguise some of the crueler assumptions of the free-enterprise system, and I often feel that econ is no more than a subtle way to get us to buy in on a businessman's vision of the world. What do you say about a system of thought which presumes that everyone acts out of self-interest?

A sociologist with years of econ, Stephen is an outright skeptic. He thinks economics does little more than repeat what is already known. He told me a joke to illustrate the point. Three men are starving on a desert island when they find a can of beans. The first, a strong man, wants to tear the can open with his teeth. The second, an engineer, proposes that they open the can by dropping a heavy rock on it from a great height. The third is an economist and he has a plan of his own. "First," he tells the other two, "you must assume we have a can opener."

Be that as it may, I've too often had the feeling that the professors are saying, "Assume you've had economics."

Ames went on. The 1Ls gave most of their attention to research and writing, and the professors seemed to make allowances. Nicky tailored his assignments to conform to the competition's schedule. Perini suddenly began to lecture, rather than calling on a student to serve as target or foil. As the due dates for briefs neared, attendance fell off in each of the courses. In Property, where absences had been high from the start of the term, as many as a third of the students were sometimes missing. At the start of one session, Fowler looked around the room and said, almost sanguinely, "Well, let's see who's here."

For all the hard work that students put into Ames, those labors seemed to reflect genuine interest, rather than the normal patterns of panic or pack-running aggressions. There were the familiar extremes, of course—people going so hard they missed sleep for three nights, others who claimed to have written their briefs without reading any of the cases they'd cited— but most of my classmates seemed to take Ames as a welcome diversion. As opposed to exams, moot court offered a real opportunity to demonstrate and to see for yourself that you had acquired some competence with professional tasks. And the process of working through the cases firsthand and shaping your own argument provided a novel vantage on the law at a time when the daily preoccupations of the classroom had begun to seem routine.

"It's the only damn thing in law school that makes sense,"

Aubrey said about Ames. He was increasingly disenchanted with school and professorial abstractions. "It's the only thing all year that prepares you for practice."

I shared much of the general enthusiasm for Ames. The First Amendment issues in our defamation case—the questions of which citizens were public figures and why speech about them should be less restricted—turned increasingly subtle and challenging as I worked them through, and I took real pleasure in the research. There were of course some aspects of Ames I was less keen on. One of the purposes of moot court was to acquaint us with the proprieties of the case citation—the shorthand notations used in all legal writing to indicate in which court a decision was made and the volume in which the case is reported. A judge, or opposing counsel, will often want to review the cases you point to for support, and accurate citation is thus another of the dull, lawyerly skills you cannot go without learning. Our Ames briefs were required to conform to the scheme of citation developed by the *Harvard Law Review*, and as I prepared to begin drafting, I found myself spending hours deep in the library stacks checking on nerve-wrackingly small details, such as the page number on which quotations I'd be using appeared in each of the two or three report series issued by different publishers.

But on the whole, I enjoyed the work of moot court. The brief provided another of the opportunities we seldom had to try legal writing and to gain more familiarity and control over the law's impersonal rhetoric. I was beginning, I thought, to feel a little more comfortable with it.

The only large difficulty I encountered with moot court had nothing to do with what was required of us. The problem was personal, for I was having trouble dealing with Terry. He had never mustered much excitement about Ames, and I'd only dimmed his enthusiasm further by unwittingly grabbing off the part of the case, the Constitutional issue, which he later admitted had interested him more. As a result, Terry appeared to become even more determined to do things his own way and at his own speed. He paid little attention to external requirements. His work was listless and sporadic, and much of the research he did was careless. In the memo conference, Margo had given him suggestions on ways to approach his end of the case, but he refused them, preferring an erratic legal theory of his own. He seemed to have a vague idea of winning the case by concocting an entirely new approach to the law of defamation, relating it to the concept of fault, even though his thinking was unclear and there was little support for what he was saying among existing authorities.

"Look," he told me a few days after our conference with Margo, "that girl is all wrong. She doesn't really understand this case. The issue is all different."

I asked him if he had the cases to prove that.

"There're pages of cites in the legal encyclopedias," he told me.

"Have you read any?" I asked.

"There're hundreds of cases," he repeated.

In the following weeks he did not seem to read many of them. As the deadline for the draft brief approached, it became apparent that he would never complete work on a part of the case that he'd promised to cover. I took over the research and writing myself, without much overt complaint. It wasn't worth it, I figured, to strain a good friendship. I had to pull my only all-nighter of the year in order to get my portion of the brief ready, and when I reached school on the day it was due I was disgruntled to learn that Terry had not finished his half. We had the long President's Day weekend ahead, however, and Terry assured me that he'd finish the brief in the next day or two and get it to Margo, who would still have two days to look it over before our next conference, scheduled for Tuesday.

Annette and I left town for the weekend, but Terry found

me by my locker as soon as I got to school on Tuesday morning. He had a funny smirk as he approached.

"Hey," he said, "that girl's gettin' a little impatient with me."

I asked what that meant. He explained that he hadn't finished the brief yet and that Margo, angry now, had called him the night before.

"Terry," I said, "this isn't funny. You've got to get that done."

"It'll be done, man," he said, "it'll be done. I'm goin' to the libe right now. I'll write it this morning. She'll have it by noon. We don't meet her until two."

"Just get it done," I said again. "I don't want to end up flunking this thing." That seemed like a vaguely realistic concern now. Word was that each year there were a few 1Ls who took Ames too lightly and ended up having to repeat the entire Legal Methods program the following year. I was happy to let Terry go his own way so long as I was not going to get dragged down with him, but now I was beginning to worry. He seemed stranger about the whole business daily.

I met Terry at two and together we went toward Pound, where we were scheduled to see Margo in a conference room on the third floor. I asked if he'd finished the brief and Terry assured me he had; but as we rode up in the elevator, he was obviously agitated, fidgeting, rolling his shoulders.

"Hey, listen," he said. "I'm pretty bugged about this. I went in to see that girl, what's-her-name, Margo, at the BSA office, to make sure she got the brief, and, man, she was reading my thing and when she saw me she really went through the roof. I mean, she told me I was going to have to do the whole thing over again, that I was wrong."

That was what I was afraid of. "What did you say?"

"I told her it wasn't my life," Terry answered.

"Look," I said, "that's not a subtle approach." When I

looked at Terry I could see a hard gleam coming into his eyes. He was powerfully angry.

"Well, it's not my life, man, is it?" he asked.

I agreed that it wasn't, backing off. We went down the hallway in silence. Outside the conference room, Terry grabbed me for a second.

"You go first in this thing," he told me. "I'm still hot. I've gotta get myself under control."

My half of the conference was fine. Margo raised points with me, trying to make sure I understood the dimensions of my argument. I didn't agree with everything she said. But by and large I appreciated most of her suggestions.

When she turned to Terry, however, it was obvious they had remained irritated with each other. Margo handed Terry back his brief. It was handwritten—typing was required—and her remarks appeared in a large scrawl across the back of each page.

"I'm sorry my comments sound a little nasty," she said, "but I was really angry when I read that. You cite two cases. And you never stated the facts. That's supposed to be at the start of your half of the brief," she said to Terry. "I told you guys before that how you state the facts is important."

Terry answered again that there was nothing to stating facts.

"You said that last time," Margo told him. "It was supposed to be done now. And how can you hope to convince the court when you only cite two cases?"

"I cite CJS, Prosser, ALR," Terry answered.

"Those are encyclopedias," she said, "hornbooks. They're not cases. They're not law."

For a moment, the two of them debated with increasing heat. Terry insisted he had done things the right way and after briefly attempting to maintain an icy restraint Margo became slightly sarcastic. As they replied to one another, each would look to me for support. Margo was right, I knew; but I also recognized how much Terry valued loyalty. I tried to show nothing.

Finally, Margo decided to be plain.

"Your arguments are just incredible," she said to Terry. "They make no sense. Really. This thing with defamation and fault—you're going to embarrass yourself if you say that in front of the court. You'll embarrass Scott."

Terry popped. His eyes filled with the same outraged gleam I'd seen in the hallways and he leaned forward in a belligerent animal posture. His hands were in fists, and now and then he struck the table. For an instant, I was afraid he might hit Margo.

"You're just making up rules," he told her. "I don't care if everybody who's ever done this sees it your way—they're all wrong. You're wrong! You're just abusing your power as an advisor. You're trying to *push* me around. You give me cases in black and white. You show me! You don't know *what* you're talking about!"

At last he bulled away from the table and pounded from the room. A moment after he left, Margo began crying.

"I'm just trying to *help* you guys," she said.

I sought to comfort Margo as best I could. I apologized for Terry, but I felt badly shaken by the way he'd reacted. He'd frightened me, and obviously Margo as well.

I didn't see Terry until the next day.

"You tell me what you think," he said. But then he added his own version of the events. "I was wrong," he told me. "I mean, I shouldn't have backed off. I mean, I was too apologetic."

I stared at him, incredulous. Then I called him a name and walked away.

Late in the year, when I described HLS to a friend who is a doctor he compared it to a hospital ward. He said that both were places where the inmates frequently found it hard to stay close with anyone. People were under too much tension, in extremity, often too busy saving themselves to think about preserving relationships.

I think that's true. My friendship with Stephen never quite recovered after first-term exams. With Terry, Ames remained a barrier between us. We both cooled off in a couple of days and Terry even agreed that he was too harsh to Margo. But he never apologized to her. Instead, he became determined to justify his behavior, to prove that the screwball theory about defamation he'd designed made sense. As the final brief and then the oral argument approached, he worked furiously to locate cases or law-review articles which lent some credence to what he maintained. He never found them. I tried at first to dissuade him from his reasoning, then finally attempted to understand what he was saying, but I failed on both counts. As we went through the remainder of Ames, I often told myself that it was just Harvard Law School, now and then it made all of us nuts. But in the deliberateness of my efforts to objectify, to be fair to Terry, I recognized a distance which had not been there before.

2/17/76
(Tuesday)

I saw Stephen today after Law and Public Policy. He had read a notice on a bulletin board and when he informed me of what it said, a little wiggle went through my belly.

"Grades tomorrow," he said.

I will not pretend that in the weeks since exams, I haven't spent a lot of time thinking about grades. Tomorrow will be when the music gets faced. Like everyone else, I can't help assuming that the results will be highly predictive of my future law-school performance, which in turn will dictate much of what happens to me when I get out of this place.

One of the most immediate effects of tomorrow's marks is that they will serve as a first cut for Law Review. I admit that the more often I think about being on the Review, the better I like the idea. Over time, it is hard not to be taken with the prominence of the *Harvard Law Review*. It is quoted in judicial opinions, relied on, deferred to throughout the legal world. In keeping up with Morris's course, I now often go to the Libe to consult the journal articles and I've begun to realize that I would probably enjoy being part of their production.

Not that I expect that to happen. Anybody who gets two Bs tomorrow will probably be out of the running, and I suspect I will be in that category. The word is that almost everyone at HLS gets Bs, although the precise distribution of grades is one of the most closely guarded secrets at the place. The registrar keeps the information under wraps to prevent any efforts at top-to-bottom-of-class ranking, which was dropped in the 1960s. It is generally known, though, that the registrar sends a record of past marks in first-year courses to each professor. Hypothetically, the teachers are free to disregard those figures, but it's a safe bet that most keep the past distribution of grades in mind. The students tend to think in terms of a fixed curve, with a lot of speculation about the ratio of grades. One kid I met in the gym locker room informed me authoritatively that only ten percent of the grades are As. But Wally Karlin said that Nicky Morris had told him that the usual distribution broke down twenty/sixty/twenty, As, Bs, and Cs, with a smattering of Ds and Fs. Whatever the curve in each course, the kind of consistently high performance which leads to Law Review is rare. One thing I know for sure is that after three years, no more than eight or nine percent of each class has the average of A-minus or better which is required for graduation *magna cum laude*.

Exams were too crazy for me to feel I could predict my grades with any accuracy. I imagine Torts will be higher than Crim. In the past weeks, I have tended to strike little bargains with myself, trying to hold off my dread of Cs, by not thinking too much about the possibility of As. On the whole, I guess I'd feel good about a B and a B-plus. It would put me on the track toward graduation with honors, which would be a nice reward after three years of slaving. The real goal, however, is to resist the familiar HLS vibes and to be comfortable with myself tomorrow, no matter what the results.

At the end of Civil Procedure the next day, Nicky Morris gave us a little speech.

"I don't think you should be getting the grades you'll be receiving this afternoon. I've always thought that the first year should be pass/fail. None of you are far enough along for these grades to reflect with any accuracy any of the permanent, highly ineradicable differences between people which are measured by exams. So I urge you not to take these grades this afternoon too seriously. Absolutely nothing that you would like to do in the future in the way of a legal career will be determined by them. Nothing. Not teaching. Not jobs with firms."

Phil Pollack, sitting next to me, leaned over and whispered, "Notice he doesn't mention Law Review."

I noticed. We were all thinking the same thing. Though an admirable effort, Nicky's speech did little to relieve the prevalent anxieties. By the end of the day many people would feel that limits had been fixed.

The plan the registrar had hit upon for the distribution of report cards required all 1Ls to present themselves at two o'-clock at one of two classrooms in Langdell, to receive their marks. Many of us could picture the stampede to those rooms and resented having once more to submit to the mass. The registrar later explained that that had simply seemed the fastest means of getting the reports distributed. As it was, 1L anxieties about grades had appeared to her so pronounced that she'd sped things in her office, so that first-year marks were coming out weeks before those of second-year and third-year students.

I played squash in the afternoon and showed up late in Langdell to avoid the two o'clock crush. At the hour, apparently, there had been a long line. I was told that people had filed into the room and emerged expressionless, the grade sheet clutched against their chests while they mumbled that they had not looked at it. By the time I arrived the crowds had dispersed. Downstairs there were a few people from another section standing around. I heard one ask another how he'd done and the reply: "I won't make the Law Review."

As I headed up toward the room where the grade reports were being handed out, I saw Stephen coming down the staircase. There was more in his face than a smile—his expression was animated by something wild, a profound kind of glee. I did not have to ask.

"You did well," I told him.

He laughed out loud. "A-plus and an A."

"My God," I pumped his hand. The grades were astronomical. "That's wonderful."

I asked him to wait and hurried on up. The huge classroom was quiet. The woman from the registrar's office removed a long computer slip from a book of them.

"Very nice," she said before she handed the sheet over.

An A-minus in Criminal, a B-plus in Torts. I would not make the Law Review, I thought at once, but I had done well. I felt light-headed, just from meeting the reality of all of this after worrying so long.

I headed down to find Stephen. Sandy Stern had now positioned himself at the foot of the stairs, asking people their grades as they sifted past. Sandy himself had done quite well, an A and an A-minus, but he was not satisfied.

"I'm not sure I'll make Law Review," he explained. Apparently, he'd decided to survey everyone whom he considered competition. When he asked me how I'd done, I felt almost flattered. In the days before, I had not been certain whether I would discuss my marks. Talking about grades seemed a lot like talking about how much money you make—there was no way to be tasteful. Speaking freely risked envy or contempt. Remaining silent seemed to magnify the importance of something I wanted to treat as meaningless. In the end, I made no conscious choice. When Sandy asked, I just blurted.

Behind me, Myra Katchen came down the stairs. She was a former grad student in philosophy, good in class—another of the people Sandy would consider a hot competitor. He asked how she'd done.

"Okay," she answered, "but I won't make Law Review."

Down the hall tunnel, I found Stephen and walked him to Harkness, where I bought him a congratulatory Coke. As we sat in the lounge, Aubrey appeared. There was no need to ask how he'd done. He looked gray. He put the coffee cup he was carrying down on the table.

"Smack in the middle of the class," he said. Bs of some kind, that meant. Aubrey had worked doggedly first term, unafraid of confessing his ambitions. He wanted the most selective firm, the highest salary, the Review. I felt he deserved better for his honesty. And after going bust out in LA, he would, I'm sure, have savored some great triumph now, reaffirming all his best hopes for himself.

The three of us tried to make conversation, but it was self-conscious and strained. Stephen eventually told Aubrey his grades and Aubrey congratulated him. As I stood up to leave, I told Aubrey that we had some consolation—at least next year we'd be able to join Stephen for bag lunch over at Gannett House, where the Law Review is located.

Stephen smiled then murmured almost to himself, "I guess I will be over there."

I checked on Stephen for some sign of humor, but there was none. Four exams remained in the spring, and we had all heard stories about 1Ls who received two As first term and never saw

As again. But looking at Stephen I could see he had caught a whiff of a high ether. He knew what he wanted, now. He knew where he belonged.

I walked Aubrey back to his locker. Willie Hewitt came by, bragging about two Bs.

"Not bad for a screw-off, huh?" he asked me as he passed. Aubrey seemed to wince. He stared into his empty locker.

"I'm so tired of being competent," he said suddenly. "I've been competent all my life. I wish I could be either the best or the worst. This is just so goddamn dull." He shook his head and laughed a little. I clapped him on the back.

Up in the library I tried to study, but I was still in a daze of contradictory emotions—shame, envy, pity, pride. I had put such confused feelings into grades and exams that a tangle was bound to emerge. I felt an ugly and powerful jealousy of Stephen, but I realized my grades were good. I had heard enough from 2Ls and 3Ls before to know that along with many others I remained vaguely in the running for Law Review, if far from the front of the pack. Much of the hallway commentary and my own first reactions were really expressions of regret at a diminished chance.

Mike Wald came up to me as I sat there. "The 1L grades come out?" he inquired.

I said yes, why did he ask?

"Lots of red faces." Mike gestured toward the rest of the library. "People crying."

Incredibly, Mike was right. That afternoon and in the next few days I found that many of my classmates had taken grades hard; they were glum, disconsolate, and indeed, occasionally teary. Virtually all of us had been outstanding students, accustomed to the reward of high grades. Those high marks had been the means by which we'd made our way through the world—to famous colleges, to Harvard Law School. They were success itself, the underpinning of self-images, taken, over time, less as limited reflections of our abilities than as badges of personal merit. Now, as predicted, most people had received Bs, grades many had rarely seen, having gone to college in an era when straight As were not uncommon. For several, the step down was a terrific blow and the reactions were sometimes extreme. Clarissa Morgenstern, I was told, had had two B-pluses and had become hysterical. She wept wildly and swore to leave law school. Others seemed mammothly insulted. Kyle had grades like mine.

"I couldn't believe it," he told me. "I looked down there and I thought, No, there must be something wrong, one of them's not an A."

The day after grades came out, we all spoke of nothing else. It was another of the times Annette had come with me to school, and when we got home she told me how offended she had been by the constant gossip about marks, the ceaseless comparisons. It seemed to her ugly and obsessive and adolescent. No doubt it was. But most of us—aside from the few with two As—needed the reassurance of knowing how others had done, just to be certain that a B was not a sign of incompetence. Phyllis Wiseman was in her early thirties, a wife and mother who even as a law student had continued to place her family first. She was widely admired in the section for holding that kind of distance on the law school's demands. But when grades came out, even Phyllis felt she had to take part in that great show and tell.

"I've never been a busybody," she told me, "I've never been a gossip. I don't care what my neighbors do. But I'm just crazy to know how everyone did."

As it was, few people spoke of Cs, although it was well known that a large number were always given. Most of the students who'd received Cs seemed to have been shamed into silence. And there was an even more disquieting indication of how deep the discomfort over grades ran. As the comparison of marks continued, I heard several comments to the effect that the number of high grades seemed disproportionate. Some of that was a statistical quirk. Given the queerness of the exams, the results on individual tests were bound to be somewhat random. With only two grades in, there were a lot of people who, like me, had received one A, but would not over the long haul find themselves making As half the time.

Yet even taking that into account, the grades seemed peculiarly high, particularly when one considered what we'd heard about the strictness of the usual HLS curve. I asked Mike Wald about it one afternoon in the library when we had a longer talk about grades.

"People lie," Mike told me. "That happens a lot around here. Some people just can't deal with not being at the top. They lie to their classmates and they lie to employers. It's gotten so bad," Mike said, "that firms are thinking about requiring a transcript before they hire."

Eventually, the talk in the section about grades, and the craziness which surrounded them, began to subside. But a wake of bitterness remained. People recovered from the hurt of being in the middle, of being cut out of the race for the Law Review, but few seemed to regard the whole process of examination and grading, law-school style, as any more sensible. So many of the results had appeared irrational. Terry, for instance, had banked everything on Criminal. He put all his study time into it, and more or less wrote off Torts as a subject he would never comprehend. Yet in Crim, he'd only gotten a B, while from Zechman he'd received a straight A. There were many stories like that. And there were also a number of people who'd demonstrated real insight into legal problems in class but who somehow had not done well on the exams. Ned Cauley was one. In a case like his, I was left wondering if the law school's system of blind grading—with a student's entire mark based on a test identified by a number and not by name—was worth it, or if it forced professors to ignore knowledge obviously relevant to their evaluations.

Most persistent among my classmates seemed to be an anger that there had been grades at all, that persons who were all demonstrably talented had been subjected to this terror of minuses and pluses, divided from each other, stacked up in tiers. I myself was willing, at moments, to concede that at either pole there might have been people worth noting. If someone really could make great sense of those exam narratives, then he deserved some commendation—he had a talent I didn't have. And at the other end, if students seemed not to have learned, it was appropriate to warn them of that. But for the great majority of us in the middle, it was hard to believe that these levels of fine discrimination, A-plus through B-minus, C, D, and F, could be made with much accuracy. A few years before, Harvard 1Ls had been given the opportunity to opt for pass/fail grades or simpler evaluation schemes—High, Satisfactory, Low, and Fail—but in an inexplicable reversal, the faculty had abolished those options a year before we arrived. We were left in a system which seemed close to capricious and which was often unavoidably painful when you considered its real-world effects.

On the afternoon I'd spoken with Mike Wald about grades, I'd asked him if there really was any justification for all of it.

"A lot of people will tell you," Mike said, "even a lot of professors, that grades are essentially for employers. The alumni give quite a bit of money to this law school, and most of them are members of the firms which interview here. They want to have some way of believing they're making meaningful distinctions between applicants. They see somebody for what—a twenty-minute interview? They know they need something else to go on. If a firm does a lot of real-estate law, then maybe they can pick between two people because one had a B-plus in Property and the other one had a B-minus. It's all crazy," Mike said, "but I can tell you that the firms are the ones that really scream when the faculty talks about pass/fall."

I looked at Mike a second.

"That's commerce," I said, "not education. That's just product packaging."

"Some would say," Mike told me. He smiled first, then he shrugged.

————

In recounting the February commotion surrounding grades and future membership on Law Review, it is well to note that at about the same time some interesting changes were taking place among those students already over at Gannett House. Late in February, the Review announced that Susan Estrich, a 2L, had been appointed president. It was the first time in the eighty-nine-year history of the Review that a woman had occupied the position, essentially that of editor in chief.

It had been a good year for minorities and the Law Review. Earlier, Christopher Edley, another 2L, had become the first black member since the late 1940s. Considering the Review's standing as one of the legal world's great points of arrival, both developments went to underline the gains being made by minorities at Harvard Law School and in the law world at large.

In the America of a decade or fifteen years ago, it is all but certain that many members of my class would not have been there. In the recent past, however, there has been an astonishing rise in the enrollment of women and racial minorities in American law schools. There are three times more black and Spanish-surnamed law students in U.S. law schools than in 1969, and the growth in female enrollment has been a kind of social miracle—an 1100 percent increase in the past twelve years. Nearly a quarter of American law students are now women. In my class at Harvard ten percent of the members were black, three percent Latin, twenty-one percent female. As the year had worn on,

I had watched with some interest to see how those working their way up from the short end of the stick were doing around HLS. The answer, in brief, was very well.

Racial relations at Harvard Law School are probably better than in any setting in which I've found myself for many years. Even compared to the hip racial scene in the Bay Area, HLS seemed remarkable for its lack of tension. There are black and Latin student organizations at Harvard Law School, and my minority classmates were active in dealing with the special problems that faced them. Yet there was little of the effort I'd seen around other universities by blacks and Latins to keep themselves icily separate. We all felt free to be together without strain or self-consciousness. That was probably a product of the outgoingness of HLS's minority students, who are as gregarious as the rest of us, and also of the fact that few people enrolled at Harvard Law School, no matter what the barriers of the past, can think of themselves, in relative terms, as deprived.

Which is not to say that everything is gravy for those students. In the entrenched legal world, there continues to be significant discrimination in hiring and, after that, in promotion. Most employers, the great majority, are anxious to find good minority lawyers, but there are still large corporate firms which are exclusively white and where the absence of black and Latin and Asian lawyers is excused for a variety of reasons, including the prejudices of clients who must be served. This year the interviewer from one large all-white Chicago firm allegedly explained to a black 2L that the firm was just being outbid by competitors who "have their quotas too." That remark, and others, led the 2L to file a complaint with the placement office, where the law school has instituted a program to end hiring discrimination. Each interviewing firm is required to submit data on the number of its minority partners and associates, and the law school has promised to exclude any employers shown to be biased.

Some black students also complain of a quiet prejudice within the law school itself. Minority candidates are admitted with grades, and especially LSAT scores, sometimes lower than those of their white classmates. While the LSAT has been shown to be a far less effective measure of a minority student's likely law-school success, the discrepancy, combined with the failure of minority students to get the consistently high grades required for Law Review, has sometimes fed insinuations that minority students at HLS are not as capable as their white peers. Yet even conservative faculty members like Perini have given up any skepticism about the ability of minority students to thrive at HLS. "Blacks and women have achieved parity in the law school," he told us the day we had lunch with him. "There was a period at the start, when the admissions push began, when you would find the lowest grades going to minority students, but there's very little of that now."

Despite the good spirit of his remarks, Perini was one of the few professors who seemed actually self-conscious in his dealings with blacks and Latins and women. He was inevitably softer in his interrogation of all of them, and he'd had an especially hard time bringing himself to call on females. It was December before he asked a woman to state the case, and that was only after rumblings about his failure had been heard in the Women's Law Association, the female students' organization.

That women would complain of something like that—unequal footing on grounds stalked by terror—is indicative of the relentless feminist spirit abroad at HLS. WLA is active in recruiting female applicants as well as in encouraging the hiring of more female faculty (at the moment, four women teach at Harvard Law). On the whole, women probably insist on their rights more aggressively than any other minority group at HLS, but that may well be because they have more to complain about.

The law has always been one of the most overtly sexist professions around. Courts and law firms have long been known for a concerted old-boy atmosphere, like that of an English gentlemen's club, and women still encounter significant resistance to any role for them in law when they seek jobs and clerkships. Nor has the war been fully won within the law school itself, even among fellow students. Some men are self-conscious in dealing with women on an equal footing—I keep wanting to say, "Now in response to the remark of the little filly in the first row,'" Ned Cauley told a group of us one day, "but I know that just *wouldn't* go over"—and others seem to cling to old patterns of response with no self-consciousness at all. Karen Sondergard said she quit one study group because she felt her opinions were ignored solely because she was a woman. And another classmate bluntly told me, "I'm glad to have all these women here. Just gonna make our degrees that much more valuable when they're all at home raising babies."

The degree to which women traditionally have been excluded in the law world is illustrated by the fact that Harvard Law School did not admit women until 1950, long after male minority-group members of all shades and religions had been welcomed on campus. Even after the sudden jump in female enrollment of recent years, many WLA members continue to believe that it is lower at HLS than it should be. Another Boston area law school, at Northeastern University, now admits an entering class each year that is half female, and WLA has encouraged the Harvard admissions office to follow suit. At present the law school has a more conservative policy, following a program of what they call "sex-blind" admissions, which means that applicants are evaluated without reference to gender. In recent years the percentage of women in each entering class has correlated closely with the percentage of females in the applicant pool.

The long-standing prejudice against women among the male legal establishment may well be due to the competitive nature of the law as a profession. In the courtroom, there are always victor and vanquished, and a gentleman is not supposed to feel at ease engaging in combat with a lady.

At moments during the year, it sometimes appeared to me that my female classmates were not themselves entirely comfortable with the open aggression that law and law school demanded. In class, they tended to be retiring. Clarissa and Myra Katchen both spoke up often, but the rest of the twenty or so women only rarely volunteered. Moreover, if I could believe Gina, many of the women were sometimes even more uncomfortable than the men when they were called on.

"I know how this sounds," she told me once, "but a lot of the women say the same thing. When I get called on, I really think about rape. It's sudden. You're exposed. You can't move. You can't say no. And there's this man who's in control, telling you exactly what to do. Maybe that's melodramatic," she said, "but for me, a lot of the stuff in class shows up all kinds of male/female power relations that I've sort of been training myself to resent."

The general reticence of women about the aggressions of law-school life and the legal world is probably a current handicap. It may even account for the fact that women, like the racial minorities, have tended to be underrepresented on the Law Review. But the more conscious I became of the problems endemic to the law school and the law, the more I saw that aversion to aggression as one of the great assets women bring to the legal universe. By custom the law world has been rigidly patriarchal. Many of the psychological articles I read about law school accounted for the harshness of relations between professors and students by relating them to the stereotypic Freudian struggle between fathers and sons. A powerful figure parades before a group that always before has been made up primarily of young men. The older male flexes his muscles, assails the young ones, demonstrates his control over them, while they grow both eager to imitate him and increasingly resentful. In a way, those patterns of envy and subjugation are repeated throughout the legal world, with the old men always standing on the shoulders of the young ones. Law Review members do cite-checks for professors' articles; clerks write opinions to which judges put their names; law-firm associates slave over the most tedious aspects of the partners' cases. It all continues until one day you suddenly are a professor, a judge, or a partner—doing what was done to you.

The reluctance of the women in the law school about participating in these traditional and often unjust relationships was to me one of the happiest portents I saw all year. We are moving toward a time when today's numerous female law students will be female lawyers, and a prominent force in the legal world. It is to be hoped that they will bring with them sensitivities to the uses of power, of the kind which Gina described. If they do, they can make the legal world a fairer one, a place less distorted by some of the hard things men alone have tended to do to each other in the past.

3/13/76
(Saturday)

The Ames competition finally came to a conclusion for Terry and me on Thursday night, when we gave our oral argument. As usual I approached the event with trepidation. Terry was determined to stick to his half-assed theory about defamation and fault, and I couldn't imagine what the judges were going to do to him. In addition, there were complications now on my end of the case. Last week, the U.S. Supreme Court handed down another opinion relating to the First Amendment issue in *Gantry* v. *Wilson*. The Court had redefined "public figure" again, and from what I'd heard, the new formulation would all but exclude the minister. It sounded like disaster for us, kind of a bitter pill after all the work.

Had this been a genuine appellate argument, the court would have rescheduled it to allow my opponent and me to familiarize ourselves with the new case. BSA was not that generous, and so I spent much of Wednesday slogging through the opinion. I wanted to be prepared. I didn't care that much about winning or losing, I told myself, but I had no wish to leave the room feeling as faltering, careless, and inarticulate as I had after the Methods motion in the fall. I drew up a long outline of what I wanted to say.

Thursday night, I put on my three-piece suit—another fall lesson—and drove to school. After evincing blitheness earlier in the day, Terry seemed to be having second thoughts and was now trying to write out his argument word for word. We met our opponents, both from another section. Terry's opposite was friendly, small, quick-witted. The guy on my issue, however, looked crooked. His brief had seemed good and Margo had praised it when she'd given us a copy. But consulting his cases, I felt he'd often gone over the line from advocacy to outright distortion. Looking at him now, I thought I detected the same kind of cosmetics—nice suit, neat hair, and dirty fingernails. It may well have been a battlefield reaction.

At 8:00 precisely, our three judges filed in. Ames is sometimes pretty formal, and I'd heard about one group of student "counsel" who were bawled out for not standing when the court entered. Our judges were a little more casual. One was a student from BSA; he figured to be the toughest judge, since he'd been the best informed on the case. The second was a Boston attorney, an HLS alum. The third, and the heavyweight on the panel, was Judge Clarence Mealy, a sitting Superior Court judge who also teaches Trial Practice courses given for upper-class students at HLS. David had told me that Mealy was an exceptionally well-respected judge in Boston and I was glad for the realistic touch, even though I was a little more intimidated.

Terry began, "May it please the court." He was terribly nervous. He was wearing a gold sharkskin suit and he shifted uneasily as he spoke, choking, wetting his lips. To start, he was able to read from what he'd prepared. Oral argument usually commences with a brief recitation of the facts and questions of the case. This is to refresh the memory of the judges.

Terry did not get much beyond the facts, though, when the court started hitting him with questions. Like everybody else, they were having trouble making sense of his argument relating defamation to negligence. He'd finally found a case that offered some support, but it was from a minor court and from the nineteenth century, and the judges seemed to ridicule him for using it.

"Counsel," the BSA judge told him, "I don't even understand why you argued this point." Judge Mealy, a tired-looking Irishman, appeared somewhat amused. He rocked in his chair, smirking now and then in my direction. You got stuck with this palooka, he seemed to be saying, I feel for you. I tried to remain impassive, watching Terry instead. He was getting angry and frustrated. He began smacking his fist into his palm and he took on a tough, sulky look like that of a bad schoolboy. He'd become downright surly by the time they let him go back to his seat.

I went to the podium next. I had the usual lump in my throat, but most of the time the preparation helped me through. When questions were asked, I felt like I was able to move with the flow. I had composed a broad argument to incorporate the new Supreme Court case. I claimed that the general thrust of all the Court's opinions was that a person was a "public figure" whenever he or she was somehow involved with the well-being of a community, and that within that community communication about that person should be largely uninhibited. I think it was a pretty good argument. The judges sort of threw my points back at my opponent when he came to the podium later and he seemed to have a hard time handling them. "You're just making this worse," the Boston lawyer told him at one point.

When he finished, there was a round of rebuttal; then the four of us left the room to allow the judges to consult. It is usually weeks before a real appellate court announces its decision in a written opinion, but in Ames we'd be getting the word after a few minutes. BSA gives students the option of getting what they call a "competitive decision." If all the students consent, the judges not only say which side won, but also rank the four, one against another, on the quality of their arguments and their briefs. Terry and I discussed "competitive decision" in advance and ruled it out as being more Harvard Law School sickness. Victory or defeat seemed competitive enough.

In the hallway, the four of us drank beer, which BSA had provided, while we waited. Terry was feeling bruised about his treatment and I tried to console him, agreeing that the court had been rough. The guy who'd argued opposite me kept saying, "I'm just glad it's over." I agreed with that, too.

Ames cases are constructed such that they can go either way, but in most instances this year the teams which handled our side of the *Gantry* case seemed to win. Generally, they lost on my point but carried Terry's, thus overturning the lower-court verdict. We won too, but the opposite way. The decision, when we were called back in, was to reverse the lower court on the grounds that Reverend Gantry was indeed a public figure. I guess I had sounded pretty good. As we headed back to the hallway with the judges for more beer and a postmortem, there was a lot of praise for my argument from the judges and from Terry and even from our opponents. The Boston lawyer seemed to be offering me a job for the summer, repeatedly asking me what my plans were. It had not hurt me any, I knew, that none of the judges had yet actually read the Supreme Court decision.

Out in the hall, Terry soon got into another hassle with the BSA judge, repeating a lot of the things he had told Margo. I just walked away. I'd been listening to all of that for a month and I felt too good now to spoil it. It was moot court, a mythical state, a mass of frictions; but boy, did I enjoy winning. I haven't felt that kind of outright glee in victory in years. Maybe it's something else law school's done to me—more childishness—or a sign of how praise-starved I am. Maybe I just felt I'd finally done something roundly good with the law.

Anyway, I still felt high when I got out of bed yesterday morning and a trace of the tingle remains today. I can see now what makes a trial lawyer's life go round. All those victories in the courtroom, clean and unequivocal, and the sweet purring of your ugly little enemy when he is finally satisfied.

Because of the tension, HLS is a place where people are usually hungry for a laugh. In mid-March, two of the customary events for poking fun at what goes on around the law school took place.

On a Friday shortly before spring vacation, the April Fools' issue of the law-school newspaper appeared. The edition carried articles reporting that turnstiles had now been installed in the faculty office building to stem the tide of students seeking to speak to their professors, and that a second campus publication, noting the Law Review's choice of a female head, had taken affirmative action one step further and installed a dog as editor in chief. ("Streaky woofed, 'My species had nothing to do with my being elected.'") Another piece said that because students had proved so unreliable in relaying their grades to prospective employers, the registrar would now send marks directly on to the firms, from whom students could request a report in case they wanted to know how they'd done. The April Fools' issue came out on March 19. No one seemed deterred. As I say, at HLS a laugh is always welcome.

At about the same time, the Law School Show was closing its run. The Show, a musical, is an annual event. If this year's production was typical, then Harvard Law School is one site which can be safely skipped by Broadway scouts. The number of persons within the law school with both interest and time enough to take part in the Show is so low that many in the cast come from outside. Nevertheless, the Show goes on.

For such a supposedly sober institution, HLS is a place where grade-school-style dramatics are relatively frequent. One L sections often perform skits like the one we had given for Zechman in the last Torts class. In time I realized that all this playacting is a way that students manage to make clear the emotions that are not expressible amid the formalities of the Socratic classroom. Students can show affection, as we did with Zechman, not to mention other feelings more securely demonstrated in the guise of drama. Each year the Law School Show is the student body's most extensive opportunity to ridicule the faculty, and no doubt that has something to do with the Show's continued production.

Many of the faculty felt that this year's offering went beyond the limits of good taste. The sexual habits of some professors were called into question, and there were a couple of teachers who took the brunt of most of the humor. The Incident was often recalled. In one scene a "Professor Preening" took a meat-ax to a student who'd answered "unprepared."

Perini was sensitive enough about the Incident that he was rumored to have regarded the Show without much joviality. That was unusual for him. In class, humor was the only form of student rebellion he tolerated happily. He had a mild sort of banter going with Sandy Stern all year. Usually he would goad Sandy good-naturedly and Stern, flattered by the attention, would try to respond. In general, Perini had far the better of it, even when the class began to come to Sandy's aid. One day he called an answer of Sandy's "predictably confused." After he'd been hissed, Perini remarked, "I didn't know you had that many friends, Stern." But Sandy had his day. Late in the year, Perini was reminding us once more of the importance of precision in lawyer's work. Be careful of details. "Of course, you can overdo it," Perini admitted. "You don't want to go into court looking like the German army marching into Poland in nineteen forty-one." It was Sandy who shouted out from the back of the room, "Nineteen thirty-nine."

Other professors displayed a more controlled wit. Stumped by a question in a Criminal Law class, a student told Bertram Mann he was feeling uncomfortable. "I think that's the nature of the Socratic method," Mann replied; "we stand here and make each other uneasy." Fowler, on occasion, could rise up out of his gloom and be almost silly. "Everyone knows what *laches* means," he told us in defining a term which had appeared in an opinion: "No one knows what *laches* means."

Among students in the section, by far the most graceful sense of humor belonged to Ilene Bello, a tall, cheerful woman who wisecracked her way through most of the year. In the middle of the second term, repairs were made on the classroom in which we normally met for Civil Procedure. The class was shifted to another room, twice the size of the other, with seats in different order. Nicky found the seating chart useless. Instead, he called on us by shouting out digits, with students responding or passing when they heard their seat numbers. People were sitting scattered throughout the huge classroom and Nicky often struck on empty seats.

"Ninety-one," Nicky called out one day.

On the far side of the room, Ilene Bello stood up. She picked up her purse, her books, moved over a space, and sat down again. Then she looked sweetly down to Nicky at the podium.

"No one," she told him, "is sitting in seat ninety-one."

Ilene's greatest triumph, however, came with Perini. Ilene had grown up nearby in Boston's Italian North End. One day Perini was discussing a case styled *D'Angelo* v. *Potter*. D'Angelo, a layman, had drawn up his own complaint in the suit, claiming Potter had breached a contract with him.

"Now in the first paragraph," Perini asked Andy Kitter, who was on the hot seat that day, "what does D'Angelo say the contract concerned?"

"Four dozen bathroom fixtures," Andy answered.

"And how many fixtures is that? Give me the number."

"Forty-eight," Andy said.

"Just wanted to be sure," Perini told him. "Now look at the third paragraph of the complaint. How many fixtures does D'Angelo say he wants delivered?"

Andy looked down to his book for a second. "Forty-six," he said.

"Forty-six," said Perini. "Typical Italian mathematics."

The next day as class was about to begin, Ilene suddenly shouted out, "Professor Perini," and got to her feet. She had a red rose in her hand and she came to the front of the class. She put the rose in Perini's pocket, then kissed him on each cheek.

"D'Angelo says he'll be in touch," she told him.

———

One of the sages I was regularly running into in the law-school gym had issued a prophecy to me early in February. He was a 3L, a strapping man from Texas.

"You just wait 'til those first-term grades come out," he told me, "it'll be a *whole* different ball game after that. They'll be those fellas with two As who think they've sprouted wings and a halo, and they'll be a whole lot more folks who won't give one little god*damn* after that. Brother, it is not the same."

Nearing spring vacation, most of those predictions had come to pass. There were people whose grades had not been what they hoped and who now showed little concern about school. Aubrey was one of them. In the aftermath of grades, he'd fallen into deep despond. When he emerged, he'd more or

less written off Harvard Law School. From then on, he was going to be serving time until they let him out to do something
useful. Ned Cauley's case was far sadder. Middling grades
badly shook his self-confidence, and his clever, elegant remarks
were rarely heard in class after mid-February. I once tried to
encourage him, mentioning that he'd been silent lately and
that I'd valued what he'd said in the past.

"Well," he answered, "I feel as though I shouldn't be wasting everybody's time. There are a lot of people in there. Maybe
somebody else has something better to say."

The effect of grades was not always as dismal. Either because
of improved self-images or demolished pretensions, some classmates seemed more approachable. Harold Hochschild, rumored to have fallen far short of the grades he'd expected, was
now almost a likable fellow. There were others—people who
suddenly developed a sense of humor about school and themselves, a few who just stopped running and now revealed that
they were attractive persons.

In the wake of grades, there was also growth in a peculiar
phenomenon that had been with us all year: an inordinate concern about the quieter students in the section. During registration week, Peter Geocaris had first recited to us an HLS
shibboleth: "People who don't talk make Law Review." As a
stereotype, it possessed less than complete accuracy, but the
line and the many repetitions of it I heard were revealing of a
deep suspicion of the few persons among us who were not especially outgoing. They were the unknown, the unsounded in a
closely run race. Inevitably when a professor would call on one
of them, there would be a round of speculation later in the day
on whether so-and-so was really a secret genius, or just bright
like the rest of us.

When grades came out, word eventually got around that a
gentle, retiring guy from Missouri named Rick Shearing had
had two A-pluses. That development seemed to exaggerate all

the more the fear that there was a group of silent, all-knowing automatons hidden in the section. As estimates of who would make the Law Review became regular, I'd often hear people say, "You've got to watch out for the quiet ones. They're back there taking all of it in. People like Shearing." By and large it was mass psychopathology. On a couple of occasions I heard people who'd been fearfully identified as "quiet ones" engage in the same kind of worried guessing about others.

There was now much more of that open talk about who was going to make Review. The students who'd done best wanted to believe it would be they, and of course the odds were on their side. Frank Brodsky was one of the few people in the section who'd maintained the kind of ecstatic interest in the law throughout the year which many of us had felt at first. Frank was usually with a quieter man named Larry Jenner and they were always talking law. Always. I remember one day standing by my locker and hearing Brodsky's voice—full of the usual furious, highbrow excitement—echo through the airshaft, resounding out of one of the stalls in the men's room: "Now I think Justice Jackson was right in *Willow River*; he put it exactly the right way."

I imagine Frank was eager for the Review, and there was no question in my mind that he had both the talents and interest to warrant it. A day or two before grades came out, I had spoken with Frank about exams. We'd both agreed they were silly exercises. After receiving a couple of As, however, Frank had changed his mind. There seemed to be a correlation of some kind, he said. It seemed most people had had similar grades on the two exams—an A and an A-minus, a B-plus and a B—so they must have meant something. It had not seemed that way to me.

Stephen, who obviously was another of those people at the top of the section, had his doubts now and then about the meaning of his marks. "If it weren't for Terry," he told me one time on the phone, "I might believe it. But looking at how much Crim he knew and how little Torts, and then at his grades, I sometimes think we all just got potluck."

Most of the time, however, Stephen was not as dubious. He talked to me often about whether or not he should "take Law Review." Gently, I'd try to remind him that things weren't quite in the bag. He'd agree, but the Review always circled back through his conversation like a point on a Möbius strip.

"Oh, yeah, oh, yeah," he'd say. "My feelings are, this is nice, I'm glad I got high grades because now I can relax, I can't have a bad year. But, you know, I do think about the Review. Forty, fifty, sixty hours a week. I'm still not sure I should do it."

With Stephen, I had to read that as meaning he'd decided he should. There were indications that he wanted to pull out all the stops. At the beginning of March, he said he wanted to get the study group back into gear. With Ames, very few of the groups had gone on meeting, ours included. But Stephen had a plan now—another outline, this time of Nicky's course. Again, the arguments for the group effort were persuasive. The course was too theoretical and idiosyncratic to be covered by any commercial civil-procedure guide. But in March, with exams not until late May, I was not willing to throw myself into preparations. I had finally managed to find some time away from law—I'd taken off each weekend for three or four weeks now—and I was reluctant to give up that freedom so soon. Nevertheless, Terry, Aubrey, and Stan Kreiler, a quiet, handsome man from California whom Aubrey had brought into the group in place of Kyle, all agreed with Stephen. I conceded, but reserved the right to do no work on it until April.

Stephen was hardly the only one who was already looking ahead to exams. Many people had announced plans to study for them over spring vacation. With the whittling away of about two thirds of the section as contenders for Law Review, some of those still in the running were now willing to put out an extra effort to get themselves that much closer to the promised land. On the other end, some people who were unready to accept the first grades as a permanent verdict had become determined to prepare even more thoroughly this time.

I was still working at staying cool. I told myself not to think about Law Review—I was too long a shot. Again and again, I reminded myself that exams measured none of the things which mattered most to me. But an event in Perini's class reminded me and everyone else of the real power our grades could wield over us in the future.

Early in the second term, Perini announced that, as he did annually, he would be hiring a few members of the section as summer research assistants. Several people were hopeful of getting one of the jobs. Most 1Ls have a hard time finding legal work over the summer, and being students, many people needed the money. After grades came out, Perini announced he would be receiving résumés.

"They should include," he said, "all relevant information." In case anybody doubted that that meant the two fall-term grades, Perini went on. "I'm very proud," he said, "that so many of my summer people make the Law Review. I have a very high batting average."

Perini's announcements concerning the jobs were always made during class, and the race to work for Perini became another of the dramas and competitions within the section. One time I overhead two men commiserating because, with two Bs each, both knew they'd be wasting their time applying. Eventually, Perini narrowed his choice to eight candidates. He wrote their names on a piece of paper which he affixed prominently to the seating chart. When people saw that Cauley, who'd so long pleased Perini in class, had been excluded, the criterion of selection became clear: These were the eight applicants with the highest grades. In the last two weeks before spring vacation, Perini gave each of the eight a workout in class, interrogating them on cases while the rest of us looked on. And in the end, the jobs were awarded anyway to the three men with the best marks.

It had been a vulgar episode in all respects. Once more he'd used the classroom for his own purposes, turning a private matter into a public spectacle. He'd glorified himself and the job of working for him. He'd rubbed our noses in the crucial effects of grades. And once again, he'd played on our worst vulnerabilities, everything from status fears to the need for money. It was a thoroughly contemptible performance and it doused whatever weak light of regard I'd maintained for Perini. I hated him now, and I thought less of Harvard Law School because he was there.

3/29/76

Spring vacation. Lord, how often I wondered if I'd ever make it this far.

In the past two weeks, the weather, after sporadic temptings, has lolled into spring. The gray is out of the sky and the feeling is pure liberty.

A week away from the Mighty H: Harvard, Harvard, Harvard—I cannot describe how sick I am of hearing that name. The whole university is suffused in such crazy pretense, a kind of puritan faith in the divine specialness of the place and its inhabitants. It's upper-class parochialism. I was told a story recently about a secretary who was fired after her first day on the job because she did not know how to spell the name of the university's president.

The law school is hardly immune from that kind of snobbism. It is an education in itself, learning to worship HLS. A few years ago the man then dean would instruct each student entering to refer to it as *"The* Law School." Much of that attitude seems to carry over to the present faculty. Fowler recently presented a problem in mortgage law which, he said, "you won't find troublesome when you encounter it in practice, unless, of course, the other side is represented by a graduate of the Harvard Law School, or perhaps Yale."

Harvard-love at HLS even goes so far as to amount to a kind of prejudice in favor of the law made by Harvard jurists. Perini never fails to mention it when an opinion he likes was authored by a judge who is a graduate of HLS. Most revered is the late Justice Felix Frankfurter, now a sort of Harvard Law School idol. Frankfurter was an HLS professor when he was elevated to the U.S. Supreme Court, and I guess he is the embodiment of half of the faculty's lushest fantasy. In addition, many profs were his students; a number—including Fowler— were his clerks. Frankfurter, in truth, was a giant, but his opinions are all treated like biblical texts and his style of jurisprudence, now probably dated, is uncritically endorsed in most classrooms.

Amid the adversities of the first year, we have all been particularly susceptible to this kind of thinking about HLS. It must be special, you tell yourself, why else, in God's name, am I going through this? Our presence at Harvard Law School is for many of us the only thing left on which to rest our self-esteem and we have all at one time or another gone around assuring ourselves how fortunate we are to be here, how smart we must be. The standard of excellence stuff feeds on all of that— makes us run harder to prove that we are worthy, really are the best.

Of course all of HLS chauvinism would be silly, as well as offensive, were it not for the fact that over time people at Harvard Law School have made believers of so many others. It might all be a snow job, but there is still that aura which draws the firms and the politicians, and even the tour buses on the weekends. (In the latter case, it may be nothing relating to the law which is the attraction. I was standing in front of the law school recently when three young women piled off one of the buses and begged me to point out the dormitory where the young hero lived in *Love Story*.) In the legal world, with its formalities and stratifications, people cannot resist thinking of a top layer of law schools, and Harvard and Yale are pretty much it.

As a result, it is simply assumed at HLS that a Harvard J.D. is a stepping stone to big things. Mann often told us he was addressing us as a group of future judges and law profs. Guy Sternlieb goes even further. We are now doing a section on what Guy calls "political analysis." We dissect political environments and evaluate options for actors within them. Sternlieb will often issue challenges to the class. "Damn it, there's a reason I teach this course. You people are going to be congressmen and mayors and State Department officials in twenty years. What will you do in these situations? What will you say?"

I am glad Guy asks those questions, but I am still a little discomfited by a place which is so cheerfully assumed to be the training ground for the power elite. That peculiar pride represents an incredible, if tacit, stake in the status quo, and also amounts to a quiet message to students that their place in the legal world should always be among the mighty. It produces the kind of advocate who is uncommitted to ultimate personal values and who will represent anyone—ITT, Hitler, Attila the Hun—as long as the case seems important.

Am I saying, then, that I'm sorry I'm at Harvard Law School? I don't think so (although looking ahead to spring exams, which are always thought of as the pit of the first year, I reserve judgment). None of my observations on the law school are meant to be wholeheartedly damning. It's just that three quarters of the way through the year, I have realized that HLS, with its great size and wealth of resources, is a place where you must always pick and choose. I see myself in these last few months making an effort to regard the place more realistically, to keep myself from looping into either ecstasy or despair as I meet up with the diverse range of what is offered. And the arrogance of HLS is one of the things I am most eager to escape. It makes the environment even more claustrophobic and consuming and leaves me grateful for whatever few reminders I get that Harvard and the law school are not really the center of the universe. I had a nice one last week, a letter from a poet friend, a professor at a southern university, to whom I'm sure the Ivy League has always been a kind of distant mystery. The letter was long delayed in reaching me because it had been addressed care of Harvard Law School, Harvard University, New Haven, Connecticut.

APRIL AND MAY

Exams (Last Act)

Back in school after vacation. I know a little bit now of how the astronauts feel, snatched out of free flight and returned to earth. Even today I could feel the incipient pressure of exams. My stomach already is tight as a fist.

At the end of my vacation, Annette and I had gone to Cape Cod. It was our fifth anniversary and we'd spent the weekend in a romantic old country inn, hand-built in the eighteenth century. We'd walked on the beach. Sunday we flew a kite. I would not have another day off until exams ended on the first of June.

I didn't plan, of course, to let exams overtake me that thoroughly. On April 6, the first test was still more than five weeks away. But I had ignored work during Ames, and had eased off in March. Now, in the first days back, I saw that I was going to have to pay. In Property, for instance, I had never mastered the Estates in Land, a set of medieval rules which still govern many aspects of the conveyance of real estate. Fee simple, fee tail, remainders, reversions, life estates—I'd let it all go, hoping the ideas would somehow settle in over time. They hadn't. In April the concepts were still more foreign to me than anything I'd encountered since the physics formulas of my first term in college.

Obligations outside the regular course work also began to crop up. Sternlieb gave us a pass/fail take-home test on the analytic material covered in the initial weeks of his course. That ate up one weekend. Perini scheduled a practice exam on the first term's material, and preparing for that consumed another. Perini's test was not required, but I knew I needed the review. Another thing I'd recognized in the first week back was how difficult it was going to be to put together the two year-long courses, Contracts and Procedure. My classmates had returned from their vacations talking about terms from the two classes which I'd all but forgotten: quasi in rem jurisdiction, the parol evidence rule, promissory estoppel.

So, suddenly and without the zest and excitement I'd felt previously, I had reverted to the first-semester schedule—five hours sleep, work all weekend. In the second week of April, Eric Varnig, a professor from Harvard Business School, took over the teaching of Law and Public Policy from Sternlieb. Varnig lectured on management techniques in government, condensing what was a semester course at the B School into five weeks. He did not, however, cut out much of a term's worth of reading and by the end of his third lecture I was nearly three hundred pages behind. It was again a race to squeeze the most out of every day. I was always looking at my watch.

The biggest burden was probably the study group Procedure outline. Once more Stephen was administering an exacting standard, but it was difficult now to quarrel with him, for the outline had taken on undeniable importance. In the week before spring vacation, Nicky Morris had discussed his plans for the final with the section; he wanted our reactions before he began composing the test. Nicky told us that he had decided to try an even more pronounced departure from issue-spotting exams. "People never get beyond reciting rules," he said, and admitted that students had criticized him in the past for giving a rule-oriented test in a formidably theoretical course. Instead, this year he planned to test knowledge of the rules with a single issue spotter. The remainder of the exam would be comprised of more open-ended questions.

Even while Nicky was detailing what the other questions would be like, I heard Stephen call my name from behind. His arms were open and his face was full of the glee I'd seen the day he'd received his grades. "We've got it," he was mouthing, "we've got it." What he meant was that the Procedure outline on which we'd now all begun work provided a nearly ideal organization of information for the exam Nicky was describing. The test would be another eight-hour affair, and with that amount of time, it sounded almost as if we'd be able to pull the answers out of the outline verbatim.

Our plan for the document had been entirely inadvertent, but in April word spread through the section that our group had craftily devised the "perfect" outline. As the month wore on, I became aware that we were the objects of a quiet resentment. Most groups had never resumed operation in the second term, and several people seemed vaguely offended that we had continued engaging in cooperative efforts. Even those groups still functioning would find it hard to duplicate what we had done. We'd started a month ahead of them and also before the hectic term-end reviewing had begun.

In a few instances there seemed to be outright irritation, a sense that we had gained some unfair advantage.

"How's the machine doing?" Jack Weiss regularly asked me, referring to our study group. Jack was another two-A man, a strong contender for the Law Review. By mid-April he'd become twitchy and taut, chewing up Maalox by the box. He seemed nearly obsessed with our damn outline. I'm sure that rumor had turned it into a virtual Rosetta stone of Civil Procedure. Jack was probably certain we'd all make As, and he knew he was working against a curve with top grades for only so many.

Terry had had the same treatment from Jack.

"Look," I suggested to Terry one day, "maybe we just ought to announce that anybody who wants to Xerox our damn outline can."

Terry did not like the idea. It did not fit in with his bootstrap philosophy. Nobody had ever given him much of anything, let alone at Harvard Law School. I was not sure I liked the idea myself. We'd all done a good deal of work on the outline by now. I wasn't sure what compensations there'd be in making a gift of those efforts to the whole section.

As for Stephen, he did not seem to notice any of this air of mild controversy about the outline. He was in a kind of blind panic now, preparing for exams. Over vacation, he had visited St. Louis, where he'd gone to graduate school. He liked the city and he had a weak hope of finding summer work there. But when he displayed his résumé to a number of law firms he found that the customary prejudice against first-year law students as summer clerks did not apply in cases like his.

"I'll tell you something," he said to me when he returned with four or five offers for the summer, "grades don't talk— they scream."

Anybody would be taken with that kind of sudden new attractiveness. Stephen—lonely, bereft—was especially susceptible. He seemed desperate not to let any of that slip away. He'd spent all his free time over vacation reviewing, and now he was going at it even more intensely. He was literally outlining the commercial outlines—"distilling," was the way he put it— he'd already finished a complete digest of Perini's hornbook. He would excuse himself from lunch after eating in minutes. He was even going off by himself to study in the brief breaks between classes.

In the process, he seemed also to have grown more beguiled by the trappings of success, Harvard Law School style. He was talking less often about teaching when he finished school and more about practicing law. That, I'm sure, was a response to the real interest in law he'd discovered in himself. But he also frequently talked about the financial differentials between the two careers and said he was thinking about working permanently for the private firms of which he'd been so contemptuous in October.

"I never thought it would be him," Terry told me after watching Stephen for a while after spring vacation. "I mean, I've been around people, I know what goes on. But I didn't think he'd get sucked in. Man, he bought the whole trip."

I probably should have spoken to Stephen. I saw him being taken away from himself. But I remained confused about how much of what I recognized in him was a reflection of my own jealousy. I stayed silent, while my friendship for him veered toward pity.

On occasion, Stephen would still take the time to call me, especially when he was down. There were a lot of moments now when he seemed to be borne on heavily by the pressures, the contradictions, in everything he wanted. The conversations were more or less soliloquies by Stephen, alternating tones of fear and ambivalence and denial.

"Well, I'm working away here," he told me one Sunday when he called. "I have the Procedure outline going and I've really been getting down on Con Law. I figure Contracts I'll have pat; he won't be able to touch me. Property's the only thing. We're hanging over the cliff in the course." Like me, Stephen had been having his trouble with the Estates in Land. Recently, he'd told me with real concern, near panic, that he was sure he'd flunk the course. He had instants like that when all his fears seemed to open up. Usually he allayed them with more work.

"You'll be okay," I told him now.

"Oh, sure. I figure—the hornbook, the outlines—I'll get up in the B range. From there, who knows."

"Uh-huh," I said. I asked about his weekend.

It was okay, he said. He'd gone to a party Friday night. Sandy Stern was there and they'd spent the evening talking about who was going to make Law Review. Stephen had categories all marked out. At the top were "sure ones," which meant Shearing. For some reason he didn't include himself in that group. He was one step below, among the "good possibilities." There were others who he'd decided were clearly "out," because they were not working hard enough. Andy Kitter was "out" because he had fallen in love.

"I figure people who make Law Review deserve it," Stephen said. "What a prize, huh? Fifty hours a week in hell."

I made a sound of assent.

"I hear the firms really get down on you if you quit," he said. "I don't know. You've got the grades anyway. Well," he went on, "these exams really aren't bothering me. Not like first semester. I felt like hell then. I figure I'll be cool about these. I don't feel any anxiety yet," he said. "Not yet," he said, before he got off the phone.

————————

Late in April, the registrar's office made available forms and pamphlets so that the 1Ls and 2Ls could register for courses for the following fall. Amid the gathering fears roused by exams, it was nice to know that someone actually thought we would reach the second year.

Like many of my classmates, I had frequently looked forward to being an upperclassman. For one thing, there would be more free time. We'd all be beyond that struggle to familiarize ourselves with the law's strange language and logic. The work would be easier, and there'd also be less of it to do. At HLS, second- and third-year students are usually not allowed to enroll, even voluntarily, for as many course hours as are required in the first year.

For 2Ls and 3Ls, much of that unoccupied time goes into extracurricular activities, including a wealth of student organizations that work on law-related problems which affect the world beyond HLS. Three student-edited legal journals cover developments in the specialized fields of civil liberties, international law, and legislation. Student research groups, like the Legislative Research Bureau, harness the free legal manpower floating through the law school's halls to delve, at the request of those affected, into contemporary legal problems. There are also organizations, such as the Legal Aid Society, involved in the direct delivery of legal services to the poor.

Nearing the end of the year, many 1Ls were eager to participate in those groups next fall. And we could see other appealing freedoms in the year ahead. Often we had spoken wistfully of the more relaxed atmosphere in upper-year classes. In some, the Socratic method is forsaken. Professors lecture, taking questions from the floor when they finish. Where the Socratic method is employed, it is sometimes treated with disdain. In December, Gina reported that she had sat in on a Commercial Transactions class in which nine persons consecutively had passed. The professor had employed the screw-your-buddy tactic, calling on the student beside the one who'd failed to respond, and had ended up going down an entire row. "Pass." "Pass." "Not me." "Not me, either." "Sorry." "Maybe next time." Gina told the story to a group of us at lunch and we were all gleeful. Those would be the days.

Most important, the curriculum in the second and third years is far more flexible. About 150 upper-year courses are offered, and not one of them is specifically required. Every student decides on his own what he or she will take. For the second year, the faculty recommends a series of what they call "basic courses"—Constitutional Law, Accounting, Corporations, and Taxation, which is essentially a study of the provisions and policies of the U.S. Internal Revenue Code—but you are free to disregard those suggestions. Some students view the inclusion of Corporations, Taxation, and Accounting in the faculty's recommendations as an effort to direct students into business law. But even professors like Nicky Morris, politically radical in their perspectives, agreed that the basic courses dealt with material important in almost every area of practice. Even a criminal prosecutor, for instance, could not handle many kinds of fraud and embezzlement cases without knowing something about a corporation. Morris, however, was not as encouraging about the courses themselves.

"You have to *take* Corporations," he explained to the study group one day late in April when we had lunch with him, "because the stuff is so boring that if you aren't *threatened* with an exam you'll never make yourself read the hornbook."

Nicky's attitude toward Corporations was symptomatic of sentiments toward the work of the second and third year in general. It may all have looked rosy to a 1L, but 2Ls and 3Ls seemed to regard the last two years as being little more than a forced march, and many of the faculty had not much more enthusiasm for what went on.

Problems in the second and third years of law school are not unique to Harvard. Professors Herbert Packer and Thomas Ehrlich, both of Stanford, writing for a Carnegie Commission study on legal education, pointed out a sense of shortcomings in upper-year education everywhere, and named that as one of their prime considerations in recommending that law school be abbreviated to two years.

As a first-year student, I am hardly able to pose as an expert on the inadequacies of the second and third years. I can, however, after my months in the hallways, report the consensus of upper-year students' complaints. One problem is that the subject matter is often far from compelling. Usually the courses are much more specialized and technical than in first-year classes—Corporate Policy Planning, Labor Arbitration, Maritime Law, are examples. Another difficulty is that employers are knocking on the door, calling students out, and many are eager to move on. Classroom doings are likely to seem abstract, dull, and inactive when compared to what happens in practice. New clinical courses, which give upper-year students detailed instructions and experience in trying cases and representing clients, are often far more popular than traditional classroom fare.

But what looked to me to be the biggest trouble was also the most obvious. In order to reach the second and third years, students must pass through the first year, and by then many have already had the stuffing kicked out of them. They have been treated as incompetents, terrorized daily, excluded from privilege, had their valued beliefs ridiculed, and in general felt their sense of self-worth thoroughly demeaned. If you get knocked down often enough, you learn not to stand up, and after being a Harvard 1L, a silent crawl to the finish line looks to many students to be the better part of valor.

Looking around the hallways, I often saw the 2Ls and 3Ls as a sad, bitter, defeated lot. I met repeated instances of those attitudes all year: Peter Geocaris's wounded ruefulness about the Law Review; the many 2Ls and 3Ls I consulted in the spring who told me that there was not a course at HLS worth taking; or the entire third-year class, who on the eve of graduation elected as Class Marshall a man who had pledged to remind every class member annually of the degrading manner in which they had been treated, so that none would ever give a dime in alumni contributions to the Harvard Law School.

The 2Ls and 3Ls recover, I'm certain. David has told me that most of his classmates reported a great thrill in starting practice and in discovering again that they were the talented people they had thought of themselves as being before they came to HLS.

But I'm not sure if that is not too late to dissolve some of the ill effects.

"It makes me so unhappy to see what happened to all the people Sonny started with," the wife of a 3L friend said to Annette and me one night near the end of the year. "They're all such good people, and they're all so cynical now. They just do everything they have to and they ridicule it at the same time. They all swore the first year they'd never go to corporate firms, and now they just took the job because it was sort of expected. And most of them have already promised themselves they're going to hate it. It's just classic alienation."

As for me, I knew enough now about HLS and myself not to vow that I wouldn't fall into any of those typical attitudes. I would just do my best. I tried to select my courses for next year carefully. A lot of 2Ls and 3Ls told me that was pointless. Second-year and third-year registration is often a large-scale repetition of what went on with first-year electives in December: oversubscribed courses, waiting lists, the registrar pushing students out of classes like checkers. I had heard the same rumor a number of times that one 2L had been bumped from so many courses the preceding fall that he'd simply withdrawn from school for a year.

Still, I persisted. I checked on each professor, conferred with upper-year students, sought faculty advice. I registered for the basic courses and also for classes in Legal History, Evidence, Law and Philosophy, Antitrust, Labor Law. As I prepared my schedule I followed two ground rules, which seemed to me the most important in making law school palatable: One was that I would not submit myself again to a teacher who ran his classroom like the Star Chamber. I did not care if a professor was known as the greatest formulator of the law since Hammurabi—if he was said to treat his students harshly, I passed him by. Second, I tried as often as possible to choose classes with small enrollments. Upper-year courses are often taught in groups as large as 250. Facing numbers like that, I knew no professor could deal humanly with students.

Maybe my plans for next year would not work out. But I saw no point in conceding early. As it is, if the folklore is in any way accurate, I have two years to learn all about feeling hopeless, feeling bored.

———————

In the last week of April, Nicky Morris made an announcement in the wake of which the year dissolved into disgrace. That was no fault of Nicky's. He meant well. But it was typical of the reactions which had attended him all year that things did not play out straight.

As we neared the end of the year, I had come to regard Nicky Morris as a teacher of exceptional generosity. He was more aggressively concerned with his students' well-being than any other professor I knew of at HLS. He was unflinching about sharing his time with us, in his office or after class. In the practice exams he gave occasionally, I saw a sincere effort to lessen our anxieties and provide the feedback we so badly needed. With his frequent criticisms of the HLS grading system, I felt Nicky was hoping to demystify and lessen in importance what was for many of us the most painful aspect of the year. And in his classroom approach to Civil Procedure and law in general, I perceived Morris as attempting to make legal education a richly intellectual enterprise, provocative and appealing to those going through it.

I admired Nicky Morris enormously, and many members of Section 2 shared my sentiments. But more students—although they enjoyed the class—had less regard than I for Nicky personally. They found his hipness phony, and in one of those inevitable student slanders referred to him as "Beat Nick." His frequent talk about grading, they said, was a deliberate attempt to add to grade pressures, an indication of how much stock Nicky himself put in academic standing. And in his classroom conduct, despite the easygoing procedures like passing, those people insisted that Nicky was egotistical and insensitive, eager to put his students down.

It was true that there had been moments when Nicky was less kindly than he should have been. He frequently seemed to belittle the best student remarks, implying they were unoriginal or routine. I never wholly set aside the feeling that Nicky was competing with us, trying to prove that he was still, as billed, the greatest law student at HLS since Frankfurter. Yet over time I'd also recognized that competition between professors and students is just within the nature of the Socratic method. In May, I went to an open meeting on legal education in which one young professor characterized Socraticism as "placing a premium on being able to outdraw a student at twenty feet." I imagine that it is a taste of that kind of daily confrontation which draws many former law students back to become law professors.

In singling Nicky out for criticism on this score, I thought I saw in my classmates a reaction which mirrored what had gone on with me after I had been called on by Perini. Only when I was less desperately frightened could I feel my resentments of him; only toward Nicky, the least fearsome of our teachers, did many people dare express their anger over some of the most consistently offensive aspects of law-school life—the antagonism between teacher and student in the classroom, their distance outside of it, the indignity of being examined and marked. It was dangerous to feel hostile toward Perini or Isaac Fowler—they seemed capable of any retaliation. Nicky, on the other hand, was committed to liberal tolerance; and like me with my Contracts reading, there were students in the section who could not resist the temptation to abuse. Whenever time was short, it was Nicky's assignments that were ignored. People would pass when called on, smirking like adolescents. And because Nicky was so patient, students brought him grievances that never would have been aired elsewhere. They pushed him. They challenged him. They tried to manipulate. And Nicky remained good-hearted, responsive, sincere, which was what led to his announcement on that last Friday in April, at the start of class—the announcement which sent the year into decline.

"There is a lot of concern," he said, as he paced at the front of the room, "that some study groups are producing huge outlines and course guides for the exam. A lot of people apparently feel that they're really up against it, competing with these collective efforts. So, if the class agrees, I have decided to change the plans for the exam a little bit to allow the collectives and the individuals to go at it more evenly."

Nicky's purpose was to ease tension, but as had happened so often, his effect was exactly the opposite. Much of that had to do with the state his audience was in already. By the end of April things were rapidly becoming overheated within Section 2. Although we now had experience with exams, the demands were greater this term. There were four courses to review for, not two. And the schedule was a more formidable obstacle. Exams would begin only a few days after classes ended on May 14. In January, most of us had had the comfort of Christmas vacation before the tests. That had given us the opportunity to escape the trips and neuroses we all laid on each other. Now there was no release. Exams would begin a few days after classes ended. In the dormitories, I heard, they were already crawling the walls; we were all feeling considerable heat. Gina claimed that the only way she was keeping herself whole was by leaving school promptly after the day's final class so she could escape the anxiety-ridden conversations now so frequent in the hallways.

Under that pressure, the bonds within the section were starting to yield. For much of the year, the members of Section 2 had been strongly supportive of each other. True, there were petty jealousies, but we'd held together well enough for Mann to pay us that compliment about mutual protectiveness, in the last Criminal class of the first term. But to a significant degree, I think that first-semester grades had had an atomizing effect. We were no longer on equal footing. There was genuine envy now, and a real race for the Review, and in the next ten days, I would see and hear of and take part in conduct which was shameful.

And Nicky's announcement sent us off in that direction. The actual content of what Morris said fit the intent he'd described—to even things up between groups and individuals. He restricted the scope of the potential questions he might ask on the exam and that, in theory, should have made it easier for people to prepare without the aid of study groups or group outlines. But in the section's current state of anxiety, it was more the emphasis, the implications, of Nicky's announcement that people took hold of. By his calling attention to what study groups like ours were up to, students felt as if Morris had tacitly endorsed, even urged, group work. And by altering his plans for the exam, Nicky seemed to acknowledge the potentially powerful effect of the study-group outlines.

Thus panic set in at once. People who'd remained convinced that groups were no longer worth it for them, quickly lost that conviction. Within twenty-four hours some groups long dormant had revived, and other persons were casting about nervously for groups to join. Now everyone began outlining Civil

Procedure, as well as some of the other courses, especially Property, where it was becoming clear *nobody* understood Estates in Land.

The most vigorous new study group was headed by Kyle Schick. Over the first weekend in May, Kyle put together a huge sixteen-person cooperative which became busy at once outlining Property and Procedure. Some people thought that was treacherous—because, as I later learned, it was Kyle who had gone to Nicky in the first place to complain about the group outlines.

As exams neared, I was told many times that Kyle was openly confessing his desperate desire to make the Law Review. He felt Review membership was indispensable in getting where he wanted to go in a career as a law teacher, and I imagine that he was driven to Nicky by a fear like Weiss's—that those with outlines had an advantage he could not overcome. Before exams were over, Kyle had lodged similar complaints about other people with other professors. In each case, I'm sure that Kyle got a good hearing, because he had gone to great lengths to cultivate our teachers all year. He'd involved a number in consultations concerning his on-campus business; he'd had the teachers to his house for parties. He'd even tried to assuage Perini's wounds, sending him—as only Kyle would dare—a long congratulatory note after Perini had finished a series of lectures in our class on "conditions," a complicated subject involving questions about those contract terms whose violation creates a breach.

I know that Kyle did not like Nicky Morris much. He'd told me that. He voiced the familiar complaints about Nicky's ego. But he still invited Nicky out on weekends to play softball, and visited him in his office to talk over deep issues in Procedure. I'm sure Nicky trusted Kyle; and in case he didn't, I was told that Kyle induced Phyllis Wiseman, who was normally quite reticent, to come with him the day he lodged his objection about the group outlines. Phyllis was a sympathetic figure. She had a family to look after, kids. Nicky had kids too. When Phyllis told Nicky that these study-group efforts frightened her because she could never spare the time to match them on her own, I'm sure Nicky understood. Phyllis's problem—genuine, sincere—made the situation clear. Nicky did what he should have, and I imagine Phyllis was grateful for his announcement. I imagine Kyle was too.

Kyle then formed his study group. He built it around a nucleus of his friends from Harvard College, but he seemed to choose the people for it very carefully. Gina told me that he reached her by long distance in Vermont to ask her to join. And Kyle never included Phyllis Wiseman.

As I had listened to Nicky Morris on that Friday when he'd announced his change in plans for the exam, my heart had sunk. Not because I felt we'd wasted all our work. The Procedure outline would still be quite valuable. But that was not the first thing on my mind. For some reason, I had not noticed the deepening discomfort in the section over our outline. I had realized that people were growing tense; I realized that one or two persons like Weiss were irritated with us. But as Nicky spoke, I suddenly recognized that my friends and I, and the few other groups engaged in similar projects, had apparently been the cause of great anxiety. I felt guilty and badly embarrassed.

Stephen received Nicky's announcement in a different mood. He took the altered design of the exam as a new challenge. He came charging back to my seat at the end of class.

"All right," he told me, "all right. Now, we've worked hard on this thing, but now we have got to *hit* it; we have got to give it the fanatical intensity it deserves."

I tried to calm Stephen as we went to lunch. Aubrey and Stan and Terry were also there, and together the four of us ac-

quainted Stephen with the news he had still not absorbed—
that it was we and our outline and "fanatical intensity" that, in
good part, had led to all of this.

Stephen puffed out his cheeks and shook his head.

"People are scared of us?" he asked. "I'm incredulous."

"Scared and resentful," Aubrey told him. He was nonchalant. Both he and Stan felt that the outline was our business.
We weren't trying to harm anybody and owed no apologies for
wanting to reap the rewards of our perseverance. But Terry felt
sheepish that we'd thrown everyone into such consternation.
And I was increasingly upset by the whole business. By the
time I left school on Friday, my reactions to Nicky's announcement had broadened. In the intensified atmosphere I felt a new
pressure to do more work. And more surprisingly, I also found
that much of my initial embarrassment had begun to give way
to some resentment of whoever it was who had gone to Morris.
For some reason the outline was important to me. Throughout,
I'd assumed I was doing it mostly for the sake of my friends in
the study group, but now it seemed to have been converted to
a purpose far more personal. I realized that I might even have
been trying to overlook that rising current of resentment.
Stephen, too, was disturbed, now sorely in conflict with himself. He is a kind man, no matter how consumed, and it bothered him a great deal to think he'd been the source of anyone's
discomfort.

"It's my grades," he told me before I left school Friday, explaining—I think correctly—why there'd been such attention
to our group and thus to our outline. "I wish I'd never gotten
those goddamn grades."

By that Monday, Stephen had hit upon a more tangible expression of his concern. It had been quite a weekend in the dormitories. Members of Section 2 who had no access to outlines
and study groups were becoming desperate. They were certain
they'd fail. Even if that was not so, I'm sure it was no picnic to

feel that panic abroad and to know you were in this on your own. On campus on Sunday, Stephen had been approached at different times by two men, John Yolan and Malcolm Bocaine, who, according to Stephen, almost begged to be added to our group. On Monday, at a study-group review session before class, Stephen proposed that we indeed invite John and Malcolm to join.

Terry agreed quickly. He saw it as imperative that the study group add members, just to provide others with the aid and peace of mind. Aubrey and I were also willing. So was Stan, the man who'd replaced Kyle in the group, but he had a proviso.

"I want a quid pro quo," he said.

What Stan meant was that he wanted new members of the group to do some work in exchange for a copy of our outline. Stephen had considered that point, too. In March, when we'd divided the Procedure book for outlining, we'd never assigned anyone to the last chapters of the casebook. There seemed no need, since the material would be fresh. But Stephen, in his tireless preparation for exams, had been bothered all along by that omission, and now he proposed that John and Malcolm do that work. He had a kind of comprehensive plan concerning John and Malcolm, I saw. He had found a way to reconcile his worst impulses and his best. We all had. Let them in, but make them work. Quid pro quo. We quickly agreed.

As I went through the day on Monday, I saw that the section seemed to have gone wild. People had been cramming all weekend, already pulling all-nighters, memorizing, outlining, reviewing. Nobody seemed to have a moment now for conversation. We were all jumpy as cats.

I was no more collected than anybody else. I had gone through April feeling stable. I was working hard and there seemed to be no more to ask of myself. But Nicky's announcement and the attendant pressures had thrown me for a loop.

That congested fear of failing and screwing up, and on the other side, of wanting desperately to do well, had knotted inside me again, more powerfully than at any time since last November. Over the weekend I began to smoke again. I woke up one night in a sweat.

And today everybody's panic seemed to be working on me and making all that worse. My control over myself was deteriorating rapidly, and somehow the business with the outline was still at the center of it. When Stephen brought the news that John Yolan had no time now to do outside work, I replied, "Screw him, then. He wants dessert without making dinner. You heard Stan. Quid pro quo."

Stephen nodded cautiously. The next morning he announced that Ned Cauley had enlisted in the study group in the place of John. Ned and Malcolm were now busy working on their portions of the outline, and indeed, in the next few days, the two of them appeared to have virtually dropped out of school in order to get it done.

Other dealings were in the works. Stephen was gossiping with everybody now, perhaps so that he would not miss any other ground swells of feeling like that which had occasioned Nicky's announcement. Tuesday afternoon he consulted with Jack Weiss. Jack was still concerned about our outline.

"He wants to trade," Stephen told me Wednesday. "Their group's got a Property outline. I saw a little. It looked pretty fair. What do you think?"

I could see Stephen was interested. It was more information, one more angle, a little more security. And there was another complication here. Terry had not gone to Property classes all term. He considered Fowler a waste of time. He had promised himself that he would master the stuff on his own, but he'd put it off too long. The Estates in Land were hard to pick up out of Gilbert's. I knew he would have valued a comprehensive outline.

"What happens once we give the outline to them?" I asked. "They Xerox it and hand it all over the section?"

"Maybe," Stephen said.

"No dice," I answered. "We've worked too hard."

"What about Terry?"

"Terry took the gamble. He'll just have to pay."

"You're right," Stephen said after an instant. He laughed a little. "Hochschild's in Weiss's group. Can you imagine what would happen with our outline in Hochschild's hands?"

People were skipping classes now to outline. Everytime I passed the copy center under Langdell, I saw another member of Section 2 in line there with a sheaf of papers and a distrustful look—people whom I'd felt close to. We were in warring camps now, different study groups.

Late Thursday afternoon, following classes, Stephen and Terry and I stood in one of the Pound classrooms talking about how bizarre it had all become.

"Man," Terry said, "I've been thinking. We should give everybody who wants it a copy of our outline."

"With a quid pro quo," Stephen added.

"Screw the quid pro quo," Terry said. "I mean, hey, I asked myself why we did this. To review, right? To learn. That's all we have to worry about." He looked at me. "Right?"

"I don't know," I answered. I was still overwrought. It had been a miserable week.

"Man, you're the one who was sayin' give it away."

"But look at the situation," I said. "Kyle's trying to screw everybody. Half the people in the section think we're crazy."

"Hey, listen, what do you care about Kyle?" Terry asked. "What's the difference, if we can help some folks out?"

I thought a second. Then suddenly I was speaking from the frenzied center of everything that had gripped me in the last week.

"I want the advantage," I said. "I want the competitive advantage. I don't give a damn about anybody else. I want to do better than them."

My tone was ugly, and Stephen and Terry both stared at me an instant. Then we quietly broke apart to find our separate ways home.

It took me a while to believe I had actually said that. I told myself I was kidding. I told myself that I had said that to shock Terry and Stephen. But I knew better. What had been suppressed all year was in the open now. All along there had been a tension between looking out for ourselves and helping each other; in the end, I did not expect anybody—not myself, either—to renounce a wish to prosper, to succeed. But I could not believe how *extreme* I had let things become, the kind of grasping creature I had been reduced to. I had not been talking about gentlemanly competition to Stephen and Terry. I had not been talking about any innocent striving to achieve. There had been murder in my voice. And what were the stakes? The difference between a B-plus and a B? This was supposed to be education—a humane, cooperative enterprise.

That night I sat in my study and counseled myself. It had been a tumultuous year, I decided. I had been up. And I had been down. I had lost track of myself at moments, but because of whatever generosity I'd extended my own spirit, I had not lost my self-respect. But it would not stretch much further. I knew that if I gave in again to that welling, frightened avarice as I had this afternoon, I would pay for a long time in the way I thought about myself.

It's a tough place, I told myself. Bad things are happening. Work hard. Do your best. Learn the law. But don't suffer, I thought. Don't fear. And for God's sake, don't give up your decency.

The madness in the atmosphere, the battle between the study groups, persisted. People continued to surreptitiously hand each other outlines in brown-paper bags. Jack Weiss kept making insulting remarks. Our study group met one afternoon to go over one of Perini's former exams and we soon discovered that none of us could even begin to answer it; for a day Stephen fretted that we would all fail Contracts. In Kyle's group, Gina reported, there had been an insurrection because no one could understand Kyle's remarks on collateral estoppel, a crucial subject for the exam. Karen Sondergard cried one day when she decided she preferred to be in our group rather than another. Fearful rumors spread that a group had stolen a copy of one of the exams. At another point, Stephen became convinced that Aubrey and Stan had made a backstage deal with Kyle's group and were receiving information which they were not sharing with the rest of us. And all along our own group continued to swell. Stephen always found ways to employ the new members. By the last week of classes the group had grown to eleven or twelve.

"John Yolan has changed his mind," Stephen told me one day in the library.

"Fine," I said, "give him the outline."

"With a quid pro quo?" Stephen asked.

"With or without," I said. "Just give it to whoever wants it. Terry is right."

After that Thursday afternoon in that classroom, I tried not to let myself fall into that tangle of fears again. There were times I felt it happening and would work hard to resist. One day I found myself pacing back and forth in the law-school gym, muttering, "I'm okay, I'm okay," trying to keep in mind that I had some worth which would outlast exams. But I felt it was important not to give in. I knew where I stood now. I knew what I was against.

I had finally met my enemy, I figured, face to face.

Last Contracts class with Perini. He has been fearsome all week, complaining about absences and roasting the people he's called on. He does not want us to go out with the impression he is soft or that the exam will be easy.

Today, though, he was mellow. Students have been collecting gifts for him. They were presented at the beginning of the hour—a portrait of a famous Contracts commentator, a large rusty steel coil so he would "have a nice spring." Then the class rose to sing to him:

> *Offer, acceptance, consideration,*
> *The peppercorn theory, a free-market nation,*
> Mills *versus* Wyman, Klockner *"v"* Green—
> *These are a few of our favorite things.*

He followed with a rousing lecture on assignment of contracts—the procedure for selling your rights under an agreement to a third person—then closed with a schmaltzy peroration. It had its nicer moments. He apologized to Sandy Stern for past insults; he told us not to panic on the exam and said—as no one else has—if we do just blank out with fear, to come see him. He told us what a good group we were, but he could not resist a parting crack about the Incident, and its transformation to a public event. "It's been hard," he said, "to be constantly defending my behavior to people who don't understand what goes on in here." And he also resorted to a heavy sentimentality which approached bathos. He told us that we were all his family, that we were all his friends.

"He's got a lot of nerve," Gina said afterwards, "terrorizing me all year, then saying he's my friend. He's not *my* friend."

Wade, I understand, compared today's remarks to Nixon's farewell speech.

I don't know why I can't forgive Perini for his excesses; he has his talents as a teacher. The cruelty, I guess. The class rose to give him a standing ovation as he left. I could not bring myself to get to my feet.

5/14/76
(Friday)

I'll never enter a classroom again as a first-year law student. Final classes today.

Fowler, with rare warmth, offered some fatherly advice about the exam before he finished: "You people worry too much about these examinations. I'm still not sure what we test—time management, perhaps. Your problem is that you all want to be number one and no one can be in this kind of group. Oh, someone will be, by the numbers, but not really."

Half an hour later, Nicky wound it all up. He told us he has worked for years to teach law in a way which he feels reveals the inherent interest of the subject matter. He warned us of the stultification we would likely feel as upper-year students and offered to do what he could—supervise papers or other kinds of research.

He was walking the length of the room as he spoke.

"There is an immense amount of talent in this group," he said. "I have had my best year yet with you and I thank you for that." He kept right on strolling and went out the door. He left all of us on our feet, applauding behind him.

Then the realization: It was over. Our year together. Exams are personal, you and the books and the test you write. This was really the last moment for Section 2. I kissed Karen, hugged Gina. I shook hands with Terry and Stephen and Aubrey. I thought about the kind of wonder and admiration with which I regarded my classmates in those first few weeks, and then about what has happened to all of us of late. Harvard Law School, I thought. Oh, Harvard Law School.

I went home feeling numb and a little depressed.

Spring exams are another of the traditions of the first year of law school. A few years ago, things were far worse at Harvard, and at many other schools, than they are now. Students would take five exams in five full-year courses; there were no tests beforehand and students had no indication of how they were doing. In many instances, the exams were given on a "closed book" basis, which meant students could bring nothing with them into the examination area—no books at hand for comfort, no pretense that students weren't expected to have the body of law in a subject memorized cold. In the spring, first-year law students would go even crazier than we did. Friends who were at Harvard and other law schools in those days have repeatedly told me the same stories about suicide attempts and about students moving into motels to get away from the madhouse in the dorms.

For us, midyear exams and the knowledge that each final was "open book" lessened some of that pressure. But still it was no cakewalk. I found the experience, coming on the heels of everything else, a lot like being sent out to run a four-minute mile after just having finished the marathon. We had four tests inside of seventeen days, thousands of pages to digest and hold together. At the end of the first term, by comparison, we had nearly a month to prepare for our tests in Torts and Criminal. I had no sense this time of any elegant confluence of knowledge taking place. The house was being built, but it was a rush job, with a lot of bad corners and no fine seams. I went over outlines, old tests. The study group met on a couple of occasions. For the most part, it was just cramming, day after day. Sixteen, seventeen hours. Half an hour for dinner. Six hours to sleep.

The first exam, four days after classes ended, was in Law and Public Policy. The night before, Gina called me. She sounded kited with fear, and for an instant her anxiety seemed to travel down the wire and take root in me. I'm okay, I told myself when I got off the phone, I'm okay. I slept soundly that night, and every other. One whole year, but it looked as though I was finally getting the better of my fear.

The Policy test, another eight-hour exam, was all right. Sternlieb had handed out a case study about the Public Health Service in advance. It was the setting for one of the two questions, which asked what steps we would take inside the organization if we were trying to push a program of neighborhood health centers. Writing my answer, I felt I had finally done something worthwhile on a law-school exam—a careful, well-reasoned response. For me, I decided, these tests were a crap shoot: Sometimes I'd screw up, sometimes I'd pass; now and then I might even do something I was proud of.

I headed to school for the Property exam, a week later, feeling almost cheerful. Maybe I'd do something worthwhile today. I didn't. It was one of those four-hour jobs and I just babbled on, fueled by adrenaline. In the aftermath, there was a lot of controversy. Some years ago, Fowler had published a law-review article evaluating a proposed zoning ordinance for a town in Illinois. One question on the test asked students to evaluate a proposed zoning ordinance for a town in Michigan. An "open book" test at HLS means no holds barred, and several students had come into the exam with copies of Fowler's old article, from which they more or less abstracted their answers. Kyle had gone at once to Fowler to complain. Fowler treated the matter indifferently and asked Kyle to leave the office.

Many people had also been dogged to the end by the Estates

in Land. Terry was able to answer only two of the four questions. Stephen also felt he had not done well and was also unhappy about his Con Law exam earlier.

"You heard it here first," he told me. "Stephen Litowitz will not make the Law Review." He brightened in a few days, however, when he'd surveyed the other chief contenders—"the supercompetent people" was the way Stephen put it—and found that they too had had trouble with the test.

Nicky's exam, two days later, was more or less as promised. Everybody had his outlines and crib sheets ready. While working on the test, I looked a few times at the Procedure outline we'd put together. After all of that, I suppose it proved somewhat useful.

Facing the Memorial Day weekend there was only one test left, in Contracts on the first of June.

6/1/76
(Tuesday)

So it all comes down to Perini. It is only fitting that he provided our travail at the end.

I just could not handle studying this past weekend. The way Perini had taught Contracts—one rule followed by a million exceptions—meant prolonged efforts at memorization, nearly unbearable after this three-week grind. I pored over the hornbook, but I could only sit half an hour, forty minutes at a time. Nor do I have enough respect for Perini left to care much about his evaluation.

I saw Kyle skulking through the hallways when I got there this morning before the test. He is normally so robust, but I guess he felt it was all on the line here, and he was cowering like a wounded animal, literally walking hunched beside the wall. I did my best to rattle him, came on chipper as a sunbeam. I tried to detain him in conversation while he was obviously chafing to go look at an outline one more time. Oh, I was the very soul of menace, and I still don't feel ashamed.

Then I went into the test room. I come to these four-hour numbers with a virtual traveling commissary: earplugs, paper, four pencils, four pens, three rolls of mints, two packs of cigarettes, a cup of iced coffee, a Coke, two chocolate bars, a pencil sharpener, an extension cord for my typewriter. As I unloaded all of this equipment I took a lot of joshing from around the room. Thirty-five or forty of us would be typing. It was nice that for a minute we were all bound in laughter again.

At nine the proctor handed the exam out. It would be unlike Rudolph Perini not to give the hardest tests at Harvard Law School. The questions covered nine single-spaced pages— Nicky's exam, by comparison, was three sides doubled. Before the test I was told that we would be taking the same exam as another section, with two differences: Our test would have five questions instead of four, and the other section would have eight hours.

I went through the exam in the same desperate rush. I didn't pretend to do much thinking. At 11:15 I looked up the first time and realized it would all be over in two hours. I was giddy at the thought. The last question was a disordered series of phrases from various nursery rhymes. Perini asked us to describe the possible contract they might form, what the problems in its enforcement might be, and what common interpretative dilemmas were suggested. Perini, I thought, you are still not cool.

When time was called at one, I walked back and forth at the front of the room applauding. I hooted, I hollered. I went out to the arcade where BSA was serving beer and drank four cups fast. Aubrey was also pie-eyed.

"Well," he said, "all that stands between you and a J.D. is six thousand dollars." He meant the tuition.

With Terry, Gina, and Mike Wald, I went out to lunch. When I got back, I emptied my locker into my backpack and called Annette, who'd volunteered to pick me up.

On the way upstairs from the phone, I ran into Phyllis Wiseman. It hurt me to see her. After holding to that steadiness, that distance, all year, she had lost her grip. For her, the final holdout, the last month has been too much: the stuff with Kyle, the dismal atmosphere, and the crunch and exhaustion of the tests themselves.

She was worried that she had not done well, that her family, her friends would not respect her. She was badly depressed.

"I did a little better than so-so last term, and now," she said, "I just mixed it all up . . . It's always so sad around here."

I told her, in so many words, she was okay—to tell herself she was okay.

Annette arrived in a few minutes.

"It's over!" I shouted when I got in the car.

I've been repeating that to myself for the past few hours. It will probably take a couple of days for me to believe it. The first year of law school. It seemed sheer myth when my friends lived through it. Now I have, too. It is over. It is over.

When Roscoe Pound, who eventually became the dean of Harvard Law School, entered as a first-year student in 1889, he was required to take courses in Torts, Criminal Law, Property, Contracts, and Common-Law Forms of Action, a nineteenth-century version of Civil Procedure. He mastered the law by reading cases; in class, his professors taught in the Socratic method. In a way, things were easier for Dean Pound than they were for me and my peers in the Harvard Law School class of 1978. He was able to pass the bar exam after only a single year of legal education. And he did not have to add an elective in the spring.

But, of course, the resemblances between Dean Pound's first year and mine are striking. For nearly a century now, American lawyers have been bound together by the knowledge that they have all survived a similar initiation; it is something of a grand tradition. For me it was an experience of great extremes. What was bad was awful. But what was good often approached the ideal. I was regularly inspired and invigorated by what I was studying, and I seldom lost the feeling that I was making good use of myself. The riches of Harvard Law School—its students, its faculty, its eminence, and its traditions, which are always a presence—yielded for me a time of towering excitement and great fruitfulness. In many ways, it was the best year in the education of this person who must be counted as now entering something like the twentieth grade, and everything considered—everything—I would probably do it again.

Yet it would be a decorous pulling of my punches not to say that I believe there are many ways in which the wealth of Harvard Law School is magnificently squandered. The century-old curriculum we inherited from Dean Pound is badly in need of change. Early in May, I attended an open meeting on legal education. It had been called by a group of first-year students, and despite the pressure of exams, 175 students arrived, most of them 1Ls. The size and mood of the crowd left little doubt of common dissatisfaction with many aspects of first-year education. The students were addressed by a panel of professors who had taught in the various 1L sections. Perini was among them, but so were a number of the youngest and most liberal members of the law-school faculty. Looking at them and at the students spilling through the aisles, Perini asked his older colleagues on the panel, "Are we the Christians here, gentlemen, or the lions?"

Either way, I realized that the same array that faced Perini that evening will confront law teachers of his philosophy in the future. A new generation of law-school teachers—some of them students who were in that room, persons shaped by different experiences, and many, like Nicky Morris, outspokenly opposed to the old ways—will soon hold sway on law-school faculties. Even Perini freely acknowledged the handwriting on the wall.

"There will be change," Perini admitted. "Not even I can claim that the Harvard Law School is the greatest and most divine institution in existence."

Many of the directions for that change in the first-year curriculum are self-evident. At places more progressive than HLS there are already smaller classes, more opportunities for students to write and to make contact with the faculty, differing formats for evaluation of student performance, election to the Law Review without reference to grades. Harvard Law School itself is a far different place than it was in 1970, when my college friends entered. There was no such thing, then, as passing a professor's question in a first-year class; no teachers who, like Morris, tried to stress the broadest humanistic outlines of the law; no midyear exams. The case method, which once meant a reading diet of nothing but case reports, has given way in recent years to the addition of journal articles, of writings which make the learning of the law less a piece-by-piece puzzling through and more like the real lawyer's task: a comparison of new elements against a known context.

No doubt the changes will go on. Fresh from the front, I would add two observations about the specifics of legal education as I experienced them in my first year. That night in May, the faculty panel roundly agreed to the continuing vitality of the Socratic method. I would not differ directly, but the peculiar privilege which Socraticism grants a teacher to invade the security of every student in the room means that in the wrong hands it can become an instrument of terror. I never felt that my education gained by my being frightened, and I was often scared in class. Law faculties have too long excused, in the name of academic freedom, a failure to hold colleagues within basic limits of decency. They must formulate and enforce an etiquette of classroom behavior which insures that teachers cannot freely browbeat and exploit their students. To refuse leaves them in a subtle but persistent state of moral abdication. I know that it is hard to think of law students, headed for a life of privilege, as being among the downtrodden; and I also recognize that classroom terror has been a fixed aspect of legal education for at least a century. But the risk, the ultimate risk, of allowing students to make their first acquaintance with the law in such an atmosphere, in that state of hopeless fright, is that they will come away with a tacit but ineradicable impression that it is somehow characteristically "legal" to be heartless, to be brutal, and will carry that attitude with them into the execution of their professional tasks.

Those objections to heavy-handed Socraticism are, in a fashion, only a part of a larger concern with legal education of which I began to become conscious after my conversations with Gina last fall. The law is at war with ambiguity, with uncertainty. In the courtroom, the adversary system, plaintiff against defendant, guarantees that someone will always win, someone lose. No matter if justice is evenly with each side, no matter if the issues are dark and obscure, the rule of law will be declared. The law and the arbitrary certainty of some of its results are no doubt indispensable to the secure operation of a society where there is ceaseless conflict requiring resolution.

But a lot of those attitudes toward certainty seem to rub off on the law world at large. Many of the institutions of legal education show a similar seeking after sureness and definition, a desire to subdue the random element, to leave nothing to chance: the admissions process, where statistical formulas serve as the basis for decision; the law-school classroom, where all power and discretion are concentrated in the professor; the stratifications so clearly marked in the law-school population, with the best students segregated on the law review, and the faculty remote from all; and the notion of the meritocracy, the attempt to rank and to accord privilege by some absolute standard. All of these things amount in my mind to a fighting of the war against ambiguity and uncertainness in quarters where it is not called for, where the need which supports the custom of the courtroom is not present. Not even the law can abolish the fundamental unclearness of many human situations, but in the law schools there is precious little effort made to address the degree to which human choice is arbitrary. We are taught that there is always a reason, always a rationale, always an argument. Too much of what goes on around the law school and in the legal classroom seeks to tutor students in strategies for avoiding, for ignoring, for somehow subverting the unquantifiable, the inexact, the emotionally charged, those things which still pass in my mind under the label "human." In time, I came to take that quality in legal education as another of those forces which could make me less a person than I'd like to be, that foe I'd come here to meet.

Courses like Morris's and Zechman's which emphasized the uncertainties and contradictions inherent in the law are signs of what I consider progress. But students still see the operation of the law only in a secondhand and thirdhand way, as it is revealed in carefully prepared case reports. Learning to think like a lawyer should involve more than the mastery of an important but abstract mental skill. Were I king of the universe—or dean of Harvard Law School—I would supplement case reading with use of other devices—film, drama, informal narrative, actual client contact like that provided in the upper-year clinical courses—seeking to cultivate a sensitivity to the immediate human context in which the law so forcefully intervenes.

Reforms like that, like others which look to be on the horizon, seem to bode well for us all. A more humane and humanistic education in the law strikes me as far more fitting than a schooling characterized by terror and the suppression of feeling for those persons who, in time, will become this society's chief custodians of justice.

EPILOGUE

8/21/76

Grades came in at the middle of last month. Despite the calm and distance of the summer, the familiar apparatus of reaction set in place the instant I saw the envelope. My fingers shook and I felt the rush of all that teetering ambivalence. Please, I asked somebody, no Cs, even as I hoped for something exceptional.

The grades were the same as first term, half As, half Bs. I got an A in the Policy course, a B-plus in Property; an A-minus from Nicky, a B from Perini. Good marks, I knew; they probably put me somewhere in the upper quarter of the class. I felt lucky. And still I was nagged by a desire for more.

Within a few days, Gina, Stephen, Karen Sondergard—all scattered around the country for the summer—had called for the first time since the close of school. The conversations were

267

convivial, but each turned in time to grades. The names and marks of those who'd made the Law Review from Section 2 had leaked out by now. Brodsky. Jenner. Sandy Stern. A couple of the quiet ones I never would have guessed. But not Stephen. (He had been right about his Con Law exam and sounded as though he was already regaining his sense of humor.) Not Kyle. Not Weiss. Not Hochschild. Not Shearing. Not me. Many were nearer than I was, but I still felt cheated. My sense of jealousy and denial left me dizzy for a day.

My enemy, that greedy little monster, is still in there rattling his cage. I guess I will be contending with him always.

Knowing that, I must admit that I made many of the rough spots in the past year far harder for myself. I met up with a lot of my own ugliness, and learned more than I wanted to about how deep it goes. I suppose that is part of the education, too. Which is not to say that the first year at Harvard Law School would do to everyone what it did to me. There are many people who would be wise enough to head back out the doors after a couple days.

But those are not the people who usually come through those doors in the first place. It is those of us compulsively pursuing some vague idea of distinction who are most likely to aspire to the Harvard Law School, and for us the year is going to take its toll. In a funny way, I think law schools as institutions attract the people least suited to them at the start. We are men and women drawn to the study of rules, people with a native taste for order. The first year, when we do not know the language or how well we are doing, when professors seem only to be posing riddles every day, is bound to throw us for a loop. And at Harvard, that driven quest for prominence which brings us there, leads us, once we arrive, to an almost inescapable temptation to scramble, despite obstacles and ugliness and bruises, for what sometimes looks to all of us to be the very top of the tallest heap.

So we come vulnerable, and the place does little to protect us from ourselves. There are people who managed the year with more grace than I did; others less. But all the conversations I have had with my law-school friends over the summer have returned, almost obsessively, to the year past and the question of exactly what it was that happened to us. Something exalted. Something fearful. We all reported at least one summer nightmare about Rudolph Perini. And we each admitted to wonder—and moments of real pride—when we thought about the persons we were last fall.

In a few weeks, it will be fall again and the Harvard Law School will open its doors to another entering class. As we did, they will bring with them their academic accolades, glittering like rows of military medals; they will bring a hunger for the law. They will bring their own great talents, energy, ambition, intelligence, charm. They will bring their enemies unmet.

"It will be so strange to see them," Gina said when we spoke recently about the coming year. "They will be One Ls."

AFTERWORD

It is an honor, of course, for any writer to find that a book he wrote more than half a lifetime ago continues to attract readers—enough, in fact, that it has emerged in this handsome new edition. *One L* has been in print continuously since the day it was published in September 1977, but I take special pleasure that the book has been reissued by a publishing consortium that now includes not only the memoir's original paperback publisher, Penguin Books, but also the house that first brought out the book in hardcover, then called G. P. Putnam's Sons.

I wrote *One L* on a kind of bet, not so much mine as that of Ned Chase, now of blessed memory and then a senior editor at Putnam's. One day over lunch, in the spring of 1975, my literary agent at the time, Elizabeth McKee, showed Ned the letter I had written to her announcing I was abandoning academic life for law school. In the letter, I had observed, as an aside, that there was no nonfiction account of the daily life of a law student. *The Paper Chase*, a well-known but far-fetched novel, had been published, and there were many books by professors full of lofty advice. But there was nothing from the ground level that offered a real-life recounting of what happened day by day to a person as she or he began learning the law. I would have been grateful to read a book like that while I was pondering my own decision to go to law school, and I had said as much to Elizabeth.

On the strength of my letter, Ned commissioned the book on the spot, adding a proviso that my memoir should cover only the first year of law school, which Ned knew, based on the experience of his own lawyer-son, was by far the most dynamic period in a legal education. (I should mention, for the sake of interest, that Ned Chase has another son, named Chevy, then the lead player on "Saturday Night Live," who three years later announced the publication of *One L* in the midst of a thronged appearance before thousands on the Harvard campus. But that, as they say, is another story.)

I received $1,000 for signing the contract, with $3,000 more due when I delivered an acceptable manuscript. But the impulsive way Ned had commissioned the book was nearly its undoing. By the time I sent in my first draft a year and a half later, Ned had largely forgotten the whole matter. "I need you to remind me of just one thing," he told me, once he had read my manuscript. "Why did I ever want to buy this book?"

In response, I prophesied a booming American interest in the law, and I backed it up with statistics showing that between 1970 and 1974 law school applications had quadrupled. Much of this was due to Watergate, I claimed, and inspiring figures like Senator Sam Ervin, with his little vest-pocket copy of the Constitution, and Special Prosecutors Archibald Cox and Elliot Richardson, who all had sought to deliver justice to President Nixon's henchmen (many of them also lawyers), in the process familiarizing the nation with the mantra, "No person is above the law."

I had no real idea what I was talking about, but Ned was convinced and went forward with publication. The senior management at Putnam's were not persuaded and, in an effort to vindicate their initial judgment, failed to order reprintings of *One L*, even after the book drew glowing reviews and seemed to be selling. Given *One L*'s faltering start, I savor the irony of its long life, particularly since the president and publisher of Penguin Books, Kathryn Court, is entitled to join me in gloating. In 1978, she was the young editor who took a chance and published *One L* in paperback.

Explaining *One L*'s continuing appeal, on the other hand, is an issue I've often pondered but probably need to leave to others to fully explain. One key, I suspect, is that the book is the confession of an unabashed neurotic. Neither then, nor now, is law school the same kind of crucible for most law students that it was for me. In turning to the law after five years at the Stanford Creative Writing Center—two as a fellow in the famous Stegner Program and three as a lecturer in the Department of English—and by returning to the cheap seats after my own stint at the head of the classroom, I had made a painful U-turn in my life. I had passion and intense curiosity about the law, but it seemed to come with a cost, since I felt I had put at risk the ambition I had clung to since childhood: becoming a novelist. I'd had no luck getting several novels published. More to the point, I seemed to be willing myself toward success as an author. And yet, I remained connected to the unrivaled joys a writer can experience when things go well.

To be clinical, I was enduring exactly what Erik Erikson meant when he coined the term "identity crisis." The law ultimately helped me solidify my sense of self. It allowed me to enter a respected profession I valued greatly—one with a smoother career trajectory than the arts, where it is all bust before the very rare boom, as it certainly had been for me. In the law you can be rewarded and appreciated when you are merely good for your age.

But I had not reached even that point yet, and as a result I was questioning almost everything in my life, and often with a great deal of pain. That is not unusual for people in their mid-twenties, and I suspect my frankness about the fact that my initiation into the legal profession frequently involved a lot of hard work in holding myself together is one element that has helped the book endure. As I sometimes joke, *One L* has provided law students for decades the reassurance that at least one person has gone through the whole experience feeling a lot crazier than they do.

Whatever the attraction, I still regularly receive mail from readers of *One L*. Those who write are grateful for the book's comfort or guidance. Some say reading about my excitement drew them to law school. Others tell me that my tale of personal torment drove them away. Most express thanks for the road they took, a gratitude they owe almost entirely to themselves.

The significance of *One L* to me can never be overstated. I often say, not purely in jest, that the great break of my literary career was going to law school. I mean this not simply because I ended up a published author—something I had longed for since I was a child—but because of what I learned about myself in the process of writing. The book that gathered itself as the product of the journal entries I wrote several times every week during my first year at Harvard Law School was not, for me, principally a commercial enterprise. It was cathartic. Each line remains written inside me. I remember every word before it's read. When I turn the pages all the sensations whirl again within me: the panic and ferocious worry, the racing desire to understand, and a ubiquitous parched heat, as if the fervid pace of learning had sucked me dry.

I had been a writer and, as it turned out, would never surrender that vocation. Keeping a journal was my refuge. I wrote, as writers always do, for me, to be myself, and to join my very new identity as a would-be lawyer, with the person I had wanted to be before.

Yet despite the relative success of *One L*, I declined to go back to a career as a full-time writer, perhaps because my transition out of that world had proved so painful. As important, I had taken my own mark well when I decided to go to law school. I felt an indelible passion for the law and becoming a lawyer that drove me toward practice.

After Harvard, I was lucky enough to go directly into the United States Attorney's Office in Chicago. For eight years, I worked as a federal prosecutor, investigating and trying cases that more often than not centered on corruption in the legal profession: judges taking bribes, lawyers paying off tax assessment officials, a state attorney general who shortchanged the taxman. It was an exhilarating, demanding job, but I still snuck time on the morning commuter train to pursue that elusive dream of being a novelist, writing longhand in the unused pages of spiral notebooks my kids had taken to grade school. When I left government service, I took three months away from the law to finish the novel I had been dragging around in my briefcase and was promptly struck by lightning: *Presumed Innocent* became a number one best seller around the world and eventually a feature film starring Harrison Ford. It is generally credited with beginning the parade of novels about lawyers that have populated the best-seller lists ever since.

Notwithstanding the success of my first (published) novel, I was still not ready to give up practicing law, especially since I had just become a partner in the Chicago office of a firm now known as SNR Denton. Although the amount of time I spend practicing has tapered off slowly since the early 1990s, I continue at SNR. In the early days I did a lot of civil litigation, which I was eager to learn, as well as white-collar criminal representation. By the time my second novel, *The Burden of Proof*, was published in 1990, I began doing more pro bono criminal work, including representing an innocent man who had spent twelve years in prison, much of it on death row, for a murder he did not commit. My work on capital cases led to my appointment in 2000 to a fourteen-member commission the governor of Illinois selected to propose reforms to the Illinois death penalty system, a commission whose recommendations were, in salient part, enacted into law through the efforts of a young Illinois state senator named Barack Obama, with whom I worked. In fact, over the years I have ended up serving on a variety of public bodies, including the merit selection commission our U.S. senators asked to make recommendations for the federal bench and U.S. attorneys. In 2004, I became the first chair of the newly created Illinois Executive Ethics Commission, a good group with a very tough job in my home state, since the Commission is charged with administering the state's ethics enforcement system for executive branch employees.

Throughout the years, I have continued to write. There have been nine best-selling novels, a nonfiction book on the death penalty, and a continuing sideline writing opinion pieces for major newspapers as well as occasional magazine articles. It is hard to imagine a richer or more satisfying professional life. And I was also blessed to raise three spectacular kids who have always been at the center of my life. Except for the fact that my marriage did not ultimately survive, I have been, by almost every other measure, a fortunate person, and one who continues to relish my involvement in the law.

Because of *One L*, I am frequently asked how much law school has changed since I entered Harvard more than thirty-five years ago. I have two answers: A great deal. And not enough.

I watched my older daughter endure her own first year in law school at the University of Michigan in 2002–03 and thought she managed it with much more grace than I did. There was still considerable grade competition, but some of that was probably due to the decline of the legal economy leading to fewer jobs for graduates. But I don't recall her fearing class, or her classmates. Overall, it was an intense experience for her but not soul-splitting, and part of that was due to her being in a less severe environment than I had experienced. I think the same thing would be true at most law schools these days when the brute exertion of patriarchal authority has gotten a bad name.

Harvard, as well, is a kinder and gentler place, especially in the wake of the deanship of Elena Kagan, who worked a sea change by emphasizing that the students, not the faculty, deserved to be the first concern of the institution. For too many years, the experience of Harvard law students remained akin to mine, feeling like you were playing an unwinnable game of king of the hill, a pygmy versus intellectual giants who were ready to thwart all comers.

The period after I graduated found Harvard Law School enduring an uneasy time. The faculty was riven by struggles between practitioners of Critical Legal Studies, which involved a deconstructionist approach to law and legal texts, and their opponents who were naturally dubbed "conservatives," never a term of endearment in Cambridge, Massachusetts. This struggle played itself out in celebrated battles about the hiring and promotion of minority and female professors. Students were often left behind as the faculty's energy was directed toward their political war.

When I entered HLS, the so-called win ratio between applicants accepted at both Harvard and Yale law schools was roughly 50/50, but the proportions turned decidedly in Yale's favor over the ensuing years, reportedly as high as 90/10. Eventually, not only Yale but Stanford Law began to overtake Harvard in win ratio and also in some of the national rankings, where Yale has now stood securely at the top for decades. Furthermore, NYU, Columbia, and the University of Chicago looked like they might give Harvard competition for third place.

Thus, Elena Kagan became dean at a time when the need for change had become clear to virtually everyone, if the law school was going to hang on to some share of its vaunted standing, which is of signal importance to everyone there now or in the past. Curricular reform followed.

Today, the 1L class is divided into sections of eighty students, about half the size of what I faced. The law school provides funding for section-wide social activities to foster a culture of collaboration among section-mates who experience one another as more than in-class rivals. While the fixed menu of Contracts, Torts, Criminal Law, Property, and Civil Procedure remains in place, students are now required to take a course in Statutes and Regulations, recognizing that the executive and legislative branches, not just judges, make a considerable portion of the law with which contemporary attorneys deal. Additionally, 1Ls are offered a choice of three classes in international comparative law. There is a legal writing section of forty students as well as an optional section in Practice and Theory taught during a January interterm, a mini-clinical class that introduces to the first year the valuable question, How would a real lawyer deal with this problem? Much of the anomie and isolation that characterized life at HLS have been reduced by these changes.

And the entering classes there, like so many other places, look different too. One-third of the students are classified as "students of color"—persons of Asian, African, Hispanic, and Indo-Pakistani descent—and the gender split is roughly 50/50. The institution no longer treats public service law as an alien enterprise, as it did in my day. Every student must now do forty hours of pro bono work in order to graduate.

Finally, in a serious attempt to lessen the outbreaks of com-

petitive greed that characterized my section and were repeated
now and then over the years, letter grades have been done away
with in favor of a system in which roughly 10 percent of the
students in a given class get a "low pass," 30 percent a "high
pass," and the majority simply "pass."

All these are salutary changes and constructive responses to
the criticisms made over the years in *One L* and many other
places. Not all law schools have gone as far as Harvard in re-
forming the first-year curriculum. But, in general, the changes
there are emblematic of a more welcoming and embracing face
on legal education. Plenty of law students still go through the
first year in a state of abject terror, but that is more a product of
their own inevitable insecurities rather than of an educational
system that seemed silently committed to exacerbating them.

Nevertheless, as is ever true of well-planned reform, what
has been accomplished still does not go far enough. I continue
to lament that many of the dour hallmarks of legal education
that go all the way back to Dean Langdell—large classes and
grading based on a single exam—continue to prevail in almost
all U.S. law schools. Those features have a detrimental effect
on both the pedagogical environment and the anxiety level of
law students. Further, there is a fair chance that the educational
model reinforces a culture of distance and competition, instead
of collaboration.

Worse, Langdell's model continues to prevail for an ugly reason: money. In some universities, law schools are profit centers,
where a very small faculty teaches a very large student body, all
of whom pay a very high tuition. If nothing else, law schools
come much closer to being break-even enterprises when they
are run this way, meaning they do not create the same drag on
university endowments, as many departments in the humani-
ties and social sciences tend to do.

Size means that the scholars who teach classes of 80 to 150
students simply do not have the time to grade several papers

every semester, nor to provide much one-on-one instruction. With so much riding on finals, exam time is inevitably a mad season at law schools everywhere. There are many inspired educators teaching in American law schools, but they are still battling a system whose fundamentals work against them and which, in its unkindest aspects, encourage students to view those years as the road to an admission card, rather than as an education that can shape their values throughout their years in practice.

Furthermore, because large classes remain the norm, the Socratic method continues to prevail, still occasionally making for uncomfortable experiences for students. One Harvard professor admitted to me privately a few years ago that when a student answers "unprepared," the teacher asks the slacker to select the classmate whom the professor will call on next, a Hobson's choice guaranteed to turn the student from sloth into pariah.

But overall the justification for intense Socratic interrogation in my day—that it was intended to toughen up students for the rigors of practice—is recognized as an argument with many flaws. Most law school faculty members are not ignorant about the nature of the people who are drawn there—ambitious, competitive, aggressively intellectual—nor about the fact that it remains a tender time in the development of virtually all students. Professors enjoy the lifelong impact of their lessons, but that is a consequence of the fact that the personalities of their students are not yet set in concrete. Faculty members should bear that in mind, and these days the majority of them do.

None of this is to deny that law students should be treated as adults, but toughening them up for the combat of the courtroom or practice is not a good excuse for humiliating classroom interrogations, which are rarer in U.S. law schools now than in 1975, but far from extinct. Court or contract negotiations are usually a few years off for all 1Ls, and, in any event, those activities will be undertaken only after each student has achieved a much more solid sense of professional membership.

Nor do I believe curricular reform has gone far enough at most law schools, even though I admire the changes Harvard made. I have long urged that a course that looks directly at the lawyering process ought to be part of the basic first-year curriculum. I say this for complicated reasons that have to do with my own assessment of the practice of law.

It goes without saying, since I have continued to practice for decades now despite being blessed as a novelist, that I like being a lawyer. I have found practice, for the most part, a kick. There are finite tasks to be accomplished that require intellectual sophistication, a quick grasp of facts, and diverse personal skills—guile, judgment, persuasiveness, and the ability to project the force of personality. Every case and every client is in some aspect unique, yet similar enough that you can take predictable pride in recognizing your own increasing skill. The human settings, and the complexity of legal questions, engage me just as thoroughly as when I was 1L, wondering whether a contract was formed when I ordered a hamburger. And although saying this flouts the contemporary temper in the United States, I still believe a practicing lawyer can do a lot of good, not only on behalf of poor clients, who seldom get the same quality of representation as the well-to-do, but also in representing paying clients who often are in desperate need of their lawyer's help.

Last, I love the milieu of the law. Thirty-five years ago, one of the perceptions that drove me to law school was not only the realization that many of my closest friends from college had become lawyers, but recognizing that the same was true of new pals I was making in the Bay Area. I have loved being among lawyers and still enjoy my colleagues. I say, with no exaggeration, that I have met more "great" people in the practice of law, persons of uncommon depth and ability, than I think I would have in any other calling.

Yet whatever my pleasure in my part-time practice, my attitude is not universal. Many lawyers do not like what they do; they see themselves as imprisoned in gilded cages: highly paid, well regarded, and unhappy. I cannot count the number of attorneys who have told me that if they had my success as a novelist, they would board up their law offices in moments.

Some of this is romantic, grass-is-greener stuff. But the fact is that life at the bar is hard. The nuts-and-bolts work can be frustratingly detailed or numbingly routine—and the environment is sometimes dismal, especially in this era of the Am Law 100, where every law firm is in a tireless competition to maximize profits per partner, a necessity if the most valuable lawyers are not going to jump ship. Day by day, practice can be a grind. On one side stands the adversary, of dubious ethics and limitless zeal; on the other, the client waiting hungrily for favorable results. Between them is a stressed-out existence of economic pressure and ceaseless competition, a parade of deadlines, obdurate judges, unreturned phone messages, a hail of e-mails arriving like bullets, a life of lost weekends and evenings, a Sisyphean struggle to catch up. Worst of all, if you push the average unhappy lawyer hard enough, he or she will usually come out with something like this: *What is it worth in the end? What good am I doing?* A prominent partner in one of Chicago's most successful firms once said to me in private, "What do I care if his robber baron wins or mine?"

That is, of course, the rub. A lawyer may do his or her job very well but does not set the moral agenda. The ends are established by the client. It is the lawyer's obligation to carry those goals forward, within the limits of law and ethics. It is his or her job to be a competent professional, to do well, without regard to whether he or she is doing good.

This dichotomy between doing good and doing well, which so deeply troubles the legal profession, should be familiar to those who have read *One L*, for its roots reach into legal education. As I noted, one of the most painful aspects of law school is what students often experience as the sense that they are being taken away from themselves. Deeply developed values and beliefs are challenged and generally exposed. Students learn that for every argument there is a counterargument. The plasticity of the law is taught. Moreover, most of what takes place during the supercharged and occasionally coercive atmosphere of the first year goes to emphasize what I would call a culture of professional competence. What matters, professors tell you time and again, is not that you come up with the right answer on exams but that you reason powerfully and recognize countervailing arguments in areas where there are no accepted solutions. Rationality is a human attribute worthy of being prized. But lawyers trained in law schools generally come away with the feeling that adherence to a larger world of values is somehow discouraged. For the idealist is substituted a technocrat. The do-gooder is now someone who aspires only to do well.

So where is the path out of this mess? Thirty-plus years down the road I have learned this much: our lives as lawyers can be redeemed best by the system of which we are a part. The synthesis of the do-well, do-good dialectic is some margin of faith in the legal process. To my eye, lawyers take the greatest satisfaction from their calling when they believe at some level that the legal system aims at achieving just and rational results, no matter how far it sometimes strays from those objectives. As corny or even unlikely as it sounds, most lawyers, at root, are involved in doing justice, and their professional existence is enhanced by feeling connected to that goal.

In a way, this is not an argument at all but simply the passionate advice of experience as both a prosecutor and now a defender. I was intensely proud to stand in court every day, after first becoming a lawyer, and to announce my name to a judge and say I was there to represent the United States of America, a client whom I believed was almost always right in its desire to punish those who broke its laws. Although it took me a while to see the point, I eventually realized that defense lawyers also have a noble role. A lawyer is a client's friend within the framework of the intricate legal bureaucracy. The practice of law is gratifying at its highest levels, not only because of the status, intellectual challenge, or sometimes exorbitant financial rewards, but because there is something profoundly pleasing to all of us about being able to provide direct aid to someone eager for assistance. The classic question to a criminal attorney, "How can you represent those jerks?" has a classic answer, "Because they need me to." It is the true essence of what lawyers do to stand up for the rights of those who are despised, to tell a society, "My client may deserve serious punishment, but first prove that is the case. And remember at all times that he is a human being, which means he must be treated with minimum standards of decency, because doing so redeems not only him but you."

For a lawyer, the essential professional task is to subsume his or her own interests to the client's needs. Worthy as that role may be, it is not unique—real estate brokers and literary agents, among many others, do the same thing. But lawyers also labor with a concomitant dedication to the system of justice. The fundamental tension of the profession is the struggle between bold advocacy of the client's interests and the need to establish and hold to limits that prevent advocacy from leading to irrational and inequitable results. Thus, the lawyer's job is to be, on one hand, the impassioned representative of the client to the world and, on the other, the wise representative to the client of the legal system, and the society, explaining and upholding the demands and restrictions that the system places on them both. Every lawyer who enjoys the practice learns to recognize and embrace these conflicting imperatives, even as he or she labors daily to resolve them.

But that learning right now is ad hoc and comes on the job. Law school still makes little effort to inculcate professional values or to be the cultural center for the practice of law by instilling us all with a sense of fidelity to the lawyering process. Students are introduced of necessity to the culture of professional competence, without being taught as much about the commitments of their profession. To be sure, things are much better than when I was a 1L. In my day, clinical education was still questioned by academic purists, who believed law school should be about selecting the next cadre of legal scholars; those not fit for that task were of less interest and free to become practicing lawyers. Today, clinical training is now an accepted and often required part of virtually every law school curriculum and has provided a needed context to the theoretical education that continues to prevail, as it should, through the bulk of the curriculum. At Harvard there are also a smattering of courses that look at the profession and problems with the delivery of legal services.

But the truth is that a professional law school faculty, most of whom are principally teachers, have at best a limited interest in practice and, in most cases, have actively shunned it. Doctors are trained by practicing doctors. Lawyers are still trained initially by those who'd rather not do what most of their students will undertake for decades.

My vision would counteract that with a first-year course that would, at root, ask the question, What is a lawyer? That class would examine the rules of professional conduct in detail and explore their complex rationales along with the competing solutions to classic problems like, say, how a lawyer should react when his or her client wants to lie on the witness stand. Additionally, that class would look at the assumptions of an adversary system, including the law's concept of fact-finding and the truth, and also delve into the history of the legal profession and the role of lawyers today, who are, in this nation, the counselors to leaders in every field.

Ever since Watergate, when the nation was stunned to find that many of the felons who surrounded President Nixon were lawyers, so-called Professional Responsibility training has been a requirement for law school graduation and bar admission. But that class is usually part of the final lurch toward graduation, taken in the third year as little more than an afterthought because students have to. Putting a course on the lawyering process side by side with the other core classes would help students realize that the law is not simply about intellectual discourse but is a living system that is re-created every day by every attorney who practices. It would put the values of the profession at the center of the curriculum.

I am sure that there are those who will say that, in attempting to inspire adherence to the larger values of the legal profession, I risk becoming an apologist for the evil that lawyers do, and that the kind of legal education I endorse would teach students to be ethical but zealous advocates for leaky waste dumps, rapists, and discriminatory employers, a horde of happy hired guns, blessed by their professors to pile the bucks high in the name of the lawyering process. But understanding the values of the profession does not mean becoming an uncritical cheerleader, nor does it prescribe the ends. In fact, one of the fundamental questions of the class I envision would be whether the profession really serves its own values if quality representation is available only to the affluent. Yet I think law schools make a mistake by putting off those debates for the years of practice.

Institutions, particularly ones as hoary as legal education and the law, have their own persistent character. I do not believe much in panaceas, and certainly the proposals ventured here, individually or taken as a whole, do not amount to one. If every curricular reform I suggest were implemented tomorrow,

I know that lawyers would not skip to work down LaSalle or Wall Street whistling "Zip-a-Dee-Doo-Dah" or turn their faces to heaven to shun all temptations. The law is a tough business, full of striving souls, and our hunger and ambition will ever drive us. But law school remains the great common ground of the profession. Before we begin a life of sparring with one another, what can and should be commonly instilled is a sense of mutual enterprise, a vision of the worthy, if complicated, ambitions of the profession, and the freedom to take pride in this difficult and venerable calling. If perhaps lawyers will never quite learn to do good and to do well, the law schools, at least, can do better.

One concrete contribution that *One L* indubitably made to legal culture is the term itself. When I started my book, "1L" was the computer code that first-year students found accompanying their names at Harvard Law School. The term was well established as an acronym at HLS, but only there. The success of the book resulted in "1L" replacing the more cumbersome "law school freshman" as a term for entering law students all over the country.

Furthermore, to be a 1L now connotes to those inside the profession, and many outside, that the student in question is enduring a unique educational passage. For despite the years, and many appropriate and laudable reforms, the core experience of the first year of law school remains in many ways unchanged. Some of that is because the basic curriculum and the teaching methods are largely unaltered. Some of that has to do with the testing and grading system. Much of it is a result of the personality types drawn to the law—articulate, assertive, frequently competitive—who will inevitably make one another nervous, especially in an environment whose utter novelty guarantees that everybody is bound to feel uncertain from time to time. One Ls will always feel they have entered a new world. Consequently, despite the predictable variety of experiences, most lawyers look back at the first year of law school as a critical period in forging their personal and professional identity and one characterized by considerable emotional intensity. Something important happens then, and I believe that simple fact, more than any other, underpins *One L*'s continuing currency.

S.T.
Evanston, Ill.
2010